How To *Permanently* Erase Negative Self-Talk

So You Can Be Extraordinary

How To *Permanently* Erase Negative Self-Talk

So You Can Be Extraordinary

By

Emily Filloramo

New Chapter Press

ISBN: 978-1937559564

Published by New Chapter Press
1175 York Ave, Suite #3s
New York, NY 10065
Randy Walker, Managing Partner
RWalker@NewChapterMedia.com
www.NewChapterMedia.com

Disclaimer
This book is not a substitute for psychotherapy. The contents in this book and the healing steps are for informational and educational purposes only. The author and the publisher do not guarantee that anyone following these techniques, suggestions, tips, ideas or strategies will become mentally and physically healthy. Please seek the help of a licensed mental health provider if you are not psychologically stable. Emily Filloramo of BeMoreExtraordinary.com(Executive Image Nutrition LLC) and New Chapter Press assume no liability nor responsibility to anyone with respect to any loss or damage caused, or alleged to be caused, directly or indirectly by the information contained in this book.

All names and identifying details of the case studies have been changed.

Praise for Erase Negative Self-Talk!

"I spent 30 years developing Internal Family Systems (IFS) as an approach to psychotherapy, but with a gnawing awareness that it could be used in many other fields to help people if I only knew how to apply it to those fields. It is gratifying to have someone as talented as Emily Filloramo translate IFS with such enthusiasm and clarity into her realm of coaching. As her plethora of rich case examples indicate, she knows what she's doing."

—Richard Schwartz, Ph.D, LMFT, Founder and Developer of Internal Family System model of psychotherapy, President at Center for Self Leadership

"Internal Family Systems (IFS) is a model of psychotherapy that helps manage and potentiate the human condition. It is one of the most accessible, intuitive, effective and permanent forms of healing available. Emily has done an outstanding job of bringing IFS to the general population. *Erase Negative Self-Talk* is clear, a joy to read and highly relatable. By getting to know our parts, we can overcome life's obstacles and live life with more love and compassion."

—Frank Anderson, MD, Psychiatrist, Chairman of the Foundation for Self-Leadership

"I'm a huge proponent of alignment and Emily Filloramo's realistic, timeless and proven approach to excelling in life provides the blueprint you need to reconnect with who you truly are and surmount the challenges that exist within. Read this book, implement the profound, yet easily executable strategies and share your gifts with those you're most compelled to serve. The world is waiting for the real you."

—Steve Olsher, *New York Times* bestselling author of *What Is Your WHAT? Discover The ONE Amazing Thing You Were Born To Do*

"Belief systems are one of the most powerful and least understood forces on the planet. *Erase Negative Self-Talk* is required reading for anyone interested in living their purpose, passions, dreams, and destiny full destiny full out. If you are serious about achieving true greatness in your life, this book is a must read."

—Martin Fox, "One of the Best Leadership Educators in the USA," Founder and CEO of Center for Global Leadership, CenterForGlobalLeadership.com

"This book is a guide to figuring out your intentions and how to start getting more of what you want. Emily Filloramo's advice is to begin by healing your own stuck and broken parts, and in turn you'll achieve anything you want on your own terms."

—Joshua Rosenthal, Founder and Director, Institute for Integrative Nutrition

"There are parts of us that seem to have a life of their own, whether it be binge eating, drinking, violent outbursts or other struggles. *Erase Negative Self-Talk* confronts with boldness the way to view ourselves with a wide-eyed view. Finally a conscious and insightful way to understand and deal with our ghosts in the closet. This book takes healing to a whole new level. A must read!"

—Francesca Luca-Bastarache, TalkWithFrancesca.com, WUFC Radio 1510AM Boston, The Legends 106.1FM Newburyport

"Emily Filloramo has the ability to help you make sense of your life looking backwards and discovering your life's passion and purpose through the process. You will be amazed at how you can get unstuck and see the benefits of positively reframing your challenges."

—Joel Brown, Founder and CEO of Addicted2Success.com

"A genuine breakthrough in accessing your true core self so you can not only contribute to this world but be happy while doing it."

—Lionel Ketchian, Founder of HappinessClub.com

"Do you feel you're not living up to your potential? Are you stuck and frustrated? *Erase Negative Self-Talk* will help you understand the underlying causes for your failures and slipups. Just reading this book will give you a sense of love, understanding and compassion for yourself."

—David Wood, *The KickAssLife Podcast*, KickAssLife.com

"Emily Filloramo's coaching and advice helped me to eliminate self-imposed obstacles that had hindered my success in my adult life. I now feel unburdened and "unleashed," and it has resulted in me achieving results in my business I did not think possible even a few short months ago."

—Jonathan Twombly, real estate investor and President of Two Bridges Asset Management LLC

Acknowledgements

I am deeply grateful for Doug Osber for seeing my potential and planting the seeds (right after I was laid off in October 2011 after 27 years in corporate America) to embark on this wild, scary and adventurous entrepreneurial journey. One of the most important aspects of my journey was finding the right tribes of people to hang out with so my dreams could come true. This book and my brand, *Be More Extraordinary* would not have been possible without the existence of IvyLife (IvyLife.net), a networking group for Ivy League graduates founded by Chris Colvin and Dale Kramer-Cohen. Thank you Chris and Dale for this wonderful networking group that led me to meet key people who positively steered me towards my soul's calling.

I am very grateful for Jonathan Twombly's and Samantha Foerster's support. Thank you both for providing the unwavering encouragement to keep me moving forward and reaching for the stars. Thank you for the encouraging words I needed to hear when it seemed like I just didn't know where all this hard work was going. You confirmed everything I was feeling about my soul's purpose, the bigger mission and message that I had to get out to the world.

Thank you Ben Sturner for not "rejecting" me when I took the risk of saying hello to you first. You had no idea I wanted to write a book and I had no idea you were close friends with a publisher. The Universe put this all into place and all I had to do was show up when opportunity presented itself. It was meant to be that I stood next to Randy Walker of New Chapter Press at the reception you invited me to.

I owe my deepest gratitude to my publisher, Randy Walker, who believed in me after a single 20-minute conversation and decided that my book was something he wanted to take a risk on—publishing a first-time author.

Rosemary Sneeringer, my awesome editor was my "knight in shining armor" in this writing project. Without your guidance and your talented editing skills, this manuscript would never have been completed in six months!

I thank Jon Morrow, Glen Long, Shane Arthur at BoostBlogTraffic.com for giving me the no-holds-barred critiques of my writing, and for enhancing my writing abilities. Jon is a huge inspiration. He is a quadriplegic who runs a successful 7-figure business. If you think you have limitations (being the prisoner of your own mind), it's relatively nothing compared to what he has to go through day-in and day-out, with only the use of his voice and voice recognition software, with 'round-the-clock nurses tending to his every need. He is one of the happiest people I know. These blogging mentors helped me to become a better blogger and writer. Without them urging me on and giving me critical feedback on my writing, I would not have become a writer—something

I had never realized was in my realm of possibilities—since English is my second language and I hated the struggles I had with reading comprehension and creative writing in school.

I am also deeply grateful for my teachers in the Internal Family Systems training program: Ralph Cohen, PhD LMFT, Ann Sinko, LMFT, Rina Dubin, LCSW. Thank you for the guidance in teaching this wonderful model of psycho-spiritual healing.

And, I am very thankful for my husband Rick and my son Jason for supporting me in this entrepreneurial journey that was full of speed bumps. I love you both dearly.

I appreciate my parents and my siblings for all my childhood experiences. There was a silver lining after all to having the childhood that I had. I love you all. I now know that I was supposed to experience everything the way that I did —all in the name of finding my true calling as a *Be More Extraordinary Magician.*

—Emily Filloramo
2015

About Emily Filloramo

I am a *Be More Extraordinary Magician* who guides you to go from good to great to extraordinary so you can dream big and manifest health, wealth, awesome relationships and happiness in the journey to living to your potential.

How? Through discovering and discarding the emotional gremlins that keep you stuck. I gently guide you to erase deep-seated blocks and install new mental programming so that you can quickly and positively shift your self-image and get the courage and confidence to take your life to the next level.

When I turned 50 years old, I finally connected the dots of my life looking backwards. I realized I was purposely given my miserable childhood and adult experiences in order to heal myself and launch into my current state of unlimited passion, potential and opportunity.

We can't ignore our personal history, but once we unlock key negative memories and overturn the associated faulty beliefs, we can finally release them, make peace with the past, get out of our own way and move on. As a result, all areas of our lives blossom and we truly can become magnets for everlasting love, positive expansion, purpose and passion. If you are a high functioning individual and you are determined, you too can get unstuck, unleashed and become unstoppable, just like I have, by overturning your faulty beliefs.

My unique combination of life experiences, enthusiasm, nutritional expertise, pharmaceutical sales, and professional trainings in psycho-spiritual healing, and the psychology of achieving human potential gives me a one-of-a-kind platform to help you heal mentally and physically from your emotional scars. Now you can overcome self-doubt and confidently express your authentic, passionate and happiest self.

I earned my B.S. in Nutrition from Cornell University, grounding me solidly in the health field, and my 27-year award-winning career in pharmaceutical sales with Pfizer (10 of which were spent in the psychiatry arena) gives me a unique perspective to reveal the unvarnished truth of what it really takes to achieve optimal mental and physical health. Medications for many (not all) conditions are just Band-Aids, they are not the ultimate solution to better living. We need to get to the root causes of the beliefs that hold people back. My signature coaching technique is inspired by professional training in Internal Family System (a cutting-edge psycho-spiritual modality to heal emotional wounds) as well as Neuro-Linguistic Programming (communication and belief change tools to help people reach their potential).

You can learn more about me at www.BeMoreExtraordinary.com and contact me at Emily@BeMoreExtraordinary.com and on Twitter @EmilyFilloramo. I look forward to hearing from you.

Table of Contents

Introduction

Stop Pretending Everything is "Great!"

Get Out of Living in "Quiet Desperation"

*"If you deliberately plan on being less than you are capable of being,
then I warn you that you'll be unhappy for the rest of your life."*
— *Abraham Maslow*

Ann, 40 years old, is thinking, *I'll be happier when . . .*

- "I lose a few pounds and feel more confident and attractive"

- "I find Prince Charming or my husband stops controlling me"

- "My house is nicely decorated"

- "I'm doing something more meaningful with my life and making good money"

Peter, 45 years old, is thinking, *I'll be happier when* . . .

- "I nail the next promotion"
- "My wife stops nagging me and she finally does something about her weight so I am proud to be seen with her"
- "I buy the bigger house"
- "I get the Porsche 911"

Here's the harsh reality you probably already know— neither Ann nor Peter will be *permanently* happier when they get the better-looking partner, more money, social status and "stuff"(unless they're living in poverty).

Philosopher Henry David Thoreau famously said, "Most men lead lives of quiet desperation and go to the grave with the song still in them." One of the most important keys to getting out of "quiet desperation" and happily living a fully charged life is the courage to veer outside of your comfort zone to reach your potential. However, it's hard to be on this journey to overcome mediocrity and dream big if you are emotionally overwhelmed with fears, insecurities, worries and the stresses of everyday life—or if you are consumed with trying to release old emotional scars.

You may have heard it said that we need to be happy *first*, inside, *right now* on the journey to reaching our goals; that if we think something outside of us will make us happy, it's only an illusion or a temporary high. But what if you know this is true and you're still not happy because you're struggling to climb the ladder of success (and live up to your potential), stumbling and sabotaging yourself each time you get two feet from your goal (the "glass ceiling") because deep down inside there are parts of you that don't believe you *deserve* to get what you want. You long to sing every song that is bottled up inside of you, but there are other parts of you that hold you back from unleashing your most authentic self-expression and vulnerability. The fear of your own greatness looms large and that's why your dreams stay smaller than you you're capable of. Do I really deserve to be the leader of this non-profit?" "Do I really deserve to be the vice president of this company?" "Do I really deserve to be with this hot and beautiful woman?"

As you get closer and closer to your dreams, those voices of fear rooted in the past become louder and louder, like the dog that's been peacefully napping and all of a sudden gets startled with the noise of adulation. The dog barks to get your attention—those are your inner voices—wanting to put you back where you came from so you can live out the theme of your life you heard over and over as a child: "You're not as smart as your brother. You're never going to amount to anything. You're not good enough." These fears surface big time when you step out of your comfort zone, and then it feels too scary, so you retreat and shrink back into the small box that you've been living in, pretending to be smaller than you are, so your friends won't criticize you and reject you, and so you don't disappoint yourself when you pass on opportunities.

You desperately want to grow, but your mind—conditioned with irrational fears—keeps you stuck in "average." But if you let these fears stop you, you will derail the rest of your life, holding you back from the bigger "whys" of wanting to give yourself and your family—especially your children—a life that is happy and fulfilled.

You might even want to stay where you are because it just doesn't hurt enough to do something about it. "I'll just keep eating ice cream, I know I have diabetes, it's easier to blame my genes instead of myself." Maybe you have to get cancer or suffer a heart attack to make it hurt enough to change your ways. It might be easier to hide behind excuses. "Middle management is all I am capable of." "I'm not meant to be healthy and attractive." It's ultimately your choice of how much regret you want to have at the end of your life, when you are in hospice or when you watch someone else get the limelight in your company. "I coulda' been that leader *if only* I had the courage . . ." "I coulda' prevented the cancer *if only* I had let go of the anger and resentment I had towards my mother . . ."

Or when you do manifest one of your dreams (get the body you want, make more money, attract the love of your life), you feel like an imposter and then you sabotage and lose what you've gained. This is the hardest part of realizing your dreams—actually *believing* that you are great and that you *deserve* to get what you want.

In order to achieve more, you have to bust out of your comfort zone. Eventually you'll reach a higher comfort zone and then bust through those barriers to reach the next level. You have to want it badly enough to do something about it. Not taking risks mean you stay safe, which means you will be stuck for the rest of your life. But you don't have to stay stuck. I'm going to show you how to get rid of the negative voices and fears for good so you can get the courage to go big.

Perhaps you are financially successful and have all the trappings of success according to Madison Avenue—luxury cars, houses, beautiful designer furnishings and clothes, fancy vacations and exclusive club memberships—but you're still not happy because you're just keeping up with the Joneses while your emotional and spiritual gas tank are on empty. Maybe you've worked so hard to compete with your peers that there's very little saved for retirement or the kids' college education, and you may have even sacrificed self-care for the almighty dollar. Deep down there may be parts of you that unknowingly make you work hard, all in the name of trying to prove something to someone. You might even wonder, "Is this all there is? I thought all this money and status was supposed to make me happier."

If any of these scenarios resonates with you and you feel stuck, not heeding your truths and not living to your potential. If you're feeling like you're driving the bus of your life with one foot on the accelerator and the other on the brake, then your emotions are stuck in the past. The negative messages of old hurts contribute to your fears and insecurities despite your mask of confidence and self-esteem.

Many people are able to wear the mask of confidence to achieve in their profession life, but their relationships, emotional and physical health are a hot mess. They may even be the boss that's so rough around the edges that his employees loathe coming to work.

You can get unstuck and overcome your limiting beliefs and believe you deserve everything you dream about *if* you get the *parts* of you that are stuck in the past unfrozen and unburdened from the old devaluing experiences.

You have the power to heal these emotionally scarred younger parts of you. As a result of healing your parts, you will have the energy and motivation to go bigger and improve other areas of your life. This book is unlike many self-help books on your nightstand because this modality of psycho-spiritual healing —*Internal Family Systems,* developed by Richard Schwartz, PhD, LMFT—goes much deeper to identify and discard the roots of the "weeds" that have overtaken the garden of your beautiful and awesome life.

* * *

You may or may not know you have emotional scars, and some of them can be so subtle (like the birth of your baby sister, displacing you from getting all the love and attention, or not making the cut on the varsity team, or getting sent away to boarding school), yet these could be the very reasons why you are not feeling as alive as you want to feel. These painful memories can leave you with lower-than-optimal feelings and thoughts of *I'm not lovable, I'm not worthy and I'm not enough* and they can cause mood and anxiety issues that keep you awake at night, and relationship conflicts that cause breakups and drive friends and loved ones away. They can be responsible for the fears that stop you dead in your tracks, and make you self-sabotage and fail every time you want to improve some area of your life, such as trying to get healthier and lose weight, starting and growing a new business, making more money or becoming happier.

I meet many people who don't believe in themselves and can't sustain the conviction and commitment to go to the next level. Some are personal development junkies who attend big guru seminars and read self-help books. But their lives don't improve much after expending so much energy, time and money. They learn tactics on how to tackle the pain points on the surface level, and are often given advice that tells them to:

- Let it go, you're not in the past anymore
- Reframe it
- Go around it
- Use willpower
- Say affirmations
- Just believe in yourself and act "as if" you already have the results

The effects of these techniques are often temporary, then they go back to their old states and blame themselves for being a loser. The reason these results are temporary is because the problem is being addressed from the outside-in, like trying to get rid of the dandelions in your garden by chopping the heads off instead of getting your hands dirty and digging deep to pull out the roots and get rid of them for good.

So, if you want *lasting* transformation, instead of wasting your energy addressing the struggles from the outside-in, you need to get your hands dirty, dig into the roots, and tackle the real reasons you feel as you do—the emotional issues—from the inside-out, by accessing the parts of you that are stuck in the past. These are the roots of your "weeds" that you need to dig up and discard. If you don't address the real issues, the garden of your life will never bloom fully and you may end up living in "quiet desperation," staying in mediocrity and pretending to yourself and the rest of the world that "Everything is great!"

You may even know friends and family members who are in total denial that they have wounded parts. "Who me? I'm fine. Yeah . . . I'm a little controlling, arrogant and angry. So what? Look at the company I've built and all the money I've made." In the meantime, their employees are miserable and they do the minimum to collect their paychecks. Some of these controlling and arrogant leaders have a tendency to blame everybody else except themselves when things go wrong. All they care about is their big fat paychecks and their lofty CEO or CFO titles. "I'll show you how big I've become! I'm the kid who grew up in foster care, shamed and humiliated. I've finally overcome my obstacles! I'm going to let everyone know that I'm throwing a lavish 40th birthday party for my wife and make sure that only important people are invited. I'll show those bullies that put me down that they don't belong in my circle."

It's just too painful for these arrogant jerks to look at themselves in the mirror and admit that they are lonely and miserable. It's easy for others to point fingers and call them losers, but in reality they are not losers. They've had subtle (and not-so-subtle) cruel and heartless experiences when they were kids that caused them to be the way they are. It's the fault of their young parts that took the beatings from authority figures, bullies and peers. Those parts are acting out to take the attention away from the pain. They are essentially protecting that person from going back into old wounds. The parts will do anything to keep the lid on, so those agonizing events will not rise up into their consciousness again bringing with them the distress of the rejection, or being beaten or bullied. Yes . . . everything can be traced back to the past. When you understand this, you can have compassion and understanding for the bullies in your life.

The more unresolved wounds someone has, the more self-absorbed they may become because they don't have the emotional capacity to think about the welfare of others. Their minds are preoccupied with behaving in ways that show the bullies and others who have hurt them that "I'm better than you." Sadly, these are the same people who are charismatic, manipulative and narcissistic, and often move into leadership positions in corporate America, politics and entertainment. Their employees and peers incessantly talk negatively about them because they don't feel that their S.O.B. boss, family member or friend really cares about them.

* * *

Let me give you an example of how a part can be created and frozen in time with faulty beliefs from a day-to-day circumstance, not a crushing wounding such as the humiliation of being bullied. (I call these parts *exiles* because we all have them and try to erase them from our consciousness.) Many moms are busy with children, jobs, marriage, house, bills, etc. So imagine if your mom was distracted with a new baby when you turned two years old. You just didn't get as much attention from her after your baby sister was born. So mom not spending as much time with you gets interpreted as "I must be bad. I'm unlovable and unworthy, that's why mom doesn't pay much attention to me anymore."

The reason why you interpret her actions this way is because your brain is in a hypnotic trance between the ages of 0-7. Your negative experience with mom got interpreted literally and imprinted in your brain, and you live life through this filter, "Mom's ignoring me because I must not be good enough." This is the source of your limiting belief. As an adult, you intellectually know that mom was too busy to pay more attention to you. But you as a two year old had no intellectual capacity to understand that. So this part of you got frozen with these faulty beliefs. Mom and dad mostly likely did not have Parenting 101 classes that told them that it's very, very important to reassure you that you are not bad when you don't get attention or when you are punished with a time-out.

Another traumatic event that affects a lot of people is their parents' divorce. Kids end up blaming themselves for divorces. They don't have a clue about the stress of keeping a marriage together. "I must be bad, why else would mom and dad be breaking up?"

As you grew older, these negative beliefs of unworthiness got reinforced over and over again as more challenges came your way. Here are some examples of how this may show up. Johnny can't make friends or make the baseball team. Susie can't get a date for the prom. In adulthood, Johnny can't keep a team together at work and is fired from his middle management job. Susie still can't find a partner that treats her right and is burdened with financial issues. These negative experiences reinforce the original beliefs that, "I'm unlovable, I'm unworthy, I'm not enough" that were acquired when the baby sister was born or when the parents divorced.

These young parts of you with faulty negative core beliefs get frozen in your psyche at the time of the original devaluing experiences because no one was there to tell you, "You are not bad. You didn't cause this." These young parts end up ruling your adult life, they are driving the bus of your life (without a driver's license) to nowhere, hijacking your emotional well-being, success and happiness. These old wounded parts also unconsciously make you do things and feel things you don't like to cover up the pain of the wounds, such as:

- Shopping too much
- Drinking too much
- Eating too much or too little
- Gambling too much
- Getting angry
- Being sad, depressed and/or anxious
- Being afraid
- Staying numb
- Controlling others
- Procrastinating
- Being unable to trust
- Having affairs
- Biting your nails and other compulsive behaviors.

These undesirable behaviors and feelings are *protective* mechanisms to prevent you from accessing the vulnerable emotions and feelings of your young *exiled* parts that experienced the painful events. These behaviors and feelings distract you from the original big and little traumas, to keep you safe from going back into the hornet's nest of re-living the painful parts of your life. This is one of the reasons why there's an epidemic of addictions, sadness, depression, anxiety and other emotional disorders today.

According to The Center for Self Leadership, in the Internal Family Systems Model, the definition of Exiled Parts is:

- Young parts that have experienced trauma and often become isolated from the rest of the system in an effort to protect the individual from feeling the pain, terror, fear, and so on, of these parts
- If exiled, can become increasingly extreme and desperate in an effort to be cared for and tell their story
- Can leave the individual feeling fragile and vulnerable

These old toxic, painful experiences burden you with the heavy suitcase of faulty negative feelings and beliefs. They are the very reasons why you have self-doubt, inner conflict, fears and worries that keep you stuck from living an amazing and happy life. You've been hijacked and are blended in with the wounded parts of you. You will stay stuck unless you *do* address these *protective* and *exiled* parts in a safe way and reprogram them with positive beliefs that are in alignment with the true essence of who you are. As a result of unloading the suitcase of burdens, you can finally allow your expansive, brave and soul-based true Self to show up and reclaim the driver's seat of the bus of your life. The weeds that were strangling you from the thriving garden of life will finally be eliminated for good.

So just imagine...

- Making peace with the past, deleting the voices and the old stories, and gaining a *reprogrammed* mind that no longer holds you back

- Happily moving *forward* . . . released from being in *survival mode*
- No longer afraid, no longer doubting yourself, no longer resisting and procrastinating
- Resiliency to bounce back from challenges, disappointments and rejections
- Feeling and believing you are worthy of success and happiness
- Believing in yourself and able to express the *"you-est"* you without feeling like an impostor
- Clarity, focus and courage to go beyond your comfort zone to manifest success and make a difference
- Renewed enthusiasm and engagement with yourself, with your family (especially your kids), your friends and colleagues
- Looking and feeling more attractive by releasing the weight of the past off your back
- Having the ideal body and the health that reflects your happier and improved self-image
- Feeling sexy, irresistible and younger from the inside out
- Significantly reducing relationship conflicts
- Attracting a better and more ideal partner
- Experiencing success and happiness **now** *while on the journey* to living up to your potential and making your mark in the world

- Living your truth and not caring what others think
- Feeling alive and living happily ever after

* * *

What you believe consciously and subconsciously are reflected in the state of your body, health, and the stagnation in your career, relationships and emotional well-being. When you address the emotional burdens *first*, then the advice in all the other self-help programs will be icing on the cake of the self-help journey. This book will guide you to break the habit of being your average self and let your extraordinary Self out. The *Internal Family System* modality of healing is like "taking your brain out," rinsing off the "dirty" residues of the past and putting it back in, squeaky clean and full of self-love so you can come home to your true Self. It feels so great to be soaring with confidence and self-esteem, fearlessly pursuing the calculated risks to take your life to the next level—with a body you love, a fatter bank account and a partner you are crazy about. That's living life with a permanent grin on your face. When you feel good about yourself and are living a fully charged life, then having status and the material trappings of success will be the roses on the icing on your happiness cake. You'll have the foundation to **stay** at this level, without self-sabotage, without the pretense that "Everything is great!" because everything *will* be great. You'll finally stop settling, get out of mediocrity, live to your potential and make a difference before you die.

Setting the expectations for this book:

Unlike what other self-help books may promise, this book is not intended to give you the false hope that there are instant fixes to your struggles or that you can instantly turn into your most extraordinary self overnight.

This book is intended for psychologically healthy, high-functioning, success-driven people who are ready to go from good to great to extraordinary. If you are experiencing traumatic life events and you need tools to cope and recover, please seek the help of a licensed mental health provider.

In order to permanently erase negative self-talk and become your most extraordinary self, you have to take action and invest the time, energy and money to do the inner work through finding a coach or psychotherapist trained in Internal Family Systems (go to www. Selfleadership.org).

You have to be ready to take risks and you have to have the courage to fail in order to get to the next level. You also have to feel "safe" to unleash the full potential of who you are and not worry about the opinions of others. It's possible to overcome these fears when you work with an Internal Family Systems practitioner.

If you have been working on yourself for a while, Internal Family Systems' modality of healing and Self-leadership can be the "clean up" details to help you finish releasing the old emotional burdens for good. Getting unstuck and unleashed for self-aware people can happen in a relatively short period of time with concentrated deep-dive sessions.

How fast you get results is a function of how fast your inner landscape and your external circumstances are ready for you to change. There are a lot of fears associated with changing the status quo. That's why it's hard to overcome the fears on your own and it's best to seek professional help.

This book will give you the awareness of what it is going to take to unleash your best self. You can start the journey to greatness by following the steps in the Appendices. However, in order to complete the healing process, you need to be face-to-face (in person or via Skype) with an Internal Family Systems therapist to finish the process of unburdening yourself from the vulnerable parts of you that are still holding onto feelings from old significant emotional events. (Something seemingly as benign as getting passed over for the varsity sports team or getting rejected at the junior high school dance can hold you back from fearless self-expression and/or hold you back from getting everything you want.)

Through real client stories, this book will highlight what is possible when you get out of your own way. You will learn what it will take to be on the wild, scary and joyful journey of becoming your most extraordinary self.

Chapter One

Hiding Shame Underneath
the Mask of Perfection
How We Protect Ourselves From Getting
Hurt Again

"You can't connect the dots of your life looking forwards,
you can only connect them looking backwards.
You have to trust that somehow the dots will connect in the future."
—Steve Jobs

It's 2:00 am, and Mary, 41, can feel her heart pounding as the relentless thoughts circle her brain. Another sleepless night of tossing and turning, ruminating on how unfair life is . . . until she's had enough. She tiptoes into the bathroom to pop a Xanax, since the Ambien and Zoloft she took earlier are not helping her to sleep.

Not only is Mary experiencing conflict at work, which put her into depression and anxiety in the first place, but she's feeling even more distraught by the way a certain couple made her feel at dinner earlier that evening.

Both the work conflict and the couple she and her husband had dinner with make her feel unheard, invisible and sad. The people who trigger her tend to go on and on about themselves and brag about their latest acquisitions and trips, seldom taking an interest in what is going on in her life. She feels like she's *not good enough, not lovable enough* and *not rich enough* to belong with the proverbial "Joneses."

Mary feels angry and ridiculous for allowing others to make her feel this way. Why should she care what they think, do or say? Why does it bother her so much? She really shouldn't be affected by how others make her feel, but she can't stop the flood of overwhelming emotions that leave her feeling rejected, ashamed and unimportant. On top of that is the reality that she's created another night of angst, out of proportion to one meaningless dinner. Her anger at herself for her sleep-deprived situation fuels her adrenaline, making it even more difficult to sleep. Finally, night turns into dawn, and Mary gets up, groggy, depressed and feeling horrible, burdened with the weight of all of her confused and conflicted feelings.

Mary was me! Me, 10 years ago, in a state of depression and anxiety that I couldn't fathom. For the longest time, I couldn't figure out why the behaviors of this couple and other self-absorbed people bothered me so much. The answer came after my first visit to a psychiatrist who asked me, "What drama are you reliving from the past through getting triggered by self-absorbed people?"

I said, "Huh??? What are you talking about? It's not my fault self-absorbed people trigger me and make me sad. Why can't they show me they care about me?"

She said, "It's not normal to be so affected by other people's self-absorption."

Then the light bulb went off. I realized I kept hoping and hoping that *one day* these narcissistically inclined people would *validate* and take an interest in me, in the same way that I kept hoping and hoping and hoping that *one day* my father would *validate* me.

My biggest negative childhood trauma was *feeling* invisible and unworthy of my father's love. (I'm not saying he didn't love me; I just didn't *feel* it.) Because kids' brains take everything that happens to them literally, they believe they are the cause of others' poor treatment of them. So anytime I sense that someone doesn't give a hoot about how I feel, the little girl inside of me that had been *exiled* into the dungeons of my psyche feels the pain of invisibility.

* * *

On the outside, I seemed to "have it all," the Ivy League degree, the looks, the successful career, the family, the lovely home with plenty of "stuff" to go in it—especially plenty of designer clothing and shoes in the big walk-in closet. But on the inside, I felt lonely, emotionally and spiritually bankrupt, living in silent despair as an "Asian banana." ("Banana" is one of the slang terms for Asian Americans who have lost their heritage—yellow on the outside, white on the inside.) How did I get to this state of despair and depression? Let me explain.

I was "made in Taiwan" and exported to America at the age of nine, the oldest of four children (one sister and two brothers). My father worked for the Taiwanese government in the Information Services Department. My mother was a homemaker who took on secretarial jobs here and there. My father came home one day and simply told us, "We are moving to America next month. My job just got transferred to Los Angeles." Yikes!! A new country where we knew no one and didn't speak the language?

None of us knew English except my father because he was an English major in college and he wrote for a living for the Taiwan government. So I had to learn English from scratch in the 4ᵗʰ grade in Los Angeles. They just put me into mainstream classes and I had to figure out what was going on. Within a year, I was able to speak well enough to feel like I fit in somewhat. Trying to write an English paper was not so easy, though. It took me until high school to catch up on the reading comprehension and it was painful to go through the verbal section of the SATs. I hated my English classes! It's so ironic that I've become a writer out of necessity, because of being an entrepreneur, with all the blogging I must do, and with writing this book. But it was part of the plan the Universe had in store for me.

After three years of what seem to be relatively good memories for me in Los Angeles, my father came home from work and announced, "We're moving to New York City. My job got transferred again." My heart sank. I was just starting to feel like I fit in. It wasn't easy when I was made fun of for bringing a lunchbox filled with rice and leftovers from the night before. I was embarrassed. The other kids had the usual American peanut butter and jelly sandwiches and potato chips and cookies. Needless to say, I told my mom that I didn't want to bring the Asian lunchboxes to school ever again.

To this day, I still remember the first time I tasted Lay's Potato Chips at nine years old. I kept eating them and eating them, thinking they were the best thing ever. And in the back of my mind, I intuitively knew they weren't good for me. (Maybe that was the driver that got me interested in studying nutrition in college.) Weird how I still remember these experiences. The point is, we all have memories—good and bad—that are sealed permanently into our brain. So whatever good or bad things happened to you, they are lodged in your brain somewhere, waiting for you to access them in the future to heal them.

So I moved to New York City in the middle of 7th grade. Really? Move a kid in the middle of 7th grade and expect her to make friends easily? No way was that possible! Remember how awkward 7th grade was for you? "Where do I belong? Who likes me? Am I cool enough? Do I have the right clothes?" Just imagine trying to fit into a school where you were the new kid on the block, with no friends, and parents who were clueless about life and raising a teenager. My parents lived in survival mode. Their lives were about coping.

When we got to New York, we moved to Corona, Queens. Back in the 70's, this was a lower middle class neighborhood. We lived in a third floor walk-up, two-bedroom apartment with one bathroom and no air-conditioning—for a family of six. It would get so hot on some of those sizzling, hazy, humid summer nights that my siblings and me would fight over who got to sleep on the balcony. On top of this, we moved *again* the following year, in the middle of a school year *again*, to a two-family house in Bayside, Queens that my parents bought with my uncle. This time, it was a much better neighborhood, but we were definitely the poorest family on the block. Moving into a new home and a new school where I was one of few Asians was the start of my real childhood miseries.

Junior high and high school were hell for me in the public school system because I was teased mercilessly with Asian slurs . . . "Chink," "Slitty Eyes" or takeoffs on popular songs, "Let's Wang Chung tonight," or "Look at that China Girl." My parents couldn't afford to buy the latest fashions. I felt so inferior. And I couldn't get braces for my crooked teeth (no money) while all my classmates were getting their teeth straightened. I was embarrassed, didn't smile much and felt rejected, ugly and humiliated.

The prejudice was unbearable and unrelenting. I didn't belong anywhere. There didn't seem to be anyone who was interested in discovering the real me, they just made snap judgments based on how I looked.

I was also subjected to so much discord at home, which was filled with toxic emotionally abusive energy that made me feel invisible, worthless and sick to my stomach. The tension at the dinner table was so thick I would need a sword to cut it. Sometimes there would be criticism about how the dinner was not that delicious. I would cringe and steel myself for the fight that would follow, and eat as fast as I could so I could run away from the dinner table ASAP. Other times, I would be the shield between my father and mother when there were verbal assaults thrown at each other. Remembering this still makes me feel ill.

That same feeling would wash over me when I was singled out for ridicule at school or when I felt alone, afraid and unloved in social situations. For example, in high school, I was at the home of a boy I had a crush on, working together on a high school project. When his mother walked in, she told him to take me home immediately and I interpreted her tone and directive as, *Never bring her to our house again. She's not "white," you shouldn't have a crush on her.* This incident made the high school part of me take on the belief that I was *worthless* and that's why I was asked to leave. Unfortunately, the emotional assaults continued in college with more racially painful scenarios similar to this one, which just reinforced my belief that I was *not enough*, I was *worthless* and *unlovable*. Why else would people treat me this way?

It was humiliating then, and I replayed it in my mind for years to come—those rejection memories can stay with you the rest of your life. No wonder I *felt* ugly and grew up as an *ugly ducking*—because I *believed* I was ugly. The picture of me at 14 years old pretty much sums up how felt for the majority of my childhood.

14 Years Old   17 Years Old   20 Years Old

By the time I was a senior in college, I started to feel a little better about myself. The braces I longed for were off and my teeth were finally straight, I was wearing makeup, but mostly because I left home for good.

Today, I know those kids who teased me didn't intend to be mean, they just didn't know any better. But the other question still remains: Why was my home life so hellish?

Because there was always *lots* of fighting. The tension in my house was palpable, I could sense it as soon as I opened the door. I didn't even have to hear it, I'd know when they were fighting or giving each other the cold shoulder with their oppressive silence. Going to school felt awful and so did coming home—I dreaded them both. There was simply no place for me to have peace and feel good about myself.

As the oldest in my family, I had more responsibility, and I defended my mother every time there was a fight, while my sister and two brothers hid in the bedroom. My stomach goes into knots when I relive those memories.

It didn't help matters that we were the poorest among the middle class families in Bayside, New York. Our house was never maintained because there was no extra money to fix anything. Light fixtures were broken, railings were rusted through, the house paint was peeling, and the lawn was forever full of weeds. No wonder our neighbors gave us dirty looks—we brought the home values down in the entire neighborhood.

It was embarrassing having to walk half a mile several times a week just to purchase groceries, pulling the heavy cart home as if our poverty were on parade. No one else had to do this. Everyone else had cars. I was ashamed that we never had money to eat out as a family. The occasional "treat" was McDonald's. I couldn't wait to get my hands on Filet-o-Fish and French fries. (Now the thought of McDonald's is repulsive—especially since I'm a nutritionist.)

We never took family vacations—no money.

I never went to summer camp—no money.

We were never taken to the playground—no interest.

There wasn't even money for necessities. I was embarrassed that I had so many crooked teeth, that I didn't have the latest fashions and that my clothes didn't match. I *felt* ugly because I *believed* I was ugly. I felt unloved, neglected and ignored.

I had no idea what I had to do or say to get the validation that I craved—that I was lovable and worthy—that I was *enough*.

I was embarrassed to have friends over. The curtains in our house were panels of cheap Mickey Mouse fabric from craft store clearance bins, the rugs were threadbare and the hideous living room couch was emerald green with a fat red stripe down the middle of each cushion. The bathrooms were dated and mildewed from lack of exhaust fans and the towels were threadbare. We used one bath towel for six people.

As I observed other families, I saw that even if there wasn't perfect love, parents still took an interest in their child's schooling and their future so they could support themselves and have a home and family someday, but I never experienced any of that. I *felt* that neither parent really cared how school was going, and they didn't seem concerned that I didn't have very many friends. They may have shown they cared occasionally but the *feeling* remained that "I don't matter." Now I know that they didn't know any better, they had no idea how to parent their children. I often wondered what is must be like to *feel loved* as a child. (I know my parents loved me but that's not the point. As a kid, I didn't *feel* loved.) My father came home from work at 7 pm every day. He would eat dinner and then retreat to the corner to read his books. I don't remember him taking much interest in who I was or what I was interested in. He just wanted to tell me *his* stories from childhood, which I had no interest in hearing about. If I didn't feel so ignored, I might have had the patience to listen. And as for the "family time" we had, as I mentioned before, there would be so much tension at the dinner table I couldn't wait to finish eating and hide in the bedroom.

For most of my adult life, simply thinking of my childhood left me feeling nauseated and anxious. Now I realize through my work as a Be More Extraordinary Magician that my father was more than likely in his own misery because the wounded parts of him didn't allow him to be present for his family. To this day, I have no idea, since I don't have a close relationship with him. I didn't know my grandparents very well so I never had the pieces of the puzzle to put together.

My parents' lack of proper support for their kids meant that a devilish part of me came out when it came to my relationship with my younger sister. Looking back, I'm ashamed of how nasty I was to her. I lectured her on how to do things *my* way. I passed down the family trait, constantly reminding her that she was *not good enough* and *not smart enough.* After all, I'm the know-it-all big sister. The sad thing is she allowed me to dominate her and didn't speak up for herself. She was frozen. Now I feel sorry that she had to live in the shadow of her Wicked Witch sister. She has been forever affected by my treatment of her. Her story is more painful than mine. Let me share why.

As you can probably guess by now, my parents were a little clueless. We didn't go to pediatricians for physicals because we didn't have the money. My parents went broke as soon as we touched down in America when we moved here in 1972. My sister, 8 years old, a year younger than me, had to be hospitalized for a massive ear infection within the first couple of days of landing in Los Angeles—and we had to pay cash for the hospitalization. That was just an omen of more bad experiences to come.

My sister has a genetic disorder called "Turner Syndrome" and my parents had no idea she wasn't growing normally until she went to a doctor at 16 and was told she had the bones of a nine year old. That's why my sister is small and looks younger than her age. And I feel so bad for her that she had to live in the shadow of her older sister who seemed to be better in just about everything. I'm so ashamed for all the wounded parts I *created* in her psyche. We do have a relationship today but it's not close as some sisters are.

Since we didn't have money for doctors, we certainly didn't have money for dental care. My teeth were riddled with cavities. When the toothaches became unbearable, I went to a dentist for the first time at 14 years old. I had 12 cavities, and my sister and I desperately needed braces—she much more than me. My parents finally relented.

Secretly I used to peek inside the family checkbook . . . there was never very much money. My father had a secure job with the Taiwan government in their Manhattan office but he never took any promotional opportunities. Now I realize that my father was *afraid*. The fear he felt obliterated his own opportunities for promotion and he couldn't earn enough money to support his family of six.

As a teen I had so much anger built up inside of me that I started to yell back at my parents instead of skulking into my room to hide. Like a typical teenager, it began with arguments over clothes. I couldn't understand why I had to be humiliated at school wearing cast-off clothes. Wasn't it bad enough that I had to move twice and try to make new friends? I already felt like a freak and my hand-me-down mismatched clothes only made me more of an outcast—and a moving target for mean jokes. I got so frustrated with them, that one day, after holding it in for so long, I yelled, "Why did you bother to have kids if you don't know how to be parents and you can't afford to buy us anything?" I was as shocked as they were at what came out of my mouth, but nothing really happened. What I had just said didn't seem to sink in at all. They weren't going to change.

I was so miserable and fed up with their neglect, after all those years of listening to their fights, it was my turn to be listened to. In the heat of another battle what escaped from my lips was, "I wish you'd never had me, I'd rather be dead," and it hit me that it was true, I did feel "dead to them." Then one evening after the two of them were bickering, I blew up and finally said, "I'm so sick and tired of all the fighting. I can't wait to go away to college, I'm never coming back!"

What I said helped me blow off steam, but it didn't make a dent in how they treated my siblings and me. Ultimately I didn't want to become like them, fighting and yelling all the time, so I stopped trying to get them to be my parents altogether and I became my own.

* * *

I desperately wanted spending money to buy the clothes and accessories that would help me keep up with my peers and be accepted. So as soon as I could get a job, I did. At 16, I took on two jobs. On the weekends I woke up at 4 am to walk a half a mile in the dark to work the 5 to 9 am shift at the local bagel shop. I would get a break for a couple hours at home and then in the afternoon I worked as a supermarket cashier. These two jobs allowed me to escape the tension in the house and have money for halfway decent clothes.

I was often perplexed when I heard some of my co-workers or classmates say, "Our family didn't have a lot of money but there was a lot of LOVE." I would think: *Huh??? You can have love **without** money?*" I couldn't grasp the concept; our family had neither.

Because I hated my life, I knew that studying hard was the only way out of the depressing circumstances I was in. I finished in the top 1% in a graduating class of 1000 and got into Cornell. Cornell is composed of 7 undergraduate colleges. Thank goodness the college at Cornell I got into was designated a New York State school, this meant that since we lived in New York City, my parents qualified to pay for an Ivy League education with state tuition prices. It's like buying a Neiman Marcus education with T.J. Maxx discounts!

Because I was so ashamed and embarrassed about being poor, I faked a stomachache on the day of my high school graduation so I wouldn't have to go. I was convinced that my poverty would be evident to all when my family showed up.

I was so happy when Cornell accepted me, although I was also thinking, *they probably felt sorry for me.* My college application essay was on empathy. I think I wrote about how much I treasure empathy because I didn't feel much of it at home. It's humbling to think that the seeds of my soul's purpose were in the essay I wrote when I was 17 years old. Now my life's work is all about having empathy for my clients after what I've experienced.

Going away to college opened my eyes to another world. I met students who wanted to get to know me, and I was soaking up knowledge in a subject I loved—nutrition. But when it came time to go home on school breaks, I'd only last a day before I'd storm out of the house. I couldn't stand the fighting. I'd take the subway to Port Authority and ride the bus four hours back to college, opening the door to an empty dorm. Other kids had loving families to go home to, I didn't. The loneliness was painful and I'd cry myself to sleep. After sophomore year, I never went home again. I got summer jobs at Cornell and stayed there.

Although I loved my time in college and I enjoyed my studies (earning a Bachelor of Science in Nutrition), I had a hard time relating to the more well-to-do kids. I did my best to hide the fact that I didn't come from much. It was obvious from my naiveté that I didn't belong in the circles of rich prep school and upper-middle-class classmates.

I remember being in the girls' bathroom as one of the prep school girls came in with her care package from her wealthy parents in Greenwich, CT—brand new designer clothing, handbags and chocolate chip cookies. Ugh!! I felt so abandoned and ignored. I never received care packages, let alone phone calls. (No cell phones back then.) And to make matters worse, I tried to get into one of these preppy sororities but I was rejected. It was obvious that I didn't belong because I didn't have the right clothes or purse or shoes and didn't act the right way. I was just replaying bad memories from junior high and high school again. The saving grace was that I did manage to find a group of friends to hang out with that didn't seem to care that I wasn't wealthy.

However, I kept experiencing the racial slurs of being Asian every time I would go to fraternity parties. I would hear the boys whispering in the corner, "Are you going to ask that China girl to dance?" That triggered the little girl inside of me that was already hiding in the dungeons of my psyche from my junior high school days. She got triggered all over again with the same shame and embarrassment of being Asian. Even today, this part of me still thinks whenever I meet new people, *Do they like me? I'm different, I'm Asian. Do they have any prejudices against me? Am I good enough?* I know it's not rational to think this way but it still happens because of all of my toxic memories.

I often fantasized how much *more* I would have enjoyed Cornell if I weren't so miserable and if I had a clue about life. I don't remember learning anything about how to "make it in life" from my parents; their lives were about subsistence. When friends would talk about the wisdom their parents passed down to them, they would say, "My parents used to tell me _____," and give an insightful nugget of good advice, and I realized had nothing to finish that sentence with!

* * *

After completing my studies in nutrition at Cornell, I was not interested in working as a registered dietitian. Making menus for sick people in hospitals and nursing homes was not my idea of a fun job. I did manage to land a position in retail sales as an assistant manager for a women's clothing store, Casual Corner. This gave me the sales experience I needed to land my next job, working as a pharmaceutical sales rep for Pfizer. I ended up staying with Pfizer for 27 years, selling just about every blockbuster drug they made: Lipitor, Viagra (yes, I used to talk about erectile dysfunction every day), Zyrtec, Zithromax (Z-Pak), Aricept, Zoloft, Pristique and Lyrica, among others.

I loved being in sales. Now I realize that I loved getting the *validation* and the *attention* I never got as a kid, especially from the male doctors I called on. I felt loved. I felt that my life mattered. I felt accepted. Getting attention from men was a nice "substitute" for the love I didn't feel from my father. Again, I'm not saying he didn't love me, I'm stating that I didn't *feel* it. (In order for all of us to grow into mentally healthy adults, it's important for us to *feel* love from our parents.) I barely spoke to my parents or my siblings in my 20's, 30's and early 40's, because it simply triggered too many painful memories. It was just easier to push it all down and keep my beach ball of pain under water.

I remember when my very first boss asked about my family. I told him, "I don't have anything to do with my family. I don't talk to my parents." At that time, I didn't think about how *odd* my answer was. He dropped the subject like a hot potato and never asked another question about my family or my childhood.

Now I know through the work that I do that I numbed my painful childhood experiences by becoming an *overachiever* and a *perfectionist* who liked to *shop* for designer things. (There's a saying that perfectionism is "Self-hatred wrapped in a pretty box.") I swept the bad memories under the rug, telling myself. "I'm over it!" and just shopped until I could fill my house and wardrobe with nice things so that no one would suspect that I grew up poor. Now I know that this was my way of silently showing the rich sorority girls in the dorm bathroom who rejected and humiliated me that, "I'm 'rich' now, I can buy nice things just like you!"

Overachieving, *perfectionism* and *shopping* were the *protective* parts of me, protecting the *exiled* young parts of me from getting triggered again by the shame, humiliation and embarrassment of not keeping up with the rich kids. So by filling my house and dressing my body in the right designer accoutrements, it was the modern adult way of keeping up with the rich kids—the "Joneses"—so that the shamed *exiled* parts of me didn't get stirred up.

Two years after I started working for Pfizer in Connecticut, I met my husband Rick, an architect, on the tennis court when I was 24 years old. We decided to get married two years later. To minimize family contact, instead of having a traditional wedding, Rick and I decided to elope because I didn't want my father to walk me down the aisle. Just the thought of that made me feel sick because of all the painful memories of my parents' horrible fights. Besides, the wedding could have turned ugly if a triggered part of me showed up and decided to run the show. (On the rare occasion that I did visit my family and a triggered nasty part of me took over, my husband would say, "Who are you? I don't recognize you— you are so mean to your family!") So to minimize the agony, it was just easier to elope and to live in the suburbs, burying myself in work and forgetting that my family existed.

I made a good living as a pharmaceutical rep, and that's what allowed me to buy lots of "stuff." Now I know that inwardly I did it to show that chorus of "rich kids," "Hey, I'm not that poor little girl in mismatched clothes anymore. I have a pretty house. I have money now! See? I belong. I'm one of you guys. Please let me into your social circle." I'd get a temporary happy high and then come crashing down soon after. I didn't know then that I was buying "stuff" to bury emotional pain. Now I know now after my professional trainings in Internal Family Systems that this is what I was doing. (Now that I'm healed, I don't have the patience anymore for shopping. But if I need something, I buy it for the right reasons, not to soothe emotional pain.)

My *shopping too much* and *perfectionistic* parts were *protectors*, similar to how others have their undesirable behaviors such as eating too much, smoking too much or drinking too much. My behaviors kept me emotionally safe and *protected* from ever accessing the young and wounded *exiled* parts of me that held the shame, humiliation and rejection from the experiences of discrimination in junior high, high school and college.

The job of *shopping* and *perfectionism* parts were to make sure that I got approval from others that *I was good enough* through my *stuff* and through my accomplishments. The result of these behaviors showed that I belonged in the upper middle class and that I was no longer the poor little girl who was ashamed that she couldn't afford to dress in the latest fashions, who was ashamed that she had parents who couldn't afford to furnish the house with decent furniture.

Truth be told, I was embarrassed to be Asian. I tried to be as American as apple pie, but my almond eyes couldn't hide my ancestry. I tried to consciously erase the history of my wounded younger *exiled* parts that were hidden in my subconscious, but they wouldn't go away. The more I attempted to sweep my past under the rug, the more it insisted on haunting me. It was like trying to keep that beach ball under water with all your strength, but the beach ball keeps popping up. Or to put it another way, the anger from my old wounds was at a low simmer for a long time and in my 40's it was brought to a boil because these young parts of me had been ignored for too long—abandoned with the old memories of negativity and tension. These parts were just waiting to boil over, just like that beach ball that can't stay down forever.

Unfortunately, we can't erase our old wounded parts. We can only keep them out of our consciousness by pushing them down. These parts are just waiting to haunt us. So for me, the catalyst came in the form of a toxic work situation. This became the trigger to send me into depression in my early 40's. (I'm 52 now.) My psyche couldn't hold down the submerged beach ball anymore. It was suffocating. It had to come up for air. The depression was my *exiled parts'* way of telling me, "Do something, we're hurting. When are you going to heal us? We're stuck in the past with feelings of shame, humiliation and unworthiness."

In addition, these exiled parts also held me back from believing that I'm "a great person." I try to accept it intellectually but it is hard for me to let it soak in emotionally. It had been difficult to understand that others now see me as a happy, bright, kind and energetic person, when there was a voice echoing in the back of my head saying, "Really? You think I'm great? But I was such a nasty, angry, depressed and embarrassed ugly-duckling Asian kid who didn't fit in anywhere—never feeling lovable, worthy and beautiful." Without any validation as a kid that I was "great," the younger parts of me still wonder . . . "Really?"

So with the realization that my past threw me into depression, the psychiatrist prescribed meds to take the edge off, and then she sent me to a practitioner who helped me heal my younger exiled parts. I learned that my real soulful *Self*, full of love and compassion, had the power to heal these old wounded parts that were holding onto the shame, humiliation, embarrassment, un-lovability and unworthiness of my earlier years.

The Internal Family System modality of healing allowed me to heal myself. In this system, the coach or therapist is not the healer, they just guide their clients with the right questions. Since not everyone has access to an Internal Family Systems practitioner, the goal of this book is to give you the tools to start your own journey to unburdening the parts of you that keep you stuck so you can go from good to GREAT! (You will need to complete the process of healing through seeking the help of an Internal Family Systems' therapist. www.Selfleadership. org)

What's really ironic is that at the time I was in the throes of my depression, I kept thinking *Life is not fair! I don't deserve this. Get me out of this pain. What is the meaning behind all of this? Everyone keeps telling me I'll find a silver lining to all of this.* I didn't believe them—a silver lining?

Well . . . almost 10 years later, becoming a *Be More Extraordinary Magician* is the silver lining. (Sometimes you do have to wait several years to see the silver lining behind the traumas.) I would have no business calling myself the *Be More Extraordinary Magician* had I not gone through my painful emotional journey. Just like Steve Jobs said, "You can connect the dots of your life looking backward."

After I healed these young wounded parts by reliving my home life and the memories of being discriminated against, I gave them the love they needed. Then I took these parts out of the past and into the present with me. They are now loved by me and are no longer holding me back from being happy in the present, in the journey to living up to my potential. When my parts felt loved by me, I overcame my depression and anxiety. Depression and anxiety were just parts of me that showed up to keep me safe from my *exiled* parts that felt unworthy. Internal Family Systems (IFS) is a beautiful and powerful model of looking at your behaviors and feelings in a non-pathologizing way. (You'll learn more on the specifics of IFS in Chapter Four.) I wrote this book to share with you the concepts behind this deep, powerful and revolutionary approach to healing and Self-leadership, based on the Internal Family System modality developed by Richard C. Schwartz, PhD, LMFT.

As a result of my healing, I realized that my parents did the best they could and I have forgiven them. That means now I can be in the same room with them without getting triggered. I also have very little interest in shopping and I no longer shop for the wrong reasons. I wake up with joy every day because I have a mission to accomplish. That mission is to get the message out to you and the rest of the world about this next generation cutting-edge personal development healing technique that helps you manifest health, wealth, great relationships and happiness by unburdening the gremlins of your past.

But wait . . . there's more to my story.

* * *

My husband, Rick, was 35 years old when I married him at 26. We were living the" dream newlywed life," working in jobs we loved, living in a beautiful home (with me buying lots of stuff to fill it with) and we even had extra money to travel and enjoy ourselves. Three years later I was pregnant at 29. Five months into the pregnancy, he came running into the bathroom while I was busy in the shower admiring my pregnant belly. Then he collapsed, suffering a massive heart attack. Life changed in an instant on that fateful day in July 1992 when I had to get my naked body out of the shower with a blob of soap in my hair and call 911.

As I nervously waited for the doctor's assessment of what was going on with my husband, I kept wondering why this medical emergency was happening to us when we were so young, with our whole lives ahead of us. My mind was racing with terrified thoughts. *Will my unborn son have a father? Will I be a single parent? Could I end up on the streets?*

Fortunately, Rick did pull through and came home a few days later, but those niggling fears of poverty and abandonment came home with me too. It was a cold, harsh reality to always be wondering: *Is today the day I become a widow?*

My entire worldview had changed almost overnight. I resented Rick for not taking care of his health, and for all the times I was responsible for his caretaking. I didn't want to have any more children "just in case." Unfortunately everything became "just in case," as I no longer felt financially secure because he didn't have much life insurance. We didn't even think about buying more life insurance since the baby hadn't been born yet. And of course after his heart attack, no insurance company in their right mind was going to write an insurance policy on someone who had a heart attack at age 38.

With Rick's illness, leaving my job and staying home to take care of my son was no longer a remote option. I needed to work for the rest of my life. What if Rick dropped dead and I had a couple of kids to bring up by myself? I just couldn't fathom doing that. The fear of being a destitute single mom kept me from ever considering having another child. After watching my parents struggle financially to raise four kids, that was the last place I wanted to be—having children I couldn't afford.

My life was split into "life before heart attack" and "life after." And in the "after life" my job became the one thing I could always depend on to give me a solid foundation. I loved everything about it: the exhilaration of the selling experience, my colleagues, meeting and connecting with new people, and the fact that members of the medical community seemed to enjoy interacting with me—and quite often took me under their wings.

Yet, even though my job seemed solid, my husband's health wasn't. During the fifteen years following his heart attack, Rick was constantly in and out of the hospital for cardiac and digestive issues. He underwent two angioplasties, a quadruple bypass and another major surgery to control his acid reflux. We visited the emergency room at least five or six times a year.

I missed my sister's wedding because he ended up in an emergency room during a business trip to the rural backcountry of Bangor, Maine. He had to tap the shoulder of the man in front of him on the airplane to have him tell the pilot not to pull away from the gate, that he needed an ambulance because of his severe chest pains. He ended up with his second angioplasty. And to top it all off, a few years later, my son and I were on an airplane trying to get home to Connecticut from the West Coast while Rick was on the operating table having emergency quadruple bypass surgery. I just went numb during all these times of crisis.

I told Rick over and over again that he could improve his health with nutrition, but he didn't buy the idea that the right foods could heal his heart and severe digestive issues. Ironically, he never had any weight issues so it certainly wasn't "apparent." (It didn't matter that he's married to a Nutritionist. Who listens to their spouse anyway?) He wanted to believe that the next pill that a drug company dreamt up was going to "cure" his problems. (Doctors are not trained in holistic healing and only 10% of the medical schools require doctors to take an introductory nutrition course. Very sad.)

When Rick finally got "sick and tired of being sick and tired," he hired two separate nutritionists who essentially told him exactly what I had been telling him for 15 years—clean up the diet. The good news is he listened to the nutritionists and has made great strides in healing from his heart and digestive issues. (No one is ever "cured" of heart disease; it is a condition that is managed.)

But I still kept wondering why this trauma happened to me at such a young age—my life had been turned upside down, and Rick's condition created limitations on what we could do as a family. Events were always dependent on whether his stomach felt well, and travel was out of the question. He wouldn't step on an airplane anymore because of the old traumas of being trapped on an airplane with severe chest pains or gastrointestinal problems.

When his health emergencies kept happening, I would ask, "Why me? Why am I taking care of someone with heart disease at the same time as I'm raising a child? I thought caretaking your spouse didn't happen until you were old and gray. What did I do to deserve this?"

As I kept living life in the Connecticut suburbs after college, I knew in the back of my mind that *someday* my past was going to come back to haunt me. How, I didn't know. So by the time I reached my 40s, I was living in a numbed-out state with a husband who could drop dead at any moment and leave me a single mother. But that someday occurred, as I described in the beginning of this chapter, in my early 40's with sleepless nights triggered by a situation at work. I wish I could tell you the details of what happened but I have to keep my lips sealed otherwise the lawyers will come after me.

I'd slunk into a deep, dark depression and anxiety, and I ended up having to take three months of "mental disability" from work because the beach ball of the past couldn't stay underwater anymore. And that's when I ended up on the psychiatrist's couch and she asked, "What drama are you reliving from the past through this toxic situation from work?" My psychiatrist said that any time someone pushes my buttons, it is usually a replay of childhood traumas, especially the memories of witnessing those hideous, cruel fights between my parents and the shame and embarrassment of growing up Asian. Those *exiled* young parts of me couldn't take being ignored anymore.

Suffice it to say that because I had swept so much of my past under the rug, I was in total denial. I had no idea that I needed to address it. I thought I was *fine. There's nothing wrong with me. I'm living the good life. Leave me alone!* But my deteriorating mental state could not be ignored because it was taking a toll on my body. I had migraine headaches for the first time and my blood pressure was borderline hypertensive, on a

5 foot 2 inch, 100-pound frame. The stress of my toxic thoughts and feelings were showing up negatively in my emotional state and my physical health. My little girl parts that had been *exiled* into the dungeons of my psyche were screaming for help!

So that's when the psychiatrist sent me to a healer that had me "re-parent" my wounded parts that felt *worthless, unlovable* and *not enough*. After a few sessions, my depression and anxiety started to diminish and eventually went away for good. My exiled parts finally were unstuck from the past and were safe and loved by me. I reframed my own story: that the Universe decided to throw these *lemons* my way because it knew I was capable of handling them and eventually making *lemonade* out of these bad situations. My husband's illness and my depression sure had the effect of humbling me. Maybe it was the medicine I needed for my perfectionist tendencies, to show me that I couldn't live life the way I wanted. I was given these bad experiences so when clients tell me about their struggles, I get it, I've been there.

* * *

In 2011, another shoe dropped to shatter my already tenuous sense of security. After 27 years in pharmaceutical sales with Pfizer, I was laid off. In my working life, I'd always counted on very secure income, and I'd been close to full retirement, since I started at the company so young. Now the rug had been pulled out from under me, two years shy of a very large lump-sum pension. Ouch!

In the months that followed, I was situationally depressed, which led to exaggerated fears: No job, widowhood eminent at any moment, never enough life insurance, $180,000 left to pay in college tuition for my son (with no financial aid) . . . These thoughts circled my brain and I couldn't shake them off.

Then a close friend said to me, "Why don't you launch your own nutrition coaching business? That's what you're really passionate about." My knee-jerk reaction was to laugh it off. Start my own business? With what money? With what security if it all fell apart? No, I felt too much urgency about my situation—I had to get another job that paid well—I just had to.

I'd made myself a home in the pharmaceutical industry, it was all I had known for 27 years. So I applied for jobs similar to the one I'd held with Pfizer, but as soon as prospective employers figured out how old I was, they didn't want much to do with a 49-year-old woman who might not be around too long.

So as I searched for jobs online, my friend's words about starting a business stayed with me. The more I thought about them, the more they started to sound like a calling. After four months of job hunting, I procured an interview for a position I really wanted, yet I went into it thinking: *If I don't get this, it's not supposed to happen, and then it's "meant to be" for me to launch a business instead.*

When I didn't get that job, I wasn't totally devastated because it pointed me in the direction I needed to go. I could have stayed bitter and depressed, maybe even landing another corporate job, but instead I decided to pay attention to the signs and I took the risks I needed to launch my business. I had already spent a long, long time feeling as if the ground beneath me was unsteady. Enough was enough.

That's when the old "Why me?" negative story started to turn into "Why *not* me?" While I couldn't change the cards I was dealt, I could win with the cards I had by making the best out of the situation. Every negative experience gave me the empathy I needed to hold the space for my clients to feel understood and to heal. Without these trials, I'd have no business being a *Be More Extraordinary Magician.* I've had 50 years of a "Ph.D. in life experience" that I bring to my clients to help them heal and unleash the most confident and authentic version of themselves, so they can have the courage to leap and go big in their personal lives and in their careers.

In March 2012, I jumped in with both feet to learn everything I could about being an entrepreneur, spending massive amounts of money on mentors (we're talking high five figures here) and making connections with people who were very happy to advise me. Failure was never an option. I was willing to take the plunge because I believed in myself. (Healing from your inner demons gives you tremendous strength to "jump off the cliff" and take big risks.) Finally, in July 2012, I launched Executive Image Nutrition LLC, a consulting business aimed at tailoring personalized, sustainable, slimming and health-promoting plans suitable for each client.

While business was good, I knew it wasn't as great as it could be, but I couldn't figure out how to articulate my uniqueness in a sea of health and wellness coaches. Then, in February 2013, I read a business blog post that said, "Your deepest wound is your truest niche," and "Your mess is your message," and I knew what I had to do to shift the direction of my business. I was aware that the real reason why many people couldn't sustain a healthy lifestyle was not because they didn't know how to eat broccoli and drink green juices, but because the underlying *exiled* young parts living in the dungeons of their psyche were holding them back from adopting healthy habits for life.

Just as I had my shopping and perfectionism *protectors* protecting me from accessing my wounded young parts, my clients with chronic health and weight issues were using food to bury their emotional pains and to protect them from accessing their *exiled* young parts.

The more I watched my clients sabotage themselves back to their old weight after they finished coaching with me, the more frustrated I became. They needed to address the *real* problems: their low self-image from the emotional baggage they'd swept under the rug. They kept "pushing" themselves, and when their fitter body became better than their self image, it ultimately didn't feel right to them, and they would invariably sabotage themselves back to their old weight. This is why 95% of dieters fail again and again, and gain all the weight back and with interest after six months. And it keeps the diet industry profitable forever because the real issues are never being addressed. (You'll learn more about how your *exiles* show up as health and weight struggles in Chapter Seven.) So my nutrition clients led me to get myself trained in the breakthrough healing and self-leadership modality of Internal Family Systems so that I could be the catalyst for success and happiness in all areas of their lives, not just their health.

I finally "connected the dots of my life looking backwards" just like Steve Jobs said during his famous Stanford University commencement. I have a new narrative for why things happened the way they did. The "lightning rod" of my life purpose had struck. I had go through all of my painful childhood and adulthood experiences in order to realize that my gift is in doing the "inner demon" work with clients to unburden them of the faulty beliefs and feelings that keep them stuck in a life without true happiness. Nothing brings me more joy than when I see the positive shift in my clients' self-image, when their *exiled* young parts are healed and loved and they realize the light bulb of their real selves just got turned on. That's when so many aspects of their lives shift and fall into place, just like everything fell into place for me when my exiled parts were healed. When we upgrade our self-image, we can have the body and health we deserve, our career ceilings can be lifted, financial abundance can increase, our relationships can improve, and most importantly, our happiness set point can be permanently raised.

We don't have to leave our dreams tucked away in a drawer, waiting for the day when we become "happier, thinner, richer and prettier." We don't have to waste years asking, "Why did bad things happen to me?" when we could be asking, "Why *not* me? What are the lessons?"

Emotional and physical well-being are for the most part **not** achieved through the Band-Aid of prescription medicines, it is through *loving ourselves unconditionally.* It's kind of ironic that I'm saying this since I was in the pharmaceutical business. I'm not saying that there isn't a place for prescription medicines, there is. But if more people did the work to unburden themselves of the old traumas (some are seemingly benign but they nevertheless play a big part in keeping you stuck from playing big) and are able to love and believe in themselves, we probably wouldn't have the epidemic of mental and physical illnesses that we do. People need to *stay* sick in order for the drug companies and all the other sickness-related industries to be profitable. Because many people make excuses and don't want to prioritize their emotional and physical well-being and do the work to break free from the past, they turn to prescription medicines since slick Madison Avenue ads make them believe that the key to solving their problems is through pills. Unfortunately, it isn't.

My pharmaceutical sales experience, nutrition expertise, years of dealing with my husband's chronic illnesses and the work I did getting over my own demons means that I understand what it takes to achieve optimal emotional, physical and spiritual health. I have a deep understanding of mental health through spending the last 10 out of 27 years of my career at Pfizer selling antidepressants, anti-anxiety and bipolar medicines. So when people tell me about past or present mood challenges, I get it.

Better living is not through pills per se. Better living is through doing the emotional work of overturning our faulty core beliefs of "I'm not lovable, I'm not worthy, I am not enough" into "I'm lovable, I'm worthy and I'm enough." I love working with clients who know they could be achieving more and are ready to take the scary steps to go from good to great to extraordinary! I will share some of these fascinating stories of transformation in the upcoming chapters.

If Pfizer had not laid me off and I had my cushy pension, my original plan for retirement was to let my pension grow and go work at Nordstrom. What was I thinking? I would not be in my current state of joy if that plan happened. I would have been bored and miserable because I would have settled for mediocrity. For me, selling clothes would not have allowed me to unleash my full potential. So just as I didn't settle for my definition of a boring life of retirement working at Nordstrom, you shouldn't have to settle either for going through life with the status quo on "autopilot." (There's nothing wrong with working at Nordstroms. It's just not for me since my goals are a little more ambitious. Your goals don't have to be as ambitious as mine. It can simply be having the health to take care of your grandchildren.)

Here's what I've learned so far from my first 50 years of living:

- We can't sweep our emotional baggage under the rug . . . it will come back to bite us, guaranteed. Our body and mind remembers every negative, devaluing experience. The past will show up in the present in the form of being stuck in your career and finances, mood challenges, physical illness and/or relationship conflicts.

- When we undergo less-than-happy experiences, they are purposely given to us for the evolution of our souls.

- There's a silver lining to all the bad . . . it's just hard to see it when we are in the middle of it. We just have to trust that it will be all right in the end when we emerge from the dark tunnel of despair.

- There is a true Self in all of us that can emerge by unloading our dark pasts so that we can show up and *be present* for every opportunity and for everyone around us.

- The healing starts when we address the suitcase of emotional burdens and become more present with love and compassion instead of living life through our "wounded parts."

I've made the lemons of my life into a unique flavor of lemonade that only I can offer. If I can emerge out of my dark tunnel thinking that *Life isn't fair,* you can get out of yours too. So I hope you didn't pre-judge me because I "seemed to have it all" from the outside, because you didn't know my full story . . . until now. Underneath my facade of "perfection" were feelings of insecurity, shame and worthlessness.

The Universe has bigger plans for me and for you, that's why this book found its way to you. If you decide to take the action to go after your dreams, the dreams will be easier to realize if you heal the parts of you that are stuck in the past and holding you back, especially the parts that hinder you from being able to kiss yourself and say into the mirror "I love you! You are perfect the way you are!"

The rest of this book will focus on helping you understand why your negative toxic experiences from your youth created parts that hold you back from high self-esteem and confidence. If you feel stuck in any area of your life, it's not your true Self that's driving the bus of your life, it's your parts that have hijacked the driver's seat because they took on extreme beliefs and feelings to protect you. Unfortunately these protective parts often do so with their undesirable feelings and addictive behaviors in an effort to block out reliving the feelings of the old devaluing experiences. Internal Family Systems' cutting edge healing methodology is very deep and powerful. It doesn't put a Band-Aid over the bullets of your old devaluing experiences, it gets the bullets out and it heals the wounds at the source in a gentle way. When you get the bullets out, you can overcome your fears and self-doubts and boost your confidence and self-esteem so you can dream big and manifest the life you've always dreamed you could have.

I share my story to inspire you to see what's possible for **you** if you let the past go, get out of your own way, and *own* your uniqueness so you can unleash *all* of you. After all, "There is only **one** you, everyone else is taken!"

Chapter Two

Ghosts of the Past Haunt You in the Present
Why Your Wounded Child Parts Hijack You from Moving Forward

"Amazing things happen when you realize that your belief systems shape your reality."
-Vishen Lakhiani

As I mentioned in the introduction there are so many of us who are trying so hard to push ourselves to the next level, constantly searching for the next thing that is going to make us feel better about ourselves. Many of us reach a point where we "hit a wall" and can't go any further because we're out of energy and the our motivation has waned. We may even be pushing so that we can live up to Madison Avenue's images of the good life. It's human nature to want to do this, and continue to act like we're still in high school, comparing ourselves to others—except that the stakes have gone up—instead of the trendiest clothes, now it's the big houses and the luxury cars we purchase to impress other people, to show them that we're arrived and that we're good enough. After all, feeling we're *good enough* is the major hidden motivator for many people. You'll see how this plays out in the stories I'm going to share with you.

Some of us just seem so "perfect" from the outside but deep down we feel like a frauds, just waiting for the day the bubble bursts and someone finds out the real truth about what our lives are like behind closed doors. You are not alone, many of us do feel stuck, lonely and disconnected, playing it safe, unable to make decisions and spinning around in circles. It feels like nothing good happens to us while everyone else seems to be having a better time.

If you've been driven by the thought that happiness is always one more goal away, that "Once I make more money / buy my dream home /find a partner /lose the last 10 pounds . . . I will feel better," (only to be disappointed when each "thrill of victory" leads to "the agony of defeat") then it's time to take stock of your life. Momentary thrills can no longer stave off those deep-seated feelings of inadequacy that keep you from success.

For many, the demons of their past are driving them and they're not even aware of it. You may find that certain people push your buttons or a part of you lashes out spontaneously and you wonder, *"Where did **that** come from?"* Or you begin a new love or business relationship with joy and high hopes, only to find yourself repeating old patterns because the "old you" and the "old energy" took over and attracted the wrong type of romantic partner and business opportunity *again.*

If any of these sound familiar, you'll get some insights from the story of Matt, a client who went all the way down the rabbit hole because his wounded parts were screaming to be heard. (Matt's, and other clients' defining details have been changed to protect their identities.)

* * *

Matt is a good-looking, 47 year old with salt and pepper hair that reminds you of George Clooney, only he's carrying around an extra 20 pounds of beer belly. He looks outwardly successful, but deep down, he's miserable. Life is just too stressful. Matt has a beautiful, kind wife, and two sons, ages 8 and 10, and he lives in a lovely Colonial house in a well-to-do suburb with the proverbial "picket fence."

Matt went to Stanford for undergrad and Wharton (University of Pennsylvania) for his MBA, after which he was hired by a company that creates software for investment banks. He worked his way up for over 20 years and became one of the VPs of this company, making multiple six figures. Although he has all the trappings of success—nice cars, nice house and the ability to take luxury vacations, Matt has always been conscientious about saving 20% of his take-home pay (unlike his peers who blew every penny they made), and this cushion allowed him to follow his dreams and go to the next level of his career.

Matt was really good at his job but hated the grind of managing people and the office politics. After 20 years with this company, he couldn't take it anymore and quit to start his own firm doing the same thing. He knows he can service clients better than the company he once worked for.

It's been two years since he started his company and he has very few clients. His two clients are small banks, not enough to replace the salary he was making working for someone else. (He currently brings in $60K.) No one knows this, but fortunately he has enough savings to pay his living expenses while he tries to make himself a success.

Matt attends many high-level networking events and is often asked how his new business is going. His usual response? "It's great!" But secretly Matt prays that no one finds out he only has only two clients. At these meetings, Matt has a hard time confidently expressing the mission of his company and asking for introductions to others who could lead him to his next client. He's afraid of sounding like a pompous jerk or desperately looking for business. Because he has no confidence talking about the merits of his new firm, he is always eager to help others with their businesses to deflect how he is really feeling.

Matt is very afraid of failing at this venture. He has gotten in his own way because he never believed that he was "as great and as smart" as his peers have always told him. Negativity is his middle name. A failure like this will reinforce his **real** beliefs about himself, that *I'm a loser, I'm a fraud* and *I'm not worthy of success.*

Matt is smart and he's aware. He has spent years in psychotherapy and has read countless self-help books—and still he's not really that happy. When he thinks about it, he didn't enjoy reliving the old memories during therapy. He often felt worse leaving a therapy session than when he went in.

Deep down, he felt he was going in circles. Realistically, he admits therapy made him feel mentally stable but not authentically happy. The antidepressants he was prescribed took the edge off but they didn't solve his problems. Neither did attending self-help seminars. Matt got pumped up while he was there but went back to his old state pretty quickly. He was disappointed and discouraged that he never could implement the lasting changes he was hoping for. Now Matt has a new goal that will "save" him. He keeps thinking, *If I just made millions from my own business, I would be happy.*

Let me give you a peek inside of what is really going on with Matt that has him stuck.

* * *

Matt is only at 5 out of 10 on the happiness scale. This is a question I ask my clients to rate themselves so I get a quick snapshot of where they stand emotionally. "One" means you're ready to jump off a bridge, "10" means you're jumping for joy.

Matt would like to be happier but he has no idea what that feels like and he doesn't know if it's even possible for him. His self-loathing and low self-esteem show up in the way he treats his body. He eats junk food, too many fried and greasy things and drinks beer to soothe his anxiety. He angers easily, carries 20 extra pounds and has high blood pressure. (And a porn addiction his wife doesn't know about.)

He knows he should be taking care of himself but he doesn't *feel* like it. Besides, the pills will take care of the blood pressure. He *thinks* about eating better but he reasons that he couldn't eat salads in front of his friends on Wall Street. They'll just make fun of him for eating like a "sissy." And those steak and wine dinners sure taste good, especially ending it with his favorite—cheesecake. His thought process is, *Screw the diet, eating salad is just going to make me more miserable. Besides, everyone else is carrying around a beer belly too, I'm not alone! I don't look that bad.*

When Matt's at home, he has a tendency to snap at the kids and his wife, not every day, but often enough that they walk on eggshells, on guard, waiting for the next outburst. When he does get angry, afterwards he asks for forgiveness and hates himself when this ugly part of him comes out and makes him lose his temper. When we examined his past, it was apparent that his angry outbursts were just a reflection of the anger he's holding inside from old toxic experiences. Anger is a way for childhood parts and depression to express itself, especially in men, since men in our society are not supposed to feel many emotions, although anger and numbness are deemed acceptable for men to express.

Matt's childhood wasn't ideal. His parents didn't get along and fought all the time. They divorced when he was five. Matt never felt loved or worthy—he felt abandoned and rejected.

Matt understands why he feels this way from years of therapy. He's emotionally stable but he's not "cured" of his self-loathing. He does say positive affirmations every day and is grateful for all that he has. However, the *feelings* of negativity and the "inner voices" never quit—they haunt him like ghosts lurking in the background.

He asks himself after all those years of therapy, *Now what? I can't change the history of my past. How the heck do I use what I learned about myself in therapy to take my life to the next level? I'm just left hanging. Nothing was ever resolved. I know I'm capable of so much more but these voices get in the way.*

So these ghosts of the past show up in the present. His suitcase is overloaded with the dirty laundry of old emotional baggage. He needs to empty out the suitcase before anything good can happen to him. When the heavy burden of dirty laundry is taken out of the suitcase, there will finally be room for good things to happen. There is no bandwidth to take in opportunities when it's taken up with energies of the past. That's just the way the Universe works.

The burden of the suitcase has him going through the motions of his life. Matt dreads getting out of bed in the morning. He's tired, he's cranky and often hung over from too many beers the night before. His kids know not to engage too much with Dad in the morning—he just seems so stressed and overwhelmed. They want to share things that are going on in their lives but are afraid he might become critical instead of just being a dad who listens to them and understands. He expects excellence, and if that's not present, he'll push them to be better by criticizing them. So if the boys bring B's home from school, he'll say, "How come it's not an A? You'll never get into a top college if you don't get A's!" He's repeating the same things he heard from his dad. The boys feel like they just got stung by a bee and they retreat to their rooms to sulk.

Since Matt's always so tired, his daily routine involves downing several coffees, then grabbing a bagel with cream cheese from the local deli before taking the short 10-minute drive to the small office he rents. When Matt gets to the office, there is sooo much work that he's frozen and can't decide what to do next—it's just too overwhelming. It's easier to file papers and surf the Internet than to make the phone calls to his network to connect with the people who can grow his clientele.

So instead of doing hard work, Matt finds excuses to help others. It takes his mind off of his own inadequacies. That's why he loves going to his networking groups. It's an antidote to the misery of holing himself up in his office. He connects with others and helps them out, and they take him to lunch to thank him. The socializing is a welcome reprieve, but when it comes to his business, he's afraid to ask for help. "What will they think of me? I should know how to do this. I went to Wharton!"

Matt often meets very successful entrepreneurs in the Wharton alumni networking groups. They constantly boast about how lucrative their last deal was and how much their companies are worth. It's obvious these people are multi-millionaires by the company they keep and by the money they spend on a lavish lifestyle. During these interactions, Matt feels very intimidated. He's thinking:

- Who the f*** do I think I am?

- I feel so small compared to my classmates.

- I'm never gonna get where they are.

- I'm a total loser! I only have two clients.

- How do I get my sh*t together to produce results?

- How the hell do I get out of this state?

- I'm just not meant for something bigger.

- I need to get out of my own way.

Matt is in conflict with himself. A part of him desperately wants success and another part is telling himself he's a total loser. When he gets home late at night from these networking meetings, he drinks beer, watches porn on the computer and masturbates to relieve the stress. Yes, he makes love to his wife, but it's not that often; once very two weeks. He just doesn't feel like it. The porn is a better escape.

Now that he's trying to make it on his own, Matt can't get out of his own way to manifest success. All the emotional baggage from the past is coming to the surface to hold him back. Matt is feeling the consequences of his past as he tries to do the hard work of attracting clients, which he can't seem to do because he is *afraid*.

What Matt doesn't know (and what most people aren't aware of) is that there are hidden parts inside of each and every one of us that are silently sabotaging us, even if we had "perfectly loving parents." If we are not as happy as we want to be and feel held back, it's more than likely the result of negative experiences at home and/or at school that have us believing we are not *good enough, smart enough* or *worthy enough*. (And sometimes the things that happened at school can be even more negative and damaging than things that happened at home.)

If you are relating to Matt in some aspect of your own life, I will be walking you through how Matt finally got rid of these conflicting voices in this chapter and the next. So, there's the conscious part of Matt wants success but the stronger message of the other parts don't believe he is worthy of it.

Those negative parts are holding the beliefs of:

- *I am not worthy*
- *I am not enough*
- *I am a bad person who doesn't deserve success*

Matt took on these beliefs as a result of negative experiences from his parents, teachers and peers. Listen to some of the voices from his childhood days that still echo in Matt's ears today:

"Matt, stop it. Stop being such a pain in the butt and making all that noise and all that mess! Why can't you be peaceful and quiet like your sister?"

"Now go to your room for a timeout. I don't want to have you spank you some more. I'm not getting you that toy because you are being so **bad**!"

"You're such a disappointment. You're never going to amount to anything. You're just not special enough."

"Look at Matt, he's got sneakers from the Salvation Army. Eewww!!"

Is there any doubt why Matt *believed* and *felt* he was *bad* and not worthy of his parents' or his peers' love? He took on the beliefs that "I must be bad. Why else would mom, dad and my classmates treat me this way?"

But there's a scientific explanation to why Matt's mind soaked up the negativity literally like a sponge. Before the age of seven, the brain takes in *everything* that is told to us and that happens to us *literally*. Which means even witnessing or eavesdropping on your parents' fights has you take on the belief "I must be bad, why else would they be fighting?" There wasn't another loving and compassionate adult there for you to explain that it's not *you* that is causing the fights, it's their own issues. (It's sad that there's no such thing as required Parenting 101 Classes before people become parents.)

You've seen how hypnotized people can believe and be led to do strange things? Well, we were all in a "hypnotic trance" in delta and theta brain waves before the age of seven. As a result, we believe every positive and negative word, glance or feeling we got from authority figures and peers. This is the "programmable" state—these incidences are like programming a computer to be the operating system to run your adult life. This is why our young parts get frozen in time when negative events happen (positive events get frozen too). When we get older our brains mature and are able to better distinguish truth from fiction, but the negative events in adult life trigger the childhood feelings of inadequacy.

Not only was Matt punished often, his parents fought a lot, and they divorced when Matt was five years old. Matt would often hear his father physically and verbally abusing his mother.

- "You're a worthless bitch."

- "You're so stupid."

- "You're fat."

- "You can't do anything right!"

- "I make the money in the house, you're never gonna amount to anything."

- "Your job is to take care of the kids, not go after your dreams."

Matt would often cry himself to sleep after witnessing this abuse. The tension in the house was unbearable. Why was Dad beating up on Mom? Because their respective wounded parts were fighting with each other. Love and compassion come from our highest spiritual selves. Matt's mom and dad's loving and compassionate selves were buried underneath their wounds. As a result, Matt became another victim of neglect. It's another vicious cycle of "victims creating more victims."

We all know that kids are not stupid. They pick up on everything. Even if the words are saying something else, children still *feel* the real emotions behind the words. As a result of Matt's home environment, he didn't feel good about himself and grew into an adult who was silently full of fear and self-doubt. At school, Matt acted out and was put in timeouts in the hallway quite a bit. Matt was also an easy target for bullies.

In order for kids to grow into healthy adults, they have to *feel* and *believe* that they are decent human beings.

As a consequence, Matt's injured younger parts are now running his life: The part that didn't feel loved as a kid, especially the part that felt the sting of his parents' divorce, the part that felt humiliated from being called "bucko" because of his buck teeth, the part that felt shame from standing in timeout in the hallway as the other kids teased him on their way to recess. That's why he's *afraid* of stepping up to do the work for his business.

Matt has tried therapy to heal his past. He was clinically depressed for two years many years ago. Essentially what caused the depression were the old parts overtaking his psyche. He couldn't even think straight. The therapist patched him up the best he knew how, and after two years of meds and therapy, got him back to "normal." Even though Matt is *intellectually* over his wounds, he is still emotionally strangled by the associated negative beliefs and feelings. And it's showing up big time in how unhappy he feels and how afraid he is of his own greatness.

This is also why Matt has a hard time being present for his family, and why his wife and kids feel like they are walking on eggshells. These are the same wounded parts make Matt eat crap, drink too much and pleasure himself with porn.

So now, even though Matt is mentally healthy and stable, these old parts are rearing their ugly heads and holding him back from his full potential and happiness. Underneath his confident exterior are false beliefs, fears and anxieties that needlessly make him a prisoner of his own mind.

Matt is afraid and full of doubt more than he is depressed. His highest spiritual, centered Self has the power to drive the bus of his life without fear, but this highest Self is buried underneath his wounded parts.

The solution: These parts must be updated with new programming, by deleting the "virus" of the old programming and installing a new operating system that tells Matt he is *lovable, worthy* and *enough*.

Matt's true Self has the super-ninja power to heal the parts of him that are holding him back. But first Matt needs to reframe his viewpoint on happiness. He thinks making at least a half a million dollars in his new business will bring him that happiness.

Wrong! Happiness is **not** a destination. The Law of Paradoxical Intent says:

*"You must have goals but your happiness **cannot** be tied to those goals. You must be happy **first** before you reach your goals."*

Matt will be happy after he energetically unloads the suitcase full of baggage from the past, not when his happiness is based on the "destinations" of money, praise or more "stuff."

* * *

Psychologist Abraham Maslow's *Hierarchy of Needs* says that you can't move up from one rung to the next until you have satisfied your lower needs. So you will not be able to unleash your full potential until your basic biologic and emotional needs are met.

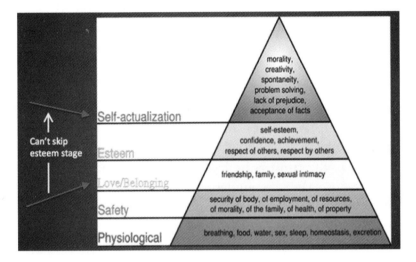

Most of us want to live a life of significance and make a contribution of some kind. Those goals are centered on unleashing our full potential or self-actualizing.

Maslow said, *"If you deliberately plan on being **less** than you are capable of being, then I warn you that you'll be **unhappy** for the rest of your life."*

That's why it is important to do everything you can live fully and go big. People who pursue self-growth don't want to die with regrets. There's an epidemic of depression and self-loathing now, and much of this is due to people not living up to their full potential. Some of us are still identifying with, still **in** and limited by the stories of the wounded parts of ourselves that lack self-esteem and confidence. As a result, the *courage* to take our dreams out of the dark drawer and into the light of day is almost non-existent. And as Maslow says, you'll be unhappy for the rest of your life because you know you are capable of more but you are not doing anything about it.

Or, there's another scenario...

Some of us do get the courage to do something to make a difference, but in that journey to self-actualization we get in our own way; we get stuck and we can't understand why.

That's because we are trying to go from the "love/belonging" stage to the "self-actualization" stage without going through the "self-esteem" stage. (See Maslow's visual.)

This **is why** Matt is stuck, afraid and unhappy. Matt is trying to self-actualize through the launching of his business but he is stuck at the "esteem" stage. He doesn't unconditionally love himself yet. Even though he "looks" successful, the truth is he lacks self-esteem and confidence. And because Matt's wounded parts lack confidence and self-esteem, they have overtaken his psyche and are sabotaging him because they are stuck in the hurts of the past.

Instead of undergoing more therapy, Matt needs to identify the wounded parts that caused his negative core beliefs in the first place. (I'll show you exactly how I guided him to heal these parts and discard the associated negative feelings and beliefs for good in the next chapter.)

When Matt is able to unconditionally love **all** of the parts of himself, he will gain the self-esteem and confidence to do the scary things and take the necessary risks to live to his full potential.

He will end up happy **now**, not *someday* when he becomes *rich*. Happiness in the present will actually bring him to his riches!

As the Law of Paradoxical Intent says, happiness is **not** a destination, happiness occurs in the **present** moment. You have to be happy **first** before you reach your goals of wealth, health, fame, etc. Happiness **now** will raise Matt's vibrations and energy and allow him to magnetize the people and the opportunities he needs for his success.

* * *

Everything is energy, including your thoughts and feelings. If you are consumed day in and day out with thoughts of, *I'm fat*, that is more than likely what you will get. What you **think** about you will more than likely get. It's the concept of "Where your thoughts go, your energy follows."

Beliefs turns into -> **Thoughts**, which turn into your -> **Feelings**, which determine your -> **Actions**, and that will show up in your -> **Results** (or lack thereof).

In Matt's case, he **believes** he is *worthless*. He **thinks**, *I'll never be able to do this*. Matt **feels** small and incompetent. Therefore, Matt **acts** like a wimp at networking meetings, with no courage to confidently tell others what a great service he provides, and ask how they can help him grow his business. His **results**—very little business, weight problem, relationship conflicts—are just a reflection of his *worthlessness* and other negative beliefs.

Here's another example. Let's pretend you or someone you know **believes** they are "fat" and that they're a "loser." Most of the time they are **thinking** about how disgusted they are with their body, so they **feel** horrible and anxious. And then they **act** on that horrible feeling by eating more junk, like ice cream or potato chips. The **results** are that they are busting out of their clothes, which in turn reinforces the original belief that they are "a fat loser." It's a self-fulfilling prophecy. But everyone can stop this vicious cycle by **believing** that they are fit and then they will act accordingly. Changing the negative beliefs into positive involves going back to the memories of the original devaluing experiences that created them in the first place.

So before anyone believes that they deserve to be fit, they have to figure out which wounded parts are holding them back from believing they are worthy of being fit and healthy.

Another consequence of not believing in yourself is that you vibrate from a lower energy. Just think about a time you met someone and thought, "I love her energy." Or, think about a time when you felt that someone had a dark cloud following them around. You feel like they suck the life out of you and you just want to avoid them like the plague. This is low energy. Our positive and negative thoughts show up in the energy we vibrate from. Think of someone you know who speaks timidly. You can feel their lack of confidence. Their low vibrations of lack of confidence and/or happiness are manifesting in the lower energy of lack of confidence in their voices. I know of a few adult women in their 30's and 40's who sound like tentative 20-year-olds. Unfortunately, it's hard to hide your thoughts and feelings. You can fake it for a while but eventually your real mood will show up. You can be saying one thing but your energy is "saying" or "vibrating" the exact opposite.

In Matt's case, his lack of self-confidence has him "vibrating" at a lower energy. People pick up on it . . . it's subtle, but they can feel it. And that's why they may not be inclined to do business with him. It just doesn't *feel* right.

* * *

So you may be wondering: how did Matt become a VP at his old job when he lacked confidence and self-esteem? Well, it's possible to "fake" your confidence and push yourself up the corporate ladder with the beach ball of the wounds of the past held under water in your 20's and 30's. But you can only hide the pains of your childhood for so lon—keeping that beach ball immersed under water with force—before your emotional and physical health take a beating. Matt faked it and made it to the executive suite of his last company but now he can no longer keep faking it in his entrepreneurial journey.

Although Matt was a good saver and didn't squander all of his money the way some of his associates did, still, his journey to find happiness did include acquiring society's definition of success: attractive wife, big house, status cars like Lexus and BMWs, and exotic vacations. By staying busy keeping up with "the Joneses," he was too busy to think about his past. After all, he'd "gotten over it," but in reality, it had only been swept under the rug. So Matt is going through the motions of life. And he is, like so many of us, not conscious of how we really feel or what is really driving us.

Until . . .

- The sh*t hits the fan when we can no longer take the grind of the job. It literally makes us sick

- The sh*t hits the fan when we try to live up to our potential and we can't get out of our own way

- The sh*t hits the fan when we realize that keeping up with the Joneses, living beyond our means, climbing the ladder of success and buying more "stuff" just to prove our worth to others doesn't make us happy

The key for Matt to overcome his desperate state is to get to know the parts of himself with the undesirable behaviors and understand and appreciate the roles they played in keeping him safe. These parts with negative behaviors took on extreme roles to shield him from the toxic experiences of his childhood. Once these parts with undesirable feelings and behaviors feel heard and appreciated by Matt's highest true Self, they will allow him to open the doors to the dungeon and access the shamed, rejected and humiliated young *exiled* parts of him that are frozen in time. Matt's true Self will be able to go back to the scene of those original devaluing experiences and give those parts of him the love and reassurances they needed that they never got from trusted and loving adults.

When these *exiled* young parts that experienced trauma are brought into the present and feel safe with Matt (and get to see what his life is like now), then the bad behaviors and feelings brought on by the *protective* parts (drinking, porn, anger, irritability, numbness, etc.) will no longer play out. These parts will no longer need to continue their undesirable behaviors and feelings and they will be free to take on new and more positive roles to move his life forward.

These parts are essentially undergoing "Chapter 11 Bankruptcy Reorganization" and they will all be getting new job descriptions. When you experience "Parts Work" through the Internal Family Systems methodology, then **you** get to tell them what their new roles are so they become part of your dream team to move you forward. They will now behave nicely as *passengers* on the bus, allowing the highest version of the Real You to drive the bus, no longer stuck and hijacked by the old wounded parts (who apply the brakes that keep you stuck and not moving forward on the bus).

Just be reassured that having these parts does not mean you have multiple personality disorder. We all have parts. They are a family. Sometimes parts get into fights because of the opposing roles they took on as a result of the wounding experiences. One part wants to eat healthy and the other part couldn't give a crap about eating vegetables and drinking green juices. When these "family members" have conflicting roles, we get stuck and can't move forward. These family members have to be heard, learn to co-exist, work toward the same goals and allow your Self to emerge and be the leader of your parts so you can drive the bus of your life forward. That's why this modality of parts work is called *Internal Family Systems*. We are working with the *family* of your *parts*.

As for Matt and the rest of us, we all have the power to unleash our greatness. No one else can do it for us. Your real true Self may have gotten pushed down by authority figures and peers through your devaluing experiences but the Self can rise again after you unburden the faulty beliefs of your wounded parts. You may already have moments of brilliance where you feel like the real you is driving the bus. But if those moments of brilliance don't last, that means your parts have hijacked you again and prevent you from going forward.

How can you tell when your true Self is in charge? When you are not afraid to be you. Self-leadership is the key to health, wealth and happiness. The real Self is joyful, peaceful, empathetic, courageous, curious, loving, fearless, honest, open accepting, confident, compassionate, beautiful, spacious, trusting, creative and connected. The Self-led person is happy and full of possibilities. This is what we are trying to unleash in Matt, the real true Self. Let's move into how I actually help him accomplish this.

Chapter Three

A Love Affair With Yourself Unleashes Greatness
You Have the Power to Release Your Emotional Scars

"Don't let your past relationships ruin your future.
Scars remind us of where we've been, not where we are going."
—Unknown

As we track how Matt overcomes his challenges in this chapter and becomes a more loving and joyful version of himself, you'll get an overview of how I take my clients from stuck to unstoppable. I am also using tools from my coaching toolbox in addition to Internal Family Systems to help Matt get unstuck. Having a juicy love affair with yourself and believing in yourself is one of the fundamental keys to moving forward and living your life happily ever after.

Since Matt has a lot of issues with the way his dad, David, treated him, he needs to step into his dad's shoes so he can understand why he is the way he is so that he can forgive him. And, Matt's *frozen* parts need to be thawed out of the past and brought into the present, to be seen, heard and validated by his true Self.

> **Emily:** Matt, we can't change the past, but I can help you understand and forgive your father. I'd like you to imagine three points of a triangle. One point is you, the second point is your father and the third point is a neutral observer such as Oprah.
>
> Step into yourself. As Matthew, please tell your father David how you feel and what is important to you. Tell him what it was like living with him. (For the sake of brevity, these conversations have been abbreviated to reveal the core essence.)
>
> **Matthew:** I feel like I was never good enough. I didn't feel you loved me for ME. I felt ashamed and rejected when I couldn't make you proud during my soccer games.
>
> I felt like you really didn't want me, that I was an accident and now you're stuck with me. I felt sick to my stomach when you yelled at and hit mom. The toxicity from the physical abuse made me feel like I was the cause of your fighting.
>
> I hated being shuffled between your house and mom's house after the divorce. I hated it when you guys talked badly about each other. I didn't want to take sides.

When I shaped up with my grades, you didn't tell me you were proud of me. I got into Stanford on a scholarship probably because they saw that you and mom didn't go to college and they wanted to give me a chance, even though I didn't have top grades like my richer classmates.

All you said was, *That's nice . . . We'll see if you can keep up with the workload. I wouldn't be surprised if you drop out.* Ouch! What's up with that? Didn't you have any faith in me? I've been in a dark place for a long time because of you.

E: Tell Dad what you wanted from him that you never got.

M: I just wanted you to tell me that you are proud of me and that you loved me. (Matt's a bit emotional with his voice quivering.)

E: Please step into the second point of the triangle. Now you are David, your father. As David, what are you feeling? What do you want your son Matt to know?

M: (speaking as his father) Matt, I did the best I could as a father. I wanted the best for you. That's why I was always criticizing you and telling you how to do things better.

I wanted you to do well so you could get into a good college. I didn't want you to end up in a blue-collar job like me. I know that plumbers are very important to society but I was ashamed of my occupation. It's *my* identity issue. There's nothing wrong with being a plumber but I just knew I was capable of more. I didn't apply myself. That's what I'm upset about. Just settling—not being more than I could be.

My temper was a result of how miserable I was because of my critical mother. I never felt I was good enough.

I'm sorry if I abused your mother the way I did. I'm ashamed but I couldn't help myself. It's that part of me that just wanted to lash out because I was angry and miserable.

I love you, I want the best for you. I am in my own misery, I don't know how to get out of it. I'm sorry for all the things I have done to you.

(Matt is emotionally raw after "feeling" his father. He never saw it from his perspective.)

E: Step back into the shoes of yourself. What do you want to tell your dad now that you've heard his perspective?

M: Oh my God! I never knew you were in so much pain. I love you! (Matt sobs and feels the pain of his Dad in his heart.)

E: Now, step into the 3rd point of the triangle as a neutral observer such as Oprah. From the 20,000 foot view, what is going on with Matt and Dave?

M: Matt has been so hurt from his past. He blames his father for his low self-esteem and lack of confidence. David is in just as much pain from his past and that's why he took it out on Matt's mother verbally and physically. Matt absorbed the negative energy of the house and concluded that he was bad and that he was a burden, and that's why they fought.

E: Now, step into the middle of the triangle. From that highest place of Spirit, what needs to happen between Matt and David in order for them to have a better relationship?

M: (speaking from a place of Spirit): Matt and David need to forgive one another. David was in so much pain from his past that he didn't know *how* to show up as a loving father. He's just repeating the pattern of how he was treated as a kid, with emotional abuse.

There is a lot of love between them . . . they just need to forgive each other.

Matt needs to let go and have compassion for his father. His father won't change but Matt can change the filter through which he sees his father's emotions and behaviors. He needs to feel sorry for his dad and all that he's gone through. Matt's homework after the session was to write a forgiveness letter to his dad, which he is not going to mail. He can burn it in the fireplace if it feels right or just tear it up. The letter will release residual negative feelings. Now that Matt has compassion for his dad, the next time he sees him, he should not be triggered.

The lesson in all of this is that many of us are "victims of victims." When we empathize with what our parents (or anyone else who has hurt us) must have gone through, the filter through which we see them changes. Forgiveness leads to compassion, which in turn leads to personal growth. If you hold onto the misery and the hate, you are only hurting yourself, not the other person. Every situation and experience is neutral until you attach a positive or negative meaning around it. So now you can neutralize what happened to you when you see it from the perspective of the other person—the reason why they did what they did. And this will allow you to forgive the other person and unshackle you from being chained to them.

At the next session, we continue.

E: Matt, last time we went through the triangle exercises you were able to empathize and forgive your dad. When you think about him now? What comes up for you?

M: I'm totally good with my dad. From all my years in therapy, I know what the issues are. I overcame the depression but I never had the chance to release the bottled-up toxic energy. Now the "Ugh!" feeling is gone.

* * *

So now comes the work of accessing the parts of Matt that are holding him back from busting through his fears to reach that next level of success.

I take him through a visualization where he imagines himself on a path. This visualization is from *Introduction to the Internal Family Systems Model* by Richard Schwartz, Ph.D. (Reprinted with permission.)

> *Imagine you are at the base of a path. It can be any path—one you are familiar with or one you have never been on before. Before you go anywhere on the path, meet with your emotions and thoughts (these are your parts) at the base and ask that they remain there and allow you to head out on the path without them.*
>
> *If they are afraid to let you go, reassure them you won't be gone long and that both they and you will benefit from the experience. See if you can arrange for any scared parts to be cared for by those that aren't scared.*
>
> *If parts remain afraid to let you go, don't go, and instead spend some time discussing their fears with them. Exactly what are they afraid will happen if they allow you to go off on your own?*
>
> *If however, you sense permission to go, head out on the path. Notice as you go whether you are watching yourself on the path or whether you are on it such that you don't see yourself—you just see or sense your surroundings.*
>
> *If you are watching yourself, that's a signal that a part is present. Find the part that's afraid to let you proceed on the path and ask it to relax and return to the base. If it won't, spend time exploring its fears.*
>
> *As you continue on the path, notice whether you are thinking about anything. If you are, ask those thoughts*

to return to the base as well so that you increasingly become pure awareness. As you continue on the path, check periodically to see if you are thinking and, if so, gently send the thoughts back.

As each part leaves you, notice what happens to your body and mind. Notice the amount of space you sense around you and the kind of energy that flows in your body.

When it feels as if you have spent enough time on the path away from your parts, begin to return to the base. See if it is possible to hold the spaciousness and energy you feel even as you get close to your parts again. When you arrive at the base, meet with your parts and see how they fared without you and what they might need from you.

When that process is complete, thank your parts for letting you go, if they did. If they didn't, thank them for letting you know they were afraid to let you go. Then take some deep breaths again and follow your breath back to the outside world.

E: So, did your parts let your Self go out on the path? What parts were holding you back from setting the Self free on the path?

M: There was a part of me that was holding onto my ankles, the part that loves to *procrastinate*. Instead of doing what I'm supposed to be doing, I just waste time on porn. It's another distraction that contributes to procrastination.

Porn chills me out. I worked on this a lot with my therapist. I've decreased the amount of porn I watch but I'm still doing it too much. I know I'm hurting my wife.

E: So the part that likes *porn* is another part we need to get to know besides the *procrastination* part. Do you want to focus on the *procrastination* part right now?

M: Okay.

E: Where are you feeling this *procrastination* part?

M: In the pit of my stomach.

E: How do you *feel towards it*?

M: I'm *disgusted* with it.

E: Can you ask the *disgusted* part to step aside so that we can get to know the *procrastination* part?

[Disgusted is another protective part that jumped in and wanted to hold us back from getting to know the procrastination part. We had to ask it to step aside. The target part you are trying to get to know has to feel that you really care about it for it to open up to you. This is no different than you not wanting to open up to someone if you sense that they are disgusted with you.]

M: Okay.

E: How do you feel towards the *procrastination* part now?

[I ask this "How do you *feel*" question again to see if his Self is present and separated from the *procrastination* part to get to know it better.]

M: Hmmm . . . I'm curious about it.

[Being *curious* about the part tells me that there's enough loving Self-energy present to allow us to get to know how the *procrastination* part has served him all of his life. Feelings such as *curiosity, compassion, and connection* are signs that the client is in a place of the Self where he wants to get to know and appreciate his part. If other non-loving feelings come out such has "I'm *frustrated*, I'm *angry*, I *hate* it," when I ask the question, "How do you *feel towards* this part?" this means another protective part (frustration, anger, or the hating part) have jumped in to prevent the Self from getting to know that part. If these parts don't want to step back, then we need to get to know the *concerns* and *fears* of the part that jumped in and understand what it is afraid of if we get to know the target part. Once the fears are addressed, then it will more than likely step aside to let us get to know the target part.]

E: When did *procrastination* first take on its job in your life? What is its job?

M: This part is young . . . right around the time my parents divorced . . . so probably four or five years old. It would procrastinate on cleaning up my room or doing homework for school. I somehow managed it all through school and college, got things done the last minute and did okay. Not always A's but I got by. I did work hard on it in the last couple of years in high school by staying up late because I wanted so badly to get into a good college and be on my own.

E: Invite *procrastination* part to tell you what it was afraid would happen if you got things done on time and didn't procrastinate?

M: It had a defeatist attitude since I always felt like what I did was never going to be good enough. Why waste extra time on schoolwork when I wasn't sure I would get the validation for my efforts from my parents? Mind as well spend time playing video games or watching TV instead.

E: So just show some appreciation for this part for the hard work it's done to keep you from wasting time on stuff you weren't going to be complimented on.

M: Yeah, it likes it that I'm appreciating it.

E: What else does it want you to know?

M: That as I grew older and needed more distractions besides video games and TV, I picked up the porn habit in college and it contributed to my procrastination.

E: Just let it know you understand how hard it's working for you. Ask what this *procrastination* part would rather be doing if it didn't procrastinate.

M: It would rather keep me on time and complete my projects without stress. Now it's so stressful to do things at the last minute and this part is really tired of staying up all night to complete stuff. It needs to get some sleep so it has the energy to keep me on time.

[It is possible for the *protector* parts to take on new positive roles in your life after you hear their story and determine which young part of you this part is protecting from getting triggered and hurt.]

E: Now that we heard how *procrastination* had a positive intention behind its behavior, is it willing to show us the little boy he is protecting underneath this behavior?

M: Whoa . . . I'm getting an image of my five-year-old self, in the bedroom, feeling rejected by mom and dad.

E: How do you *feel towards* five-year-old Matt?

[I am asking how Matt *feels* about the part to see if there's Self-energy is present to get to know him and see what he needs from him to feel safe and loved.]

M: I feel *sorry* for him.

[Feeling *sorry* for him means a *protector* has jumped in and doesn't want to let him in so easily to get to know this boy who has been hiding in the dungeons of his psyche for 42 years.]

E: Would this *sorry* part be willing to step aside while we get to know five-year-old Matt?

M: No.

[We need to address the fears of the *sorry* part so that it can rest assured that we are not going to hurt five-year-old Matt. Matt's five-year-old part is an *exile* that is living in the dungeons of his psyche, frozen in the time of the original toxic and devaluing experience. This part has been waiting for many years to get rescued out of the memory of the original negative experience with his parents.]

E: What is the *sorry* part afraid of if we get to know five-year-old part?

M: That he's going to get yelled at.

E: Let the *sorry* part know that we are not going to yell at him. We are not mom and dad. It's your adult Self coming to rescue him.

M: Okay . . . the *sorry* part stepped aside.

E: Now how do you *feel* toward the five-year-old part?

M: I'm feeling I want to *get to know him* and what happened to him that he's locked himself in this bedroom.

[Now the adult Matt is curious and in enough Self-energy to get to know his young part and to let him emerge from the faulty emotions and beliefs of the past.]

E: Is this five year old aware of you? (Matt has his eyes closed, re-living the scene from the past.)

M: He's not sure of who I am. He's a little scared.

E: Will he let you get a little closer? Maybe sit on the bed with him?

M: Yeah . . . I'm being gentle. Hey buddy . . . it's me . . . I'm all grown up. I'm back here to get to know you.

E: Does he have any idea how old you are?

M: No, he's wondering who I am.

E: Let him know that it's the adult version of you. Update him on what has happened to you.

M: Hey little Matt, I'm 47 now. I've gone to college, I'm married with two kids, I've had a very successful career in finance and technology.

E: How is he receiving that?

M: He had no idea I was so old already and so accomplished!

E: Invite him to tell you what happened that had him lock himself in the bedroom all these years.

M: Well, mom and dad were arguing again and they were fighting over who gets custody of me and my brother after the divorce. They were yelling at each other and dad got violent and hit mom across the face and was calling her an unfit mother. I got scared and retreated to the bedroom and stayed there to play with my trucks. I was so ashamed that I was causing such trouble and that I was such a burden to them.

E: What is the belief that little Matt took on as a result of the fighting?

M: That he is a bad kid and unworthy of love. (Matt is a little teary now as he is hearing the story from his five-year-old part.)

E: What does he need from you to feel loved?

M: He needs an explanation of what is going on with Mom and Dad and why he feels so bad about himself.

E: Okay . . . give him the explanation he needed to hear at the time that he witnessed his parents arguing over him.

M: Hey little Matt, Mom and Dad are not splitting up because of you and your brother. They hate each other. They should never have been married. They yelled at you and your brother a lot, not because they didn't love you, because they had so much stress with trying to live above their means. There wasn't enough money or time to go around to spend with you. They were consumed in their own negativity and had no energy left to give to you and your brother. You are lovable. You are smart. They wanted the best for you, even in Kindergarten, because they know good school habits start young. They wanted you to be the best in the class and pushed you to get A's, not B's. They are very proud of you. I'm very proud of you. I love you. You are going to do great things. You are perfect the way you are. I'm giving him a bear hug and kissing him. Yeah . . . this is really good. He feels me, he has his arms around me really tightly.

E: What else are you feeling?

M: The knot at the pit of my stomach seems to be dissipating. I'm feeling lighter. Oh my goodness! (Matt is in tears. Tears are good. They are negative energy leaving the body.)

E: Go ahead and take as much time as you need to soak in that new memory of you rocking and loving five-year-old Matt.

[As a five year old, Matt did not have the intellectual capacity to process that his parents were divorcing because of the tension between themselves, not because he was such a pain-in-the-neck kid to raise. No one was there to reassure Matt that he's not the reason why the family is breaking up. That's why this 5-year-old part got frozen in time with his erroneous beliefs and feelings that it was all his fault that his parents broke up. That's why 47-year-old Matt had to go back to the scene of the original event and rescue little Matt out of the past to be safe with him in the present.]

E: Ask Little Matt if he would like to leave the negative memory of the bedroom and be taken to a new place that feels safe.

M: He wants to go to the park and play.

E: Okay, set that up and take him to the park.

M: We're throwing the ball around at the park.

[Making new memories, this Self-led "re-parenting" is very powerful way to help Matt positively shift his self-image to someone who is quite lovable, worthy and enough.]

> **E:** Now ask him if he would consider unburdening himself of the belief that *I'm not lovable, I'm not worthy of love* that he has been carrying around since 5 years old.
>
> **M:** Yes, he's ready. He wants to burn up the burden in a campfire at the park.
>
> **E:** Set that up and let me know when the unburdening is complete.
>
> **M:** All done.
>
> **E:** Now invite those parts that we asked to step aside and see how they feel with the healing that we just did with the five-year-old *exiled* Matt that they were protecting.
>
> **M:** They are amazed at what just happened.

E: Okay . . . is the *procrastination* part ready to stop procrastinating so that you can get your work done efficiently and on time, since Matt is no longer in danger of getting criticized by Mom and Dad for not getting an A? You get to give him feedback on his work and validate him for his efforts no matter how things turn out in your business.

M: Yeah . . . *Procrastination* is ready to let me be more on time since it knows that the greater effort put into work will be appreciated by me no matter what the end result is.

E: Great! Thank all your parts for letting us get to know them.

M: Thank you, parts. I love you!

* * *

Matt had a procrastination habit he didn't like. Now he understands why procrastination came into his life—to protect the five-year-old part of him that was frozen in the bedroom with the untrue belief that he was not good enough or worthy of his parents' love. Now that the five year old is no longer frozen in time and has been "re-parented" by his Self, the procrastination part can let go of its role because there is no longer the five year old to protect.

There's one caveat to this: the *procrastination* protector part may be protecting other *exiled* parts of him that are frozen at other ages. So, if procrastination continues, then we have to find out if there are other little *exiled* parts that need to be unfrozen and melted out of the past.

It turns out that Matt's procrastination did let go of its role. (Once in a while, he will procrastinate on something, but it's rare.) Other people, instead of having a *procrastination* part, may end up with protective behaviors I mentioned in the Introduction such as shopping too much, drinking too much, gambling too much, working too much, exercising too much, etc.

Feelings are also a part of the protective system in the psyche. These feelings could be sadness, anxiety, depression, numbness, anger and irritability, etc. Undesirable behaviors and feelings numb the emotional pain, to avoid ever going back into the memories and feelings of such old hurts as humiliation, rejection and shame.

I just showed you a quick overview of how to heal the parts of you that keep you stuck from a happy and fulfilled life. Unburdening your younger parts' erroneous, limiting and extreme beliefs and feelings are the catalyst for believing in yourself and allowing your own fearless self-expression. When you believe in yourself 100%, you will attract just about everything you want into your life. Authentic happiness starts with unconditionally loving yourself, which means loving **all** of your parts, as demonstrated by Matt.

* * *

Now we'll continue with Matt's journey to getting unstuck by finding the root of why he has to turn to porn to feel good.

> **M:** I've been feeling great since I visited that five-year-old part of me that was stuck in the bedroom fighting over my custody. My energy shifted and people are noticing my positivity. Others are

noticing that I seem *brighter*, my eyes are sparkling. My procrastination has gone way down and this part is letting me be more responsible with getting things done on time.

E: Great! So, what's coming up for you now?

M: Now I want to get to know the part of me that likes porn. I want to be over it. It's hurting my marriage.

E: Let me know when you are in touch with the *porn* part.

M: Yeah, I am. I feel it as a tightness in my neck, holding the guilty feelings there.

E: How do you *feel towards* this part?

M: I don't like it.

E: Can *I don't like it* part step back?

M: Yeah, it did.

E: Now how to you feel towards *porn* part?

M: I'm connected to it, I want to get to know it.

E: When did this part come into existence?

M: In college, after a bad breakup.

E: What is its role?

M: To help me fantasize and relieve myself so I didn't have to be rejected by anyone.

E: Show the *porn* part that you appreciate the role it has played to prevent feelings of rejection when you want to be intimate with someone. What else does it want you to know? What is it *afraid* of if it didn't do its job?

M: That I would be rejected if I did the job of initiating sex. I have a hard time doing so. I made myself do it when I dated women before I met my wife. Then I let the women do the job of seducing me.

E: Let that part know how much you appreciate the protection you received so you wouldn't be rejected.

M: It's really taking that appreciation in.

E: Is there more to the story? If not, ask the *porn* part if it feels ready to show us who it's protecting?

M: I get an image of my college self that was painfully rejected by the first love of my life, Amanda.

E: Is this college part aware of you?

M: Yes, I'm with him on the park bench after he was dumped.

E: How do you feel toward the *rejected* college part?

M: I'm embarrassed by it—by the fact that it loves porn.

E: Ask the *embarrassed* part to step aside. Now how do you feel towards this *college* part?

M: I feel compassion towards him.

E: Invite it to tell you what happened when you got rejected by Amanda.

M: Amanda was the love of my life. I wanted to marry her. She cheated on me a couple of times with my fraternity brothers. Those brothers had the balls to brag to me how great she was in bed. Eventually she left me for good. She didn't like the fact that I wasn't as confident in bed as other men she slept with. I was so ashamed of my sexual abilities. I thought I deserved her but apparently she didn't think so. That's when I decided to turn to porn to soothe myself. At least no one could reject me through the computer screen.

E: What burden or belief did this part take on as a result of Amanda's rejection?

M: That *"I'm a loser!"*

E: What does this part need from you so that it can get unfrozen from the old memories of rejection and feel like he's not a loser anymore?

M: He needs a "big brother" talk from me. Hey Matt, it's not about you that Amanda slept behind your back. You were vulnerable because you were essentially the little boy who felt rejected by mom and dad. That boy made you believe you were not worthy of monogamous love. You don't know this now but 10 years after college, you are going to find out through the grapevine that Amanda was sexually abused as a kid. Sexually abused kids hold a lot of shame. She didn't believe she deserved to be loved by someone like you. That's why she cheated on you behind your back. It was her way of trying to get you to break up with her, because unconsciously, she didn't believe she deserved someone as great as you.

E: How is he taking in the information?

M: His eyes just lit up. He's thinking, wow, I'm not the loser . . . she did that on purpose because she needed validation from other men that she's good enough because of the shame she held. It's not about me. She's a hurting puppy. So I just want to tell you that you are a lovable guy. You have to believe in yourself to attract the right women to come your way. When you are your confident self, you will attract women like bees to honey. You are good enough to have a beautiful wife. In fact, you did attract a beautiful wife. Oh my . . . he just got up and jumped up and down with happiness. I give him a big pat on the back.

E: Is there anything else this part wants to tell you?

M: No, I think that's it.

[Parts need to tell their stories and be witnessed by the Self. No one was there to reassure college Matt that everything is going to turn out okay. Now this younger part of him knows that he's not bad, he's worthy of love, and that Amanda is not the right person for him.]

E: So, is he ready to release the burden of the "I'm a loser" belief he took on in college as a result of this experience?

M: Yes, let me put the damn burden in a mason jar and let the ocean take it away. (Matt imagines this in his mind.) Okay . . . all done!

E: Let's ask the other parts that step aside to come back and see if they are okay with what we just did.

[The porn part that was protecting this part has to see that this *exiled* college part has been healed and be okay with it. If not, the *porn* part can relapse and go back to its old excessive and addictive porn habit if it wasn't ready to let go and let college Matt release his past. Matt's *exiled* college part got updated with the facts about his old relationship. Now he feels relieved and porn part can release its excessive activities. Note: we don't need to get rid of our parts all together. When trauma happens, that's when some of our parts take on extreme roles such as *too much* shopping, *too much* drinking, *too much* sadness and *too much* control.]

[Not only do our negative childhood experiences create parts frozen in the past, our college and young adulthood experiences get frozen too when bad things happen—such as a breakup—that reinforces a younger part's belief that we are not lovable or worthy.]

M: Now I get that I'm afraid I might be rejected if I initiate sex with my wife. Now I see how I turn to porn to avoid initiating sex to prevent this college part of me from getting triggered.

E: So you see the connection of your present reality with your past? Your past shows up in the present relationship with your wife.

After the session, Matt is finally feeling confident enough to be more intimate with his wife. He reports at the next session:

M: My wife loves my more positive energy and the fact that I want to make love to her again. I think she suspected that I was addicted to porn but didn't say anything about it. She's such a saint!

* * *

All of these parts coming into alignment with his real Self means that Matt will be more confident about who he is and do the scary and risky things he needs to do to manifest great things for his business. So as Matt becomes more confident to talk about the attributes of his business, he starts attracting more interest. As opportunities come his way, an *unworthy of success* part shows up.

M: I know I am capable of success. But a part of me is holding back. The part that *doesn't feel worthy of success*.

E: So let's get in touch with that part. How do you feel towards that part?

M: I'm *curious* about it.

E: What does that part want you to know? How old is it? Does it know you are a grownup now?

M: It's about 8 years old. That part witnessed Dad throwing a temper tantrum at my step-mom because he was fired from a job when he messed up the plumbing in the house of a wealthy businessman. He was screaming at the top of his lungs, saying, "Rich people are bastards! Money is evil. These rich people treat blue-collar tradesmen like sh*t. Matt, don't you dare become one of those rich son-of-a-bitches who thinks they are better than everyone else." I was just frozen in the corner of the dining room, then I went upstairs, cried and buried myself in a video game. (Matt's voice is shaking as he is feeling this part.)

E: Let that part know that you are all grown up now.

M: Hey buddy, I'm 47 now. It's okay. You're safe with me.

E: What does that part need from you?

M: A pep talk on what the meaning of money is.

E: Go ahead and give him what he needs. Where are you?

M: I'm in a chair next to him as he's playing his video game.

E: What do you want to tell him?

M: Hey, buddy, Dad didn't mean to get so nasty when he lost that job. It's not about you. He was ashamed of getting fired. Because an arrogant wealthy homeowner fired him, he associates wealth with evil. His tantrum made you believe that if you got successful your dad might see you as evil and end up rejecting you. It's not true. Money is not evil . . . I'm 47 now, I've done well and nothing bad has happened to me. Dad loves you. He wants you to be successful so you don't end up miserable like he did. Money is good because it allows you to take care of your loved ones.

Come give me a big hug . . . you're gonna be okay, buddy.

E: Just soak in the new memories of love next to him at the computer. Take as much time as you need.

[With this "pep talk" from Matt's Self of today, he helped his *unworthy of success* part acquire the new belief that money is *not* evil.]

Matt was wearing the mask of confidence and self-esteem in his 20's and 30's, when most people can can get away with it. When you are older, the parts that feel unworthy creep up on us and we get stuck.

E: Matt, are you ready to get rid of the burden of this *unworthy of success* part that's been a part of you for such a long time?

M: Yes.

E: Since you acquired this belief around money that is not yours, who do you need to give this money burden back to? You don't own this . . . it's someone else's burden.

M: I need to give it back to my dad, who probably acquired it from his dad.

E: How would you like to give that burden back to your dad?

M: I've put it in a box with a red bow on it. I'm giving it back to Dad. (Matt imagines giving the burden back to his dad and his ancestors.)

E: Thank your *unworthy of success* part for letting you get to know it. Now it's been transformed into a *worthy of success* part.

M: Yeah, buddy, thanks for letting me get to know you. I love you. I am going to give you the job of Chief Financial Officer in my business.

So, Matt acquired the erroneous "money is evil" belief through a negative incident. When Matt's dad threw his temper tantrum, no one was there to reassure Matt that money was *not* evil. Since Matt left his corporate job and embarked on his entrepreneurial journey, the old money baggage held him back from confidently talking about his business because unconsciously he believed that attracting new business and making it big might mean he would lose his dad's love. With the new belief that money is not evil and that he's not going to lose his dad's love, he will be able to attract abundance without any blockages.

There are more parts of Matt that keep him stuck in other areas of his life. Matt has a part that couldn't give a hoot about his health and weight. He's 20 pounds overweight with high blood pressure and digestive issues. I take him through the same process as the other parts so that these parts can be healed of their burdens and allow Matt to improve his health. And the *eating too much* and *drinking too much* parts of him went through the same protocol. When his young parts can feel better about themselves, they will allow him to adopt healthier habits, with less overeating and less drinking.

As a result of getting unstuck from the parts of him that held him back, Mat is now confident, fearless, loves himself, loves life and feels so much "lighter" now that the "dark cloud" is gone. Others are beginning to notice.

"You look happy, Matt."

"You look like you've lost weight."

"Your eyes are sparkling."

And he's manifesting new clients and new connections that are helping his business soar. Once Matt unburdened from his past, he was able to move forward with much more ease. Matt's improved self-image, self-worth and self-love continue to contribute to his confidence and the ability to move forward without fears, self-doubts and resistance.

Now Matt can look in the mirror and say, "I love you so much! You are perfect the way you are." He has given all of his parts the validation they needed that they never received from caregivers, teachers and peers.

As a result of getting to know his parts and taking them out of the past, Matt's happiness quotient went from 5 out of 10 to 9 out of 10. He can't even get his old "state" back if he tried.

The ghosts of the past showed up in just about every aspect of Matt's life—career, relationships, emotional well-being and his health. Now that his self-image hss improved, he looks in the mirror and says, "Who is that fat guy in the mirror? That's can't be me! I love myself so much that I *want* to do the work to eat healthier to get rid of this beer belly, because that's not the real me!" So Matt happily adopts a healthier eating regimen and the weight falls off effortlessly.

He is happy **now** on his journey to making his business a success and making a difference in the world before he goes to heaven. Feeling good from the inside out means that when challenges come his way, he's not paralyzed and he has the ability to tackle them head-on. The **real** Matt has been unleashed and he is now unstoppable and **happy** on his way to living life on his terms.

It was not Matt's fault he was stuck and unhappy, it was the fault of his *parts* that were frozen in the past. They needed to thaw out and come into the present and be loved by Matt.

Nothing brings me more joy and fills my soul than to watch my clients finally believe in themselves and soar!

Please note that Matt coached with me for 25 hours over the course of 11 deep-dive 2+ hours sessions over 3 months. You need to invest the time, energy and money to get lasting transformation. The bigger you get, more fears will surface that weren't there before. (Now Matt has "tune up" sessions with me whenever any insecurities creep up.) How long it will take you to get unstuck and unleashed will depend on how connected and safe your parts feel towards your IFS therapist or coach. And it also depends on whether or not your protectors are ready to let you unburden the old stories and "change" into someone they are not familiar being, the real you.

If you are inspired to change your own life by Matt's story, but a part of you has popped up and is *afraid* to change because you don't know who you would be without your "story," then you are afraid of the unknown. Chapter Ten is devoted to fears and how to overcome them. Now let's learn more about this powerful method to get unstuck, *Internal Family Systems.*

Chapter Four

Stay Average or Kick Your Life into High Gear
Internal Family Systems vs. Traditional Self-Help Therapies

"You will never rise above how you see yourself." —Oprah

Through the story of Matt, you now have an idea of what Internal Family System's (IFS) protocol for healing and Self-leadership is all about. IFS is the next generation of powerful, cutting-edge psychotherapy and personal development. Unburdening your big and little traumas literally rewires your brain, breaking the bonds of the old memories and how you think about who you are. As a result, you can be happier, your self-image will soar and you can gain the courage to smash through the glass ceiling of your potential. As a Be More Extraordinary Magician, I use IFS to take clients from good to great to extraordinary. Many of my clients describe the transformation as "The light bulb of the real me got turned on. It's not like I have to put effort into being happy or consciously act this way, I am happy. I have come home to my real Self, I've been unburdened of the emotional pain and I'm feeling lighter with freedom, joy and endless possibilities. I just wake up this way and I can't even get my old mediocre state back. This is heaven!"

IFS is psycho-spiritual healing; letting your true Self be the agent for healing all parts of you that have been hurt. This is different from traditional psychotherapy because the IFS practitioner is not the healer, you are. Other therapeutic modalities require the therapist to be the healer.

You may have gone to many years of multiple therapists to rehash the same issues over and over again, without any resolution. You know your mother is the issue. The heavy suitcase of emotional baggage is laid out on the "platter" so to speak, but the therapy sessions haven't been helpful with emptying the stinky baggage into the trash. You've talked about mom ad nauseam for many years and you're sick and tired of still feeling angry and sad. This is where IFS can finish the "job," be "clean up duty" and empty that heavy suitcase once and for all.

Perhaps you've experienced sessions where 40 minutes into your one-hour appointment, you finally access a vulnerable memory and then the therapist says, "We only have 10 minutes left. Can you pack that thought back into the box and we'll deal with it the next time?" Sometimes you feel worse at the end of a session than when you started and you wonder why you continue the torture. You are left hanging and sobbing. That vulnerable part of you said, "What the hell did you do??!! I didn't want to come out of my protected dungeon and you've brought up the hurt again without any resolution. No way am I letting you go there again!!"

You go to the next session and you've forgotten where you left off, you can't access it (because the protectors have come out and are saying, "No, no, no, we're not doing that again!") and you never finish processing the event you started the last time. So it's no wonder you feel like you don't make much progress. Fortunately, because of the way IFS therapy is structured, even in the typical one-hour session, there's a way to put that vulnerable memory back into the box safely so that you won't feel worse than when you came in.

Some clients have even shared with me that their therapists were more wounded than they were, with low self-esteem, still living with their baggage and less-than-vibrant dim blub energy. The whole therapy experience left them with a bad taste and they just don't want to rehash all the pain yet again as they shop for a better therapist. Or they just give up altogether thinking that they are doomed to live with emotional pain for the rest of their lives.

Please be clear, I'm not bashing the therapy community at all. I've trained with many competent IFS therapists. I'm just expressing what many clients have shared with me and what I have experienced myself in traditional therapy 10 years ago. Just like any professional field—doctors, lawyers, financial advisors, therapists and coaches— some are better than others. There are so many different types of therapy and coaching models and you have no idea going in which model is going to be used on you and which one is right for you. And the traditional one-hour timeframe is not enough time to create the safety and trust necessary to access and heal vulnerable memories most people would rather resolve sooner rather than later. You have to shop around until you find someone you feel connected with.

I do things differently because I've taken heed of the frustrations of the traditional one-hour therapy and coaching models and I give my clients as much time as they need to go deep every time. We don't watch the clock, and that's why many coaching sessions are two hours long, sometimes more. I limit myself to booking only two of these intensive sessions a day so that clients have my undivided attention for as long as they need to make progress. (I'm energized after these appointments because of the progress that's been made, but I still need to decompress after holding the space for them to process painful memories.) Because my sessions are with psychologically healthy people who are ready to take quantum leaps, there is always a huge release and unburdening of something that has kept them stuck. These longer sessions are part of the reason why they are able to feel better and move forward faster.

I am amazed at the details of the shame and pain that people are willing to share during their initial one-hour consultations. I sometimes have to say "I don't need to know all the details of your backstory right now. Let's just see where you are now versus where you want to be and determine if we're a fit to work together." They feel so comfortable because they know my story, how I overcame my own "baggage" that I relate in a blog post on my website. (Now you know all the details because I've told my story in this book.) So when prospective clients know why I do what I do, and they feel a connection with me (through the videos on my website), they already trust me and feel safe with me. And because clients feel so comfortable from the outset, they are ready to unburden something during the very first session after the initial consult. Their parts trust me to be their guide. What you should know is that there's **nothing** shameful about what you have been through. Everyone's story is more or less the same (only the details are different). We don't openly talk about our emotional pain with friends and therefore we end up feeling alone and ashamed. But the truth of the matter is we are all more or less carrying the same burdens of shame, rejection and unworthiness.

P.S. When you can openly talk about the scars of the past with a positive energy that shows that you are so over it and that you don't really care what others will think, that's when you will have reached a new level of self-awareness, self-esteem and confidence. Just think about how Oprah openly shares her sexual abuse experience, and she does it to inspire others to move beyond and heal the past. There's also a well-known mind-body medicine expert who frankly reveals how much pain she experienced during sex when she was going through a really stressful period of her life. (Would you be comfortable broadcasting your sexual dysfunction to the world?) She can talk about it nonchalantly because she is no longer ashamed of it and she uses her story to show others that she was "messed up" at one point, even though everything looked so "perfect" from the outside.

I believe in IFS so much because I know the power of how this has shifted my life and the lives of my clients for good. If other books and self-help programs have not given you the results you were hoping for, then IFS is the missing piece in your personal growth journey. The majority of people trained in IFS are therapists, but there are coaches, clergy and other types of healers that know this protocol. Not all of them use the whole protocol but I am someone who does because I've seen how life changing IFS is to get clients unstuck from just about any struggles they are having in any area of their lives—health, money, relationships and happiness—it produces lasting transformation. Many of the IFS books that have been written in the last ten years have an academic flavor to them, geared more or less towards the mental health community. No books have been written—until this one—about IFS through the lens of getting unstuck and unleashed and being happy. This is the first IFS book that goes into depth on how you can erase self-doubt, get unstuck, feel joy and take your life to the next level.

Once you experience IFS, you'll see that it's unlike anything else you have tried in personal development. I put my own signature spin on top of the IFS protocol by incorporating techniques from Neuro-Linguistics Programming (techniques to help you achieve your potential), plus my own life experiences, my deep understanding of chronic illnesses from my former life in pharmaceuticals, and finally my nutrition expertise and how our low self-image is the root cause of why we can't sustain healthy habits and a healthy weight. In other words, I connect the dots for you on how to achieve emotional, mental, physical and spiritual well-being. It's a veritable inside-out makeover of your inner and outer world so you're free to express the most extraordinary and unstoppable version of you and make your mark on the world.

* * *

The *real* you is lovable, compassionate, magnetic, curious, in love with life and *happy*. It's absolutely crucial to be happy *first* through unloading your suitcase full of old heavy emotional burdens *before* trying to achieve your goals. Being happy is what will help you get what you want. Otherwise, you'll be very disappointed after expending so much energy to accomplish your goals, only to find that the happier state isn't permanent. That's because there are voices of the past telling you *you're not good enough* still haunting you in the background no matter how much you achieve.

Many of us have internalized the voices of our parents and other authority figures, especially the negative ones. "Wow, you actually got A's . . . that'll never happen again." These types of messages get played out over and over again in your adult life and you simply lack the motivation to do anything great. Your dismal state of health, money, relationships and emotional well-being are a reflection of the messages buried in your subconscious. After all, what's stored in the subconscious—all of these parts of you that are frozen in the past with limiting beliefs— runs 90% of our lives. These parts are responsible for keeping you stuck.

When we did not comply with authority figures and decided to do things "our way," they would "put you in your place" or tell you "not to get too big for your britches." Accomplishments, "being different," creating outside the box or outshining your own father, mother or siblings was shunned, and today we tend to repeat these old tapes from authority figures who told us, "Who do you think you are?" Or "You'll never amount to anything. Remember how you failed before? Getting A's is just a fluke for you. Bet you can't do it again." And you end up living out this self-fulfilling prophecy and never do it again.

Or, the opposite can happen, where you defy your authority figures and prove them wrong. You get A's and you build a successful company, make lots of money and spend lavishly, all in the name of trying to prove yourself to the people who have hurt you. Unfortunately, in the journey to building your wealth and success, you end up sacrificing your authentic happiness—all because you thought happiness would materialize with the accomplishment of the next goal.

Other times, parents unknowingly push the kids to achieve more and more just so they—the parents—can look good in front of their peers. After all, some of them need to keep up with their peer group of "Joneses" to show how great they are at producing smart and accomplished children. If the kids feel that they are being pushed by the wrong agenda and/or coerced into a field they are not interested in, they will resent their parents and become unfulfilled adults. "You're going to go to med school, law school, or business school."

This kind of upbringing can create a feeling in you of "Am I not good enough with what I've accomplished already? What about my own desires and talents? I don't want to go to med school." It can also create the drive to overachieve, "I need to accomplish more and more to show myself and others (including my parents, my siblings and those bullies) that I *am* good enough." All of these efforts or lack thereof are driven by the parts of you that urge you to move forward for the wrong reasons, exhaust you as you climb the ladder of success, and make you unfulfilled during the journey. So despite being outwardly successful, you end up staying stuck, far and away from happiness.

Some people simply may not believe how great they really are despite their accomplishments, or they may not believe they have so much potential because of the voices they heard growing up. They've got that confident exterior—but on the inside it's a different story. It's all because of the negative feelings and beliefs they took on when parents were too busy, preoccupied or stressed out to explain why they snapped at or glared at them or left them feeling *abandoned*. For instance, that time when they were transported to their aunt's house in the middle of the night at two years old because mom was hurrying to the hospital to deliver their baby brother. (Yes, sometimes things as minor as being left at a relative's house or being the last kid to be picked up at school can usher in strong feelings of *abandonment*.) Their parts are carrying all of those messages that tell them they don't believe they are worthy or able of attaining success, love and fulfillment.

Or, you may have wondered why others are more successful or have a better-looking partner than you do. "Why are they so successful? I'm smarter, more attractive, more creative . . . " The reason is that they don't have the same voices looping around in their heads, they're confident and they're shining their inner light that attracts others. But the bigger million dollar question is: Are they fulfilled and happy, even though they look outwardly successful? Do they jump out of bed with joy? If they are not happy, then it's their parts from the past that keep them miserable, despite their success. So many people are driven to be on that hamster wheel all because of unresolved emotional issues. There's nothing wrong with the attainment of success as long as it is done of for the right reasons and as long as your emotional and physical health and your relationships are not sacrificed.

Many of the clients I've worked with are outwardly successful, with important careers and multiple degrees from prestigious schools. But they are not as happy as they look. They're lonely, with few if any real friends they feel safe enough with to share their hopes, fears and dreams. It's too vulnerable for them to let their friends and family know how they really feel after all the energy they have expended building up the mask of their perfect image. Eventually they can't stand faking it anymore, and they reach a "midlife crisis," feel stuck and seek my help.

The silver lining is that all of us can show up feeling good, allowing our real, vulnerable Selves to shine, revealing our innermost thoughts, asking for what we want and deserve, and even laughing at our goofy mistakes without any feelings of shame. When we address the needs of our parts, we can be *happy* in the present no matter what is going on around us. When your parts are no longer mired in the big and little childhood traumas, they cannot pull you down anymore. Your self-image can significantly improve, your confidence and self-esteem can soar, and you can wake up contented and happy for the rest of your life. Now let's dive into how *Internal Family Systems* came about and describe what these various parts are all about.

Chapter Five

Your Outer World is a Reflection of Your Inner World
Understanding Your Parts

"It is by going down into the abyss that we recover the treasures of life. Where you stumble, there lies your treasure."
–Joseph Campbell

Psychologist Dr. Richard Schwartz, the brainchild of *Internal Family Systems,* started developing this model of healing 30 years ago because he was frustrated. The traditional psychotherapy techniques he learned in graduate school were not resolving his clients' issues. After a number of years, he perfected the process of how to overcome our big and little traumas in a gentle, safe and powerful way. This is called *Internal Family Systems* because we live with an *internal family* of our *parts*. (This does not mean you have Multiple Personality Disorder.)

When Dr. Schwartz was "testing" this model with his clients, he found that when the frozen-in-time parts were befriended, were able to tell their stories, and felt heard and unburdened of their pain, they were able to let go of their extreme undesirable behaviors and feelings and go back to their original happy and balanced roles (or take on new positive roles in their internal family of parts). These parts can finally allow our magnificent true Self—the spiritual center —to emerge from the rubble of the old wounds and be the leader of all the other parts. That's why the website is called SelfLeadership.org. Now the leader is free to drive the bus of your life to somewhere really awesome—a place you really want to go!

For the sake of simplicity, I will be describing the core essence of what *Internal Family Systems* (IFS) therapy is. I will not go into details about the complexities that can arise in some situations. If you want more information about IFS after reading this book, visit the official website of Internal Family Systems at SelfLeadership.org.

* * *

The parts of you that are stuck in the past with the burden of extreme feelings and beliefs taken on from painful experiences will eventually show up in negative way: health problems, lack of financial abundance, toxic relationships, loneliness, self-loathing, a decrease of of spiritual energy and/ or a nervous breakdown or midlife crisis. These parts start out whispering (the stomach that is always unsettled, lethargy, anxiety, fibromyalgia, unexplained aches and pains) and if they are ignored for too long, they start screaming for your help and your parts can show up in the form of diseases ("you have cancer/thyroid/autoimmune issues.")

All parts—especially the negative behaviors and feelings you wish you could just vaporize—do have positive intentions behind them. They took on these negative roles for a reason: to *protect* you, to keep you *safe*. Many of your parts are not aware you are an adult now. They still think you are that child that's been abandoned, rejected, unloved, shamed and embarrassed. Your five-year-old part could be in the driver's seat of the bus of your life with your adult Self tied up in the back of the bus. The five-year-old part can also make you afraid to dream big and move beyond your comfort zone. They can make you settle into a life of mediocrity.

Even if you had consciously aware, loving and doting parents, incidents at school, on the playground, with your siblings and/or with your peers created parts that took on negative beliefs and feelings when you were emotionally wounded. Maybe your brother or sister constantly teased you and called you a "wimp" and a "loser." You may have felt guilty, shamed or embarrassed by what they said, and you didn't have the courage to share these unkind slurs and slights with parents or others who could supply the love and reassurance you needed at the time of the injury, preventing you from feeling so badly about yourself. Maybe you did want to share but mom or dad always seemed too busy, demanding, disinterested or preoccupied. And for every one of these voices you know about and the crystal-clear moments of shame you can still visualize, there are more of them buried in your subconscious that you blocked out when you were a baby or pre-verbal. All of these *exiled* parts are just waiting for your highest loving adult Self to release them from their burdens of shame, rejection, humiliation, un-lovability and unworthiness that they've carried for so long.

Your parts can also be described as sub-personalities, little people from your past that interact with each other, sometimes opposing each other: The part that wants to move up the corporate ladder versus the part that is afraid to do so because it feels safer in the current position. Each part has its own agenda and motivation. But every part has a positive intent, even the part that likes to drink a little too much at parties because drinking soothes the part that is *afraid of rejection* when meeting new people. That *afraid of rejection* part can get activated in social situations because that part remembers being rejected by the popular clique of girls in junior high. Drinking shoves the beach ball of that rejected little girl down and keeps it under water, chills you out, keeps the fear of rejection from coming to the surface and lets you get out of the house and be social. When this part of you gets unfrozen out of the old memories through IFS therapy, she will gladly give you the courage to be unafraid to go to parties and no longer hesitant to approach others first.

What is the *Self?*

The real highest true Self can be thought of as your "spiritual center," full of compassion and love for yourself, your parts and other human beings. The Self is the head honcho in the *Internal Family* of your parts. This is the *real leader* of your life. Operating from your Self is what makes you happy, joyous and contented. You are not afraid and you are not following others—you are leading yourself— with all of your natural born brilliance.

Your Self is the agent of your healing. (In very traumatized clients who don't have the capacity to access Self, the IFS therapist becomes the Self in the healing process.) Your Self has the power to lead you to break the habit of being your non-productive self.

We are born with a Self and all of our parts. Before bad things happened, every part took on happy and productive roles to help us navigate life. (Think about how happy and fearless most babies and toddlers are, until caregivers, other authority figures and peers start criticizing them, when all they were doing was expressing their happy selves or trying their best.) In the perfect world with perfect parenting and mentoring and where we don't have conflicts with our peers, our parts help us be balanced and happy. The part that likes to achieve, the part that likes to eat vegetables, the part that likes to eat ice cream, the part that like to drink, the part that likes to be the life of the party, the part that likes to shop, the part that gets angry, the part that feels sad, and so on, are all in harmony with one another, with none of them overwhelming your system with extreme behaviors and feelings. The Self can be seen as the conductor of the orchestra filled with your well-behaved parts, playing their respective roles nicely. Everyone has a Self—even criminals—it's just buried deep because they have been severely abused, shamed and abandoned as children.

The Self has compassion for the young parts of you that are stuck in the bad memories. They want to hear their stories so that they can help heal them. The Self, through the IFS protocol, can finally safely go back into the negative experiences and *witness* what happened to the *exiles* (usually child parts of you). Your *exiles* want to be witnessed because no one was there for them when the bad things happened. After the Self witnesses what happened in the past, then the Self can "re-parent" these *exiles* and give them what they needed that they never got so that they don't feel abandoned and alone anymore. The Self then brings these abandoned and exiled parts of you into the present and they become part of the your "team" that helps you to be fearless and move you forward. When your Self is driving the bus of your life, then your insecurities, worries and fears will significantly diminish and you'll be able to relax and have fun with your life. The qualities of the Self include the C's of being calm, clear, curious, confident, courageous, creative, compassionate and connected. Parts will relax when they see Self present and sense that Self is interested in them. As the Self heals more of your parts, you'll be able to show up as your brilliant charismatic Self that draws in the right love relationships, business opportunities and friends like bees to honey.

What are *Exiles*?

Exiles are the young parts of you that experienced trauma or other overwhelming experiences and hold the burdens of emotional pain and irrational beliefs about who you are from those events. They get frozen in time if no one was there to reassure them they are not bad people and that everything is going to be okay. These events can be as "benign" as the birth of a younger sibling or being the last one to be picked up at nursery school, or as painful as being the wallflower at the junior high school dance when no one asked you to dance and you were frozen with shame and humiliation. Exiles are the parts of you that feel stupid, unlovable, lonely, abandoned, rejected, shamed, humiliated, embarrassed, guilty, worthless, neglected, frightened, not good enough, scared, empty, needy, etc.

Exiles get locked away in the dungeons of your psyche for safety, to protect you from feeling the pain of shame, rejection or embarrassment ever again. You may even have forgotten who some of these exiles are because the experiences were so painful (like sexual abuse) you blocked them out.

In IFS sessions, these *exiles* will reveal themselves when the *protectors* feel safe enough to show you the exiles they have been protecting that have been absent from your conscious mind. I've had many clients who accessed an exile and said

"Oh . . . I can't believe I just remembered this . . . I haven't thought about that little girl hiding in the closet for 30 years!"

Exiles want redemption from the person who hurt them—the parent, bully, teacher, coach, sibling, friend or romantic partner. Your exiles are the reasons why there are people in your life now that push your buttons. They remind you of the people from the past that have hurt you. So, redemption is going to happen through your Self, not through confronting the person that hurt you. **You** get to give the exiles what they needed that they never got when they were hurt. That's how you overcome the old hurts and let them go for good. And in the process, you end up forgiving the person who has hurt you.

Exiles want to tell their stories. Once their stories are witnessed by you and/or the IFS practitioner (and sometimes clients would rather go inward and witness the painful events silently), that's when they'll finally able to release the *burdens* they have been carrying for so many years. When the release happens, you'll feel so much lighter because some of the burdens in the suitcase of emotional baggage have been emptied. The more parts you unburden, the lighter the suitcase gets, and the freer you feel, the more you'll be able to grow the wings to fly into your greatness. (The beauty of IFS therapy is that the IFS practitioner does not need to know the details of the painful events. It can be private between your Self and your parts.)

An exile can even be pre-natal. I know this sounds crazy but please let me share. The healer I was working with to overcome my depression had me access a part of me that felt I was not wanted when my mother was carrying me. Every time I looked at the picture of my mom eight months pregnant with me I sensed that she was praying for a boy.

(Boys are valued more than girls in Asian society.) After I was born, I remember my grandmother scolding my mom for having girls, first me and then my sister. Grandma told my mom that she had to keeping having more kids until she produced some boys. Thankfully my two brothers were born afterwards. To heal, I had to "re-parent" this fetus part and tell her that she was wanted. It took on the belief that "I am unlovable and unworthy." It's a cultural "legacy" burden that had to be released. So everything bad that happened to me growing up—especially in junior high and high school—was a reinforcement of the original "I'm not worthy and lovable" belief that started in the womb.

Another way of looking at exiles is the *beach ball* metaphor I have been using. Consciously trying so hard to keep the beach ball down is the equivalent of trying to keep the exiles hidden under water. It just uses up so much energy to hold them down that you're exhausted and don't have the energy or confidence to take on new challenges and move forward.

Exiles are the very parts of you that make you self-sabotage when you are two feet from gold, because . . .

- They are at the root of low confidence, self-esteem and shyness.
- They stop you from dreaming big.
- They don't believe you are worthy of breaking the glass ceiling of your potential.
- They make you fat, sick, bulimic or anorexic.
- They stop you from *sustaining* healthy habits.
- They stop you from healing your addictions.

- They stop you from feeling joy.
- They stop you from having Prince Charming/Fairy Princess love relationships.
- They cause relationship conflicts and prevent you from leaving abusive relationships because they don't believe you are worthy of something better.
- They cause the "dark cloud" and angry edge in your voice, which drives others to say, "I don't like his energy . . . he sucks the life out of me."

When the exiles are unburdened, the self-sabotage can go away and your life can dramatically improve.

What are *Burdens*?

Exiles are carrying the heavy "bricks" of the burdens of faulty beliefs, emotions and negative energies they took on as a result of their overwhelming experiences.

All events are neutral until we wrap a meaning around them. Because we didn't have the intellectual capacity to understand the meaning behind seemingly negative childhood events, our brain interpreted these events as "bad" and the blame was placed on ourselves. The Self has the power to change the meaning of these events for our parts and that's why Self is the agent of healing.

These burdens are beliefs such as "I'm not lovable, I'm not enough and I'm ugly." These faulty beliefs are at the root of what keeps you stuck, tethered to your emotional baggage and unable to get out of your own way to move forward. Many people are unaware of the faulty beliefs that are underneath the mask of their confident façade. You won't know you have them until you feel stuck. These exiles' burdens are released during IFS sessions.

What are *Protectors?*

Protectors are the "soldiers" that guard the door to the dungeon filled with your exiles. Their job is to prevent the vulnerable exiles from surfacing and flooding you with their painful feelings and emotions.

Some of your parts that had healthy and happy roles in your system turn into protectors after traumas occur. So the part that was once happy became depressed and anxious instead, to *protect* you; the part that helped you eat healthy became the part that makes you eat a whole box of cookies in one sitting; the part that helped you control your alcohol intake now makes you drink too much; the part that used to let others have their voice became the part that makes you arrogant and controlling; the part that helped you shop within your budget makes you shop excessively without regard to how much debt you are in; the part that was able to take ownership for your actions makes you blame others for your failures instead. These parts protect you from going into the dungeon of shame, worthlessness and rejection.

Since we're talking protectors here, I just want you to know that when someone seems to have an angry edge to them, that anger is more than likely due to anger from childhood. Their angry part is a protector that is protecting exile(s). When the exiles are rescued, the angry part will become less angry. Anger and numbness are culturally accepted emotions for men to express. Many men have painful exiles bottled up inside. It's no wonder there are many angry and numb men who are in total denial that there's anything wrong with them. These parts of them show up and wreak havoc in their professional and personal lives.

A controlling protector also is very rampant in people who felt powerless growing up. A dad who ruled with an iron fist, "My way or the highway," causes the *controlling* protector to get erected as a way of never letting anyone control them again. "Oh no . . . there's no way I'm going to let you tell me what to do. I run the show here."

Here are some other common protectors. Parts that make you numb out in front of the TV, mindlessly eat too much, binge and purge, exercise like crazy, gamble, have affairs, get obsessed with people, work too much, sleep your misery away, smoke and do illegal drugs, become overly afraid, being excessively shy, worrying, working too much, overachieving, criticizing, being lazy, being the pleaser, procrastinating, lacking confidence and self-esteem, getting a disease—all to make sure the exiles stay safely locked away in the dungeon.

Protectors don't want you to expose these shamed and rejected parts of you to the outside world, just as I didn't want to expose the parts of me that were ashamed of being Asian and ashamed of growing up poor. So my *protectors* of *overachievement*, *perfectionism* and *shopping* kicked in to help me navigate life safely. I didn't have a need to get rid of overachievement and perfectionism completely since those qualities helped me to become really good at everything I set my heart out to do. I understand why I developed these (to show the rich girls that rejected me that "I'm good enough") but I also used the positive qualities of these protectors to my advantage to accomplish my goals.

After the exiles are healed, some protectors will drop their non-productive roles altogether, such as the depressed and sad parts, and take on the happiness role. Other parts just want to relax and take a vacation after working so hard all of these years to keep you safe.

IFS therapy sessions help you to get to know your protectors and appreciate the positive intentions they have behind the undesirable negative behaviors and feelings they are having you play out. When these protectors feel heard and feel safe, (and you let them know how their behaviors are negatively affecting your life), they will allow you, the Self, to enter the dungeon and finally give the exiles that they are protecting what they need to feel whole and loved.

Sometime we get so hijacked by our wounded parts that they take over and we feel like we're having an out-of-body experience, like drinking way too much and getting a DUI because your exiles got triggered by your ex-husband who showed up at a friend's 40th birthday party. Seeing your ex flooded you with the pain of your exiles because he criticized you the way your father did. So to relieve the triggered pains of the exile, you start to drink a little too much because your Self got shoved out of the picture. The drinking protector stepped in to make you numb out the pain of the exile that just popped up when you saw your ex.

Protector Types: Managers and Firefighters

Protectors break down into two types: managers and firefighters. A *firefighter* is a type of protector that does exactly that, it *puts out the fire* when your feelings of shame, humiliation and rejection get triggered. So this *firefighter protector* makes you eat a whole pint of Ben & Jerry's ice cream or drink more wine than you should.

Firefighters don't care about the consequences of binge drinking or eating, smoking, doing drugs, shopping, gambling and other behaviors. They don't care about getting a DUI from driving drunk or getting fat with diabetes or going bankrupt from shopping and gambling. They just want to put out the fire of shame from the exiles that comes out during situations when they get triggered. Here's an example that happens so often with women who shop too much. A friend just made you jealous with the purchase of the latest designer bag, and your shamed little exile from junior high school gets activated. So you go on a shopping spree to buy a bag that is even more expensive than the one your friend had so the little girl's shame can go away and make you feel better. This firefighter behavior doesn't care that you are $10,000 in debt. These self-destructive behaviors help put that exile back in the dungeon where it belongs.

The most extreme examples of firefighting behaviors are people who kill others and people who commit suicide. The agony of the exiles is so bad that these firefighter protectors will kill to relieve the pain, they don't care if there are four school aged children left behind.

Manager types of protectors *manage* the painful emotions of the exiles *proactively* from getting stirred up in the first place. They proactively take on behaviors and feelings to prevent the exiles from surfacing, such as working too much, perfectionism, worrying, caretaking of others before yourself, avoiding risk, procrastinating, overachieving, keeping you insecure, keeping you numb, being controlling, keeping you afraid, sad, anxious or depressed.

To keep the *protector* concept simple in the rest of the book, I will not be differentiating which type of protector is popping up—firefighter or manager—in the stories I'm sharing with you. All you need to know that it's a *protector* causing someone to feel and do undesirable things.

Do the people that push my buttons have anything to do with my parts?

Yes they do!! They are the greatest gift you can receive in your adult life. Just as I mentioned at the beginning of my story in Chapter One, people who are self-centered get under my skin and one of these people was the trigger that sent me into depression and anxiety 10 years ago. I wanted validation from these self-centered people and I wasn't getting it, just like I didn't get the validation I needed from my self-centered caregivers. By definition, self-centered people are not capable of giving me what I want because *being self-centered* is one of their protectors. (The more wounded a person is, the more self-centered they can get. They are victims too.) Being ignored by them triggered my vulnerable exiles that felt unloved, unworthy and invisible.

So now I don't waste my time wondering why self-centered people don't seem to like me. I know it's reminding me of my exiles. (After your exiles are healed, you will always be reminded of what they went through when you meet people or encounter situations that stir up the past.) Now that I know why, and even if I have to have self-centered people in my life, I don't bother getting depressed over why they can't show me that I matter.

So if you must be around people who push your buttons, thank them for being in your life. Who do they remind you of? Mom, Dad, siblings, bullies? They are the gift to help you find the source of your deepest wounds that hold you back from living your best life.

Can it Be This Simple to Heal?

Yes, **if** the protectors allow you to access the exiles to relieve them of their burdens. The easiest part of IFS therapy is healing the exiles. The hardest part of IFS therapy is getting **permission** from the protectors to **access** the exiles. Some people have layers and layers of protectors that have been erected over the years like cinderblock walls. They are guarded by many, many rows of protective soldier parts in front of the walls to make sure they don't access the dungeon that is full of cobweb-covered exiles. They are too afraid of the exiles reliving the pains.

During IFS sessions, as you get to know one protector, another one can jump in to try to stop you from going to the old memory. If you are in Self and separated enough from your parts, and the practitioner you are working with is in their Self-energy, then progress can be made. How fast you access the exiles is dependent on how ready your psyche is to unburden yourself of the old story. The fear of not knowing who you would become without your story keeps many people stuck from ever unburdening themselves. They have to work through their fears, especially the mother of all fears—the fear of being in the spotlight of their greatest selves—in order to make progress. Some people would prefer to hide behind their excuses and stay small because that way they don't have to be accountable for anything. The devil you know, full of problems, is more comfortable than the devil you don't know, full of possibilities. Chapter Ten will go more into depth about fears.

The goal of IFS therapy is for the Self to get your parts out of the extreme roles they took on as a result of your negative experiences. The extreme roles of protector and exiled parts are stuck in the past and they can be polarizing and at war with one another, and that's why it's hard to get out of your own way. Your parts are running the show, not your Self. As the Self listens to your parts' stories and gives them what they need to make it all good, then they can leave behind their extreme roles that have kept you safe and finally be on the same team as your Self—to drive the bus of your life forward. It's essentially a "Chapter 11 bankruptcy re-organization" with your parts. They get new and improved roles to drive the company (your life) forward.

Your protectors and exiles are the reasons why you are stuck from having awesome relationships, achieving your ideal body, fattening up your bank account and living happy *now*. Protectors are also more than likely the reason why people don't work on themselves—think of men who are numb and "don't do emotions." As the years go on without working on your inner landscape, the protectors can get more stubborn and extreme in their roles—more anger, more drinking, more controlling and more numbness. These behaviors become increasingly unbearable and they end up driving friends and family away and breaking up relationships. And some people live a lonely and miserable existence, sometimes watching TV all day, eating junk, a prisoner in their own house and their own minds, with no social life. These parts may end up having them go to the grave without ever coming to terms with the past, dying prematurely or living life with regrets and with emotional and physical illnesses.

Your Subconscious Runs 90% of Your Life

Another significant reason you have found your goals difficult to attain is that your conscious desires comprise only 10% of what really determines your reality. The other 90% is determined by the words, images and messages held in the subconscious. This 90% is a combination of both positive and negative *core beliefs*. Core beliefs are formed based on what happened to you, especially before the age of seven. They are the beliefs of the exiled and non-exiled parts of you. Core beliefs are what follow the words "I am…"

- I am not lovable / I am lovable
- I am not enough /I am enough
- I am fat / I am thin
- I am ugly / I am beautiful
- I am a loser / I am a winner
- I am afraid / I am fearless, etc.

A good way to test out how much emotional baggage is living in your subconscious is to look in the mirror and perform this little test. Can you honestly say to yourself, "I love you very much . . . you are perfect the way you are!" If you can't say this like you really mean it and *feel* it, it indicates that there are parts of you (from the past) preventing you from loving yourself.

We all know that nothing is sexier and more attractive than people who believe in themselves and love themselves. Self-love gives you the means to exude confidence, self-esteem and magnetism. Self-love can propel you to get everything you want because whatever you think you are, the Universe usually does its job to give you results based on your beliefs. After all, the Law of Magnetism says, "You will *not* attract into your life what you want, you will attract *who you are*." If you are thinking, *I am worried that I might not be able to keep the 20 pounds off for good,* then just thinking and worrying about it will guarantee that you will not be able to keep the weight off. That's just how the subconscious mind works. And you have this thought because it's a *part* that is holding you back from believing that you deserve to stay trim. To change this, you must reprogram your subconscious mind by deleting the faulty beliefs your parts took on when bad things happened to you, through IFS therapy. Maybe your high school sweetheart dropped you like a hot potato for your best friend or maybe your parents hit you when you didn't behave, or your teacher shamed you in front of the class after you acted out. Any of these *exiled* parts can make you not love yourself and then you end up with a *protector* part that makes you feel that you don't deserve to be thin, and this part makes you self-sabotage every time after you lose a few pounds.

When this faulty programming gets deleted and rewired with new positive beliefs—as you will see in the stories in later chapters—that's when your parts from the past release themselves from holding down the brakes and allow the Self to drive your life forward, full throttle on the gas pedal, because your parts that were stuck in the past have eased off the brakes. Those parts that used to keep you stuck in the past have now taken their seats willingly in the passenger seats of your bus. Now your subconscious beliefs are in alignment with your conscious desires to improve your life and therefore you can achieve what you put your mind to. The *internal family* of your parts are not at war with each other anymore. They have undergone "Chapter 11 bankruptcy reorganization." They are now cheering you on, giving you support and reassuring you that there's nothing to be afraid of as you jump into the unknown to pursue your greatness, including being in top physical shape, attracting loving relationships and getting that promotion.

Although you and your parts have spent many years and expended so much energy trying to keep those wounding incidents submerged, when they are released, so is all that negative energy. The suitcase of burdens you've been dragging around will finally be empty and you will have the motivation to unleash the best version of *you*. People will pick up on your new positive energy and the sparkle in your eyes. They'll want to get to know you and do business with you. The new energy is uplifting, light, joyful and exuberant. It is unleashing the side of you that is excited to know you are loveable and worthy—and that **is** who you really are at your core.

Chapter Six

Shift Your Vibration and Manifest Your Dreams
What's Possible When You Unburden from the Past

*"By choosing to be our most authentic and loving self,
we leave a trail of magic everywhere we go."*
—Emmanuel

People who are at the end of their lives, perhaps in hospice, have a lot of time to think. They're firing their internal computers, sifting through their memories, sorting them out with gratitude or forgiveness. They may seem very still and very ill, but they are quite busy within their own consciousness. There is nothing else to do but think. They are probably thinking, "If only I had done it sooner!" Some of them are positively on fire, burning up with passion, having cleaned out their storehouse of regrets, anger and pain.

Now they are ready to go forward unfettered because they don't give a damn what anyone else thinks. There is truly nothing left to lose now . . . except of course that they have so little time left.

Can you imagine feeling that sort of passion? There are no boundaries to how far you can go and there is nothing holding you back, and I want that for you. That's why I urge you to recognize and start to heal those old emotional scars now rather than later, when it can be too little too late. Begin now to detect what is stopping you as you sift through your own memories and put them to rest. Some of these incidents have obvious silver linings and some of the "whys" are still hidden in the dungeon. Others are leaving major clues, a trail of breadcrumbs in your life and your behavior. You may want to open the door to them, just a little crack . . . and we can start now by gathering some clues and by painting a picture of how far you could go if you were unburdened. Here are some common big and little emotional scars that create exiles that keep people stuck in adulthood:

- Getting spanked, shoved or any other form of unwarranted physical attack
- Being touched inappropriately—sexual abuse
- Abandonment from being left alone—last one to be picked up from school, waking up in the middle of the night at the babysitter's house
- Getting "no's" when you wanted something from an authority figure
- Feeling significantly poorer or richer than your peers
- Not feeling as attractive as your peers; peers making fun of your appearance

- Being significantly smarter or dumber than your peers or siblings
- Teacher putting you in a time-out in the hallway
- Having a different sexual orientation
- Having to fend for yourself at a young age
- Feeling ignored and neglected
- Feeling like you didn't matter

The following are a sampling of the critical voices silently looping in the minds of clients I've worked with:

- Why would anyone want someone like you?
- You're not special enough to achieve your dreams.
- There's no way you deserve love, family and a successful career. Who do you think you are?
- People will laugh at your ideas. Why do you think your ideas are so special?
- You've turned out to be such a disappointment. Why can't you be more like your brother?
- You're so average. I never imagined a kid of mine would be so mediocre.
- You're not capable of doing that.
- Once a quitter, always a quitter.
- You're ugly.
- You're so average looking, let's get some decent makeup and clothes on so you don't embarrass me.

- What's up with the B's on the report card? You're
  never going to amount to anything unless you get
  more A's.

These old silent messages rob you of joy and rob you of reaching your potential. They also make you feel confused, resentful, victimized and angry. As an adult now, consciously you know you should be "over it" but it's not your fault that you're not. These old messages are what comprise the bulk of the stuff lurking in your subconscious mind—that 90% that drives your results or lack thereof. You may have spent years in therapy and other self-help programs and still feel like there's unfinished business. Now you know it's your *exiles* that are the unfinished business. Once you hear their stories and give them what they need to get them out of the past, they won't be haunting you with these messages anymore. The messages will be rewired to the positive and you'll be set free.

These messages are the wounds underneath the confident exterior that some people erect. They keep themselves so busy that they don't even have time to think because silence and going inward may be too painful. Some even resort to numbing themselves in front of the TV or Internet so they don't have "time" to do anything productive with their lives. Watching too much TV or spending mindless time in front of the computer are *protectors*.

What are you avoiding and what are you *afraid of* if you spend your time with something meaningful instead of TV or surfing the net? Afraid of visiting your exiles? (It will be gentle with IFS therapy, I promise.) Perhaps being accountable for living to your potential? Could you be afraid of intimidating and alienating your friends and family with your true power? "Oh God, I can't risk being abandoned by my friends and family, I'd rather die." "Jeez, I can't risk making my sister feel bad if I shine my light. She'll feel even worse about herself."

Why can't I just take anti-depressants to get over my past?

If you think that going on anti-depressants and other psychiatric medicines would be so much easier than addressing the parts of you that are stuck in the past, you're in for a rude awakening. I used to sell psychiatric medicines to doctors. Yes, they work well for severe depression. For mild depression, they are only slightly better than taking a sugar pill. Yes, some people will never be able to go off of them. Yes, they take the edge off. Yes, some people have true chemical imbalances, exacerbated by the nutrient-deficient Standard American Diet. But **no**, psychiatric meds will **not** do the real healing of solving the issues of your exiles. If you only take meds there will be little growth, forward movement or true change. You might be able to numb and tune out the influence of your parts and their voices, but the reality is that you'll likely be numbing your true Self and your greatness too.

You can take meds to get functional or take the edge off while you work with your protectors and exiles. You may even be able to diminish or eliminate the use of these meds with their nasty side effects after your parts are understood and healed. IFS practitioners are seeing less need for psychiatric medicines and hospitalizations when parts are understood and healed.

Since I worked in the pharmaceutical industry, I used to joke with the IFS trainers that if everyone went through IFS healing and unburdened themselves of their faulty beliefs, many more people would no longer need meds or therapy. The pharmaceutical and psychotherapy industries could tank because we'd be stopping the cycle of "victims creating more victims." Children would grow up happy because their parents would be full of love and compassion and would know better than to say negative things to Johnny that would leave him believing he's not lovable, worthy and enough. These children would not need therapy when they grow up because they would be full of self-love. Sadly, this is not going to happen anytime soon.

What If I'm a Loser? Is it Too Late for Me?

When you understand the psyche through the lens of IFS, you will not judge yourself and others as losers anymore. The deadbeat, drug-abusing high school dropout (who was abandoned by an alcoholic mom, never knew his dad and was raised in foster care) can't get his life together due to the *protectors* and *exiles* hijacking his loving true Self. The real authentic and loving version of him is buried so deep that it would be hard for him to ever heal unless he spends a good amount of time in therapy. He is not ready to go from good to great, he is just trying to go from half-dead to good so he can cope with life. It may take a drastic negative event—like getting fired or landing in jail—in order for him to face the truth. There are trauma therapists trained in IFS and this would be the perfect step for him. Other trauma modalities can be helpful for him too.

The IFS methodology makes so much intuitive sense to people. They simply have to unburden their parts, *if* they want to prioritize their emotional well-being. We make time for the things that are important to us. Unfortunately, for many, what's more important than emotional health is more money, more stuff, buying the latest and greatest gadget and keeping up with the Joneses so that they don't feel left out. If they don't prioritize their emotional and physical health, they might end up unfulfilled with regrets toward the end of their lives because they didn't live their truth. This does not have to happen. If we prioritized our mental health *first*, our physical health would fall into place and everything else in our lives too, because we'd all love ourselves enough to want to care for our bodies and desire nothing but excellence from ourselves.

What If I Just Don't Want To Bother With Emotional Healing?

Unfortunately, if you don't make peace with the past and transform your negative core beliefs, you may be one of the people who end up living in "quiet desperation" with disastrous consequences. If you don't address the needs of your parts and you keep that beach ball underwater, eventually it will can back to haunt you in the form of mental, emotional or physical problems—depression, anxiety, gastrointestinal issues, cancer, thyroid problems, migraine headaches, skin problems, auto-immune diseases, and so much more.

Can Ignoring My Parts Really Affect My Health?

Numerous studies have shown that what you put on your fork, what you do with your feet and the emotions and feelings you carry are 80% responsible for whether or not you live to a ripe old age with diseases or disease-free. Your thoughts, feelings and beliefs (which are your protector and exile parts), your diet, lifestyle and how you manage stress has the power to be 80% responsible for whether or not your body decides to turn on the "bad genes" you inherited from your parents. (This is the science of epigenetics.) Just like eating the Standard American Diet full of unhealthy fats, sugars and starches can activate your disease genes, your thoughts and feelings and the resentment, anger and sadness from the past can be the triggers on top of your lousy diet that allow diseases to flourish.

There is quite a bit of literature on the mind-body connection to disease. Andrew Weill, MD, Deepak Chopra, MD, Mark Hyman, MD, Bernie Siegel, MD and Lissa Rankin, MD are some of the important authorities in this area. They have authored many books and you can find them on Amazon if you want to explore further.

As an example, it takes an average of 10-30 years for cancer cells to get large enough to show up on a diagnostic test or give you symptoms. So even though you may feel "fine" now, there could be many nasty illnesses developing in your body because you are not taking care of yourself emotionally and physically. So if you get sick at 60 years old, the disease genes have been fueled by your thoughts, feelings, diet and lifestyle most likely since you were 40 years old. Positive thoughts and the right diet can actually reverse the expression of bad genes and anything else that is silently growing inside of you.

I had a client who broke out in hives when she fought with her husband. The hives were her exiles showing up on her skin when they were triggered by her abusive husband. The hives stopped after the exiles were healed.

Even if you have told yourself consciously that you're "over the past" and the past is "out of sight and out of mind," the negative beliefs you acquired from old hurts are crying for your attention through some of your physical and mental ailments.

How Fast Can I Get Out of My Story and Reprogram My Brain?

The rate at which you positively shift to where you want to go in all areas of your life is dependent on whether the part of you that has held your stories is ready to allow you to emerge as your fearless, confident and authentic true Self.

There can be a lot of fear around change, good or bad. Our greatest fear is actually being in the spotlight of our greatness (and not death or our darkness). When you are living to your potential, you will be in the spotlight whether you like it or not. So you see why so many people spend their time in the darkness doing routine tasks and being run by their fearful wounded parts, wondering:

- Who would I be without my stories?

- Will my friends still love me if I am the rising star and become my greatest Self?

- What will they think of me if I reversed the shrinking I do to please others so I don't threaten them with my greatness?

- What if people leave me?

- What if I lose all of my friends because I've improved my life while they are still stuck? I'll be on stranded on an island, alone. So I'll stay where I am, even if it's not where I want to be. It just feels safe and comfortable.

There are positive intentions behind your negative behaviors. Think of the toddler who would rather throw a tantrum to get attention than not get any attention at all for being good. It's the same reason some people unknowingly keep themselves sad and/or sick with a disease so family members and friends will pay attention to them. Having a crutch like this can make you afraid to get unstuck because being ignored would be more painful.

Feeling loved and feeling like we belong are important core human needs. So if we are afraid of being thrown out of our tribe and feel threatened in any way, then it might be too painful to change, to lose weight, to get that promotion, to become healthier. After all, the devil you know is better than the devil you don't know.

If you want your life to positively shift, IFS has the ability to do that for you. With some clients, I have seen 180° shifts with just one three-hour concentrated session. Other clients needed several deep-dive sessions to get unstuck. Clients who are not psychologically healthy usually need six months or more of traditional psychotherapy sessions using the IFS model or some other modality to get to a level of stability where they can cope with the stresses of everyday life.

IFS Helps You Relate Better

IFS therapy can help everyone. From the murderer in jail to the CEO that needs to listen more and show more compassion for his subordinates. Understanding this model also makes you more compassionate to others when they are acting out because you'll understand it's just their parts that are acting out. Even when your kids act out, you can get curious and ask, "What's going on with this part of you that is slamming every door in the house?" "A part of me is curious about this part of you that likes to bite your forearms. What's the story of this part?"

This model of getting to know your parts and speaking *for your parts* is useful in everyday interactions, not just in therapy or coaching. For instance, when you are angry with a loved one, a co-worker or friend, you could say, "*A part of me* is angry that you did this . . . " instead of "I'm so angry with you, it's all your fault . . . " The emotional charge and the tone of the former is mitigated and less likely to trigger a toxic reaction from the other person. You're just blaming th*e part* for your negative feelings and behaviors. The other person just thinks "Oh it's just a part, you're not angry at *me*, it's just a *part* of you."

Or, when you see dirty laundry spread out all over the place or the dishes in the sink are never taken care of, instead of lashing out into an ugly fight, how about getting *curious?* He (or she) may very well have a good explanation of why he has a part that is not interested in picking up after himself.

"Honey, there's this **part of me** . . . that gets really irritated when I see dirty laundry piled up on the bed, the floor and the chairs instead of the hamper. This **part of me** wants to go nuts. I'm really **curious** about the **part of you** that likes to leave laundry everywhere else but the hamper. Can you tell me more about this **part**?"

This way of interacting is less charged than "Why do you leave your laundry all over the place?" Then he gets defensive and can lash back, because an exile might be stirred up by the way you are speaking. It could remind him of the way his mother used to scold him. When you come from a place of **curiosity** and **blame your part** for wanting to know, your partner will not get charged up in the same way, and he will speak for his part. It's like you have four people in this conversation—you, your part, your partner and his part. This is a beautiful and non-confrontational way of having a dialogue instead of a fight.

IFS improves how we interact with our loved ones. The more we are aware of how we need to support our children (because we've seen how our parents' treatment of us created exiles that hold us back), the better chance of having happy and psychologically healthy children. These kids will grow up with less emotional baggage and are more likely to unleash their full potential. We become better parents when we are parenting from our true Self. If you go through IFS, you'll understand how you were not validated by authority figures and/or your peers and you will be so much more cognizant of how you should interact with your own children so they grow up and become happy and productive adults.

IFS and Leadership in the Workplace

IFS therapy is the crucial missing piece in executive coaching. Some of these coaches don't have the patience or compassion to know that it **is** your past that is causing you to act out. IFS therapy is the weapon you need to shatter the glass ceiling of what's possible for your career.

The *Peter Principle* says, "You will rise to the level of your incompetency." Most executive coaches have no idea that it's your exile(s) that are still stuck in the past—they are actively holding down the brakes of your bus. Some executive coaches tell their clients to just "release the past already, just do what I tell you to do." This doesn't work! It's no different than Western medicine putting on the pharmaceutical Band-Aid to fix your aches and pains instead of finding out the root causes of your deep inner wounding.

A leader who is dysfunctional and "rough around the edges" needs an IFS executive coach (like myself), not to talk about their mother for years on end, but to unburden the exiles created by their mothers so that they can decrease conflict and lead effectively. When they decrease the dysfunction on their teams, their companies can thrive with happy and productive employees. This can be accomplished in a few concentrated sessions. Once you unveil the Self and it is allowed to drive the leadership bus, you really won't need the crutch of a coach to fake your leadership competence. You won't feel like a fraud anymore. In fact, you'll be able to lead yourself without a coach once your true Self emerges in all of its power, confidence, authenticity, creativity and inner knowingness of what which risks to take for yourself and your company.

The #1 reason why people leave their jobs or dislike their jobs is the environment they work in, especially if they have bosses that are controlling and self-centered. Bosses and employees alike can show up from a more compassionate place if they come to terms with how their protectors and exiles make them do what they do. If bosses want more productive employees, they need to genuinely care about them. People can detect if caring is authentic or not. If it isn't sincere, the bosses will continue to be the negative topic of discussion around the water cooler and the dinner table day after day.

Raise Your Self-Image, Manifest Magic

Once you release the shame, apathy, fear, anger and embarrassment of the exiles, you will naturally show up with a higher vibration and have an effect on people that you overhear described as, "I love her energy" or "He has such great energy. It makes me feel good"

Let me show you another way of looking at how your past shows up in your present reality and what you need to do to manifest great outcomes.

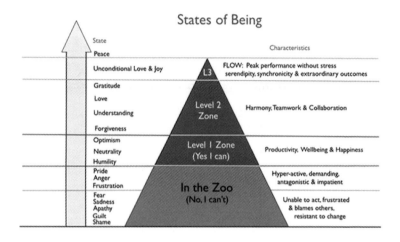

This "State of Being" scale is inspired by the *Map of Consciousness* developed by Dr. David Hawkins, author of the bestseller *Power vs. Force: The Hidden Determinants of Human Behavior.* Michelle Stanton of www.ZoneHigh.com, a company that helps you reach your potential, took Dr. Hawkins' scale one step further and translated it to everyday living. This image is reprinted with permission and it beautifully illustrates how negative energies keep you stuck from success and happiness. I am taking Michelle's concepts one step further and putting the filter of Internal Family Systems on it.

Protectors and *exiles* hold negative energies shown in the bottom levels of energy (depicted on the left-hand side and at the bottom of the pyramid) with shame, guilt, apathy, sadness, fear, anger, pride and frustration. So you are "In the Zoo" of "I can't," and may be hyperactive, demanding and resistant to change. You blame others and you can't move forward because you are stuck in your story. Others pick up on this negativity and they don't want to do business with you or be your friend or romantic partner. It's just easier to blame others for your lack of results. Since you are in this negative energy, the Universe will reflect back to you exactly what you are thinking, so you don't move forward, you're in your own way and you don't have results.

If you want to move up on the scale to Level 1 and above with joy, gratitude, trust and forgiveness and be at the top of the triangle (and be happy, productive and have synchronistic events and extraordinary outcomes manifest), then you need to release the old stories and empty the suitcase of burdens your exiles carry. When you do this, you'll be happy and feel so good about yourself. That higher vibrational energy is what will attract you to the perfect romantic partner, the business opportunities, the friendships, the fatter bank account and better health and body.

You'll end up being at the right place at the right time so you can get what you want. Synchronistic events happen and you get extraordinary outcomes. This is not due to luck per se, it's the Universe's way of rewarding you for getting out of your comfort zone, moving forward, and trusting in the unknown. Many people believe that there's no such thing as coincidences. I believe this too. You don't have to know the details of **how** you are going to get what you want. When you believe in yourself, the **how's** will magically appear. You will be at the right place at the right time, with the caveat that you *will* encounter a few speed bumps along the way. You will be rewarded when you are not afraid to experience the speed bumps. It really does work this way. This is how magical things have happened in my life (and my clients' lives) as a result of getting out of our stories. This can happen to you too. I'll share the story of how I manifested this book deal in the final chapter to illustrate this concept.

The Law of "Anti-Attraction" - The Negative Energy of Shame

Here's an example of how denying your past can show up energetically as working too hard to make your business rock. I met a Life Coach at a conference who was a nice gal but there was an energy about her that felt "off." Underneath her confident façade of "Everything is great! I love my life." She seemed like she was trying too hard to market her services. Sure enough, a few months later, she couldn't take hiding her secret any longer. She revealed on Facebook that when she was eight years old she was molested several times by her uncle. Now everything made sense to me. That "off" energy was the shame of sexual abuse. She was at the bottom of the energy pyramid depicted by the "State of Being." Now that you are familiar with IFS, you probably have guessed that if she wants to move up the scale of consciousness and attract financial abundance, she needs to release the bottom level of shame energy from the sexual abuse. This heavy burden will continue to contribute to her lack of growth in her business until she does something about this. So how she is showing up and the low energy I picked up is a reflection of her low self-worth due to the abuse.

Some people may not realize they loathe themselves. They don't know that self-loathing repels others like a skunk. It's the Law of "Anti-Attraction." And they blame everyone else around them for their lack of results. They may even have the power to suck the energy right out of you. Many self-loathing people can't even fathom moving out of their comfort zone because they are so paralyzed by their story. Remember, the Law of Magnetism says that you will attract into your life *not* what you want but *who you are*. The results of how you feel about yourself are reflected in your appearance, your bank account, the level of your career success and in your love relationships and friendships (or lack thereof). This statement can be pretty hard for some of us to swallow. But this is so true and it is expressed by all of the big-name personal development gurus. How you show up **is** a reflection of your self-worth. The results (or lack thereof) in all areas of our lives are a function of our *protectors* and *exiles*. You can change these less than optimal results by overcoming your faulty negative beliefs through IFS healing.

Makeover shows on television show contestants how they can do an outside-in makeover job with a stylist, makeup artist and hairdresser and getting slimmer through diets and plastic surgery. But is this going to last? No way! Eventually, these people self-sabotage and go back to their old habits. Nothing will change unless the inner emotional makeover is done first. The outside is a reflection of the inside. (There are people who are born beautiful and thin and they show up with great grooming and clothes. The bigger question is: How fat is their bank account, how deep and satisfying are their love relationships and how healthy is their self-esteem? Many models and other good-looking people have low self-esteem and less-than-optimal results in other areas of their lives besides their appearance.)

Now I'm going get on my soapbox and be a little in your face (like the celebrity coaches on *The Biggest Loser*) because you or someone you know may need this reality check. When we don't *feel* good about ourselves, some of us will show up dumpy and frumpy and age like a prune because we don't care about the consequences of eating junk and not taking care of our bodies. We don't care about the consequences of getting cancer, heart disease, diabetes, Alzheimer's and many other chronic lifestyle diseases because we'll conveniently blame our genes (which unfortunately are only 20% responsible for our illnesses) because it's too painful to admit that we are at fault.

We'll be jealous of others around us who seem to be more attractive, get more attention and have more money and better relationships. We conveniently "hate" them and gossip about them, wishing something bad would happen to them. This is the *awareness* we need that we have a lot of emotional baggage in this area that we need to address. They are pushing our buttons because they are making us look in the mirror to see how much we are holding ourselves back. We know we can be so much more. We wish we had the guts to be like them and get all the attention. We'll stay in our misery for the rest of our lives if we don't have the *awareness* that we are the only one responsible for our fate and we are the only one that has the key to get out of the jail we have put ourselves in. We have to understand and heal our protectors and exiles if we want to achieve great things and become beautiful, handsome and awesome from the inside-out.

It's going be hard work to accomplish this because it's pushing all of us outside of our comfort zones to do the emotional healing but it's going to be worth the trip because we won't end up lying on our death beds thinking "I shoulda', I coulds', I woulda'."

Okay, now I'll get off my soapbox. I had to be a little tough here because I care about you and I know you and everyone else have so much more to offer the world. There is only ONE you because everyone else is taken and we're waiting for you to shine your brilliance and leave a legacy. As mythologist Joseph Campbell states so beautifully, "The privilege of a lifetime is being who you are."

When you develop loving relationships with all of your parts and heal and unburden the exiles of their erroneous beliefs, when you change the "I'm not lovable, I'm not worthy, I'm not enough" parts to "I'm lovable, I'm worthy, I'm enough," your parts will finally go back to their preferred positive roles instead of working so hard to protect you and stop your progress when you are just two feet from getting the gold. When your parts are understood and healed, this is when your self-image soars and you can fathom new possibilities for yourself because you are led by the soul and spirit of your Self. You will no longer have self-doubt and your confidence, self-esteem and self-love will skyrocket as you enjoy that juicy love affair with yourself. Because you're in love with all of your parts, you can finally get unstuck and do something big with your life.

Chapter Seven

The Baggage Underneath the Love Handles and Wrinkles

How to Overcome Health, Weight and Aging Struggles

"The body is a mirror of how you heal your life."
–Lissa Rankin, MD

The state of your health and weight are a reflection of the thoughts and beliefs in your mind. The desire to get in shape to feel good about yourself is *not* a real goal. Yes, that's right, it's not a *real* goal. Real goals have substance and they spark you to jump out of bed with joy every morning like lightning just struck.

When was the last time going on a diet made you jump out of bed with joy? Probably never. **Why** do you want to go on a diet? It's not about the weight, it's about feeling good, getting noticed and being validated in the short term. What will feeling good about yourself do for you in the long term? If you are not clear on what you want to accomplish as a result of gaining confidence from having a great body, then going on a diet is futile. Getting trim for your daughter's wedding or for the old boyfriend you'll see at your high school reunion will only produce temporary results. I think you know this.

Real goals have you making a difference in other people's lives. What will having the confidence as a result of weight loss enable you to do that you are not doing right now? If you don't know the answer to this question, you'll more than likely gain all the weight back within 6 months like 95% of dieters, oftentimes "with interest." When you want to lose weight for the right reasons, you'll jump out of bed with joy and the healthy eating plan will stick.

For example, my mission is to help you and the rest of the world manifest health, wealth, awesome relationships and happiness by unburdening the gremlins of your past. Because it's a big mission with lots of things to do, I can't afford not to have high energy every day. To have high energy, I need to eat very healthy so I can concentrate and be productive. (I still allow myself that occasional scoop of ice cream. Not enough to go into a sugar coma.) And I reduce my stress by going to yoga every other day. These habits are mandatory because staying in shape and feeling good about myself allows me to take risks, to keep meeting new people and to accomplish my tasks. My mission is not about *me*, it's about leaving a legacy before I go to heaven.

Your goal may not feel as ambitious as mine. But I can assure it is you every bit as important because it's an expression of your true Self. Your goal can be as meaningful as having the health to take care of your grandchildren, modeling for them how bright and dynamic life can be as an older adult. Your goal may be to write your novel or memoir, to take dancing classes even if you have two left feet, to swim in as many lakes as you can or to make a series of instructional videos on YouTube. It can be something you've kept close to your heart and are now ready to reveal to the world.

Once you have anchored in that goal you'll realize that if you keep eating badly and don't exercise, then you might end up like one of your relatives who could barely move in "old age," consumed with talking about their ailments, how constipated they are and how they can't afford their expensive prescription medicines. If you don't want to end up like these sick relatives, you need to start healthy habits *now*, not after the doctor says, "I'm sorry, you have cancer." So take the time to really think about what being in shape and feeling good will allow you to accomplish that you can't even fathom doing right now.

From the previous chapters you understand how your parts show up as ugly behaviors and negative feelings, and how they are also reflected in how disease-free or disease-ridden you are—and in the size of your waistline. Your parts are just waiting for you to listen to them, and they are hoping to get your attention through your health and/or weight struggles, sneaking up with excess pounds, gastrointestinal problems, thyroid issues, heart disease, cancer, auto-immune diseases, high blood pressure, diabetes, skin problems, migraine headaches and many other chronic ailments.

So if you struggle in any area of your life, including weight, you need to trace it back to your negative beliefs and the hazardous self-talk that keeps running in the back of your mind all day long. These parts paralyze you from confidence and self-esteem and they get your attention through self-loathing, which could end up showing up as health and weight struggles and sagging, aging skin and wrinkles. The stress your parts are under from holding onto their burdens can make you age real fast. It's not your fault you're this way, it's the fault of your overwhelming experiences and the nonsense messages that were downloaded from caregivers, teachers and peers. These old hurts that keep you awake at night are waiting for *you* to heal them so you can heal your body.

* * *

When I initially coached nutrition clients, I was very enthusiastic and happy for them when they got results during the first three months. I kept them accountable and taught them how to restructure their meals. (Yes, some people just needed to be taught what to eat and what not to eat.) However, 90% of the people I coached had been on diets before—whether by reading celebrity diet books or joining other well-known programs that tracked their progress. While they were on these diets they succeeded and lost weight, but they couldn't sustain their healthy habits and gained all that weight back. That's when they found me online, through a friend or by attending one of my workshops.

These clients were excited about having a personal nutrition coach that was *finally* going to solve their problems once and for all. I taught them to change their diets by adding in good wholesome fresh food—lots of fruits and vegetables, lean protein, complex carbs, less "fake food" and fewer fatty animal products. They felt better, lost inches and tamed their bloating abdomens pretty quickly. I kept them accountable and I was delighted to witness their successful outcomes.

But wait, not so fast! When some of them were done with me, they eventually gained the weight back after a few months. How did I know? I'd see them in town or I'd hear through the grapevine that they were off trying another diet, sometimes even resorting to medical weight loss programs.

This was frustrating. I felt so bad for what they must be going through. I knew that some of these clients needed to address the deeper emotional issues that were underneath the surface of their weight and health problems. We touched upon it during their nutrition coaching sessions but they just didn't want to "go there" anymore. After all, they had hired me to teach them how to eat right, they didn't contract with me to do deep emotional work. They had been through therapy, they'd dealt with their pasts, it was out of their consciousness (or so they claimed). Essentially I just let it go and coached them on how to give themselves positive self-talk so they could keep up with their healthy habits.

* * *

Let me describe to you what I often heard from my nutrition clients. They generally had good dietary habits and discipline by eating minimal amounts of food during the day. And they'd feel virtuous for eating only a salad for lunch with a friend or coworker—no bread, skimping on that dressing on the side, and skipping the dessert. Then, when they got home, they'd be ravenous and pig out on whatever they could find preparing dinner. At dinner, they control themselves again (because their family is watching them eat) and pat themselves on the back for being "good." They're always conscious about eating well in front of friends and family because they want them to see that they're a healthy eater and they want them to conclude that it must be their genes that make them fat.

Then, when nine or ten o'clock rolls around and no one is looking (the kids and husband are upstairs sleeping) they start binging on anything they can find in the cupboards and fridge. They feel like an alien part of them has taken over.

(Instead of doing this at home, they sometimes hide some of these behaviors by using the drive thru and eating in the car.)

That part of them just keeps eating and eating and eating those crackers or potato chips, the cookies, the pizza, the cake or the ice cream until they feel like a bowling ball has grown inside their bellies. They might even need to pop a Zantac or Prilosec before hopping into bed, disgusted with themselves, vowing to start all over on their diets *tomorrow.* "This is the last time I'm doing this," they say. The next morning they're so stuffed and disgusted from the night before that they don't eat anything all day. But they get so hungry by late afternoon that they start the cycle all over again. Or perhaps they sustain healthy habits for a couple of days after one of these binges, but it ends up being too hard, and the old habits come back. Let me introduce someone who asked for my help and fits this profile: Sarah.

Food Covers Up the Shame of Growing Up Rich

Sarah is an average looking 48-year-old fourth grade teacher with light brown shoulder-length hair. She's been gaining and losing the same 20 to 30 pounds since she was 30 years old. She followed a balanced exercise routine in college but after she got married at 28, life just got in the way and she let herself go, gaining 30 pounds over the course of three years.

Sarah is addicted to sweets. She knows what it takes to have a trimmer body. She does well during the day but at night the munchies kick in and she can scarf down half a bag of chocolate chips cookies and/or a pint of Ben and Jerry's in one sitting. She can't stop herself. She feels good while doing it but hates herself afterward. She feels as if an out-of-body experience is happening when this part of her takes over, urging her to binge on things she doesn't want to eat.

After a few months of gorging herself on sugar, she gets so disgusted with her belly busting out of her pants and the line of flab bulging over her bra straps that she literally exercises like a madwoman on a mission. She detoxes with green juices and clean eating and stays away from ice cream and cookies.

I was hired during one of these crazy episodes of her wanting to lose weight. Her 30th high school reunion was looming and she had to look good for the old boyfriends she was going to see. She knew they were going to be there because of the Facebook conversations she'd been conducting with her private high school Facebook group. Here's is the initial consultation Sarah had with me before she hired me to help her get in shape:

> **Emily:** Why is it so important for you to lose 30 pounds?

> **Sarah:** Because I want to *feel good*, be *more attractive* and *more confident*.

> **E:** And why is *feeling and looking good* and *being more confident* important to you?

> **S:** I want to turn heads and get noticed by people.

> **E:** By men **and** women?

> **S:** Yes. I've got my 30th high school reunion coming up and a couple of my old boyfriends will be there. I don't want to embarrass myself by showing up fat and frumpy. I also want to show the girls who teased me that I turned out better than they did, to shove it up their you-know-what. The girls who made fun of me in high school will be laughing at me again if I'm

bursting out of my dress. So I can't let that happen. I'm just a little competitive.

E: It's very normal to be competitive in that arena. We all want to be noticed, no matter how old or how married we are. What else will *feeling good* and *turning heads* allow you to do that you are not doing right now?

S: Give me the confidence to finish my Ph.D. so that I can go for a higher position in education.

E: What will having that more visible position do for you? Why is it so important?

S: So I can show my husband and my peers that I can be somebody on my own, that I'm not the rich little daddy's girl who doesn't have to work another day in her life.

E: What else do you want from daddy?

S: For him to finally tell me that I'm *good enough*. (Her voice is cracking when she says this.)

E: So you want validation from everyone around you that you are good enough as you are to be Sarah, not as someone with money from her dad. What else will the confidence allow you to do?

S: I also want the confidence to leave my husband one of these days. Obviously, I can leave now since I don't need him to support me. But a part of me is very attached to being with someone. I can't stand the thought of navigating life alone. If I had the confidence by being more attractive, that might give me the courage to move forward and find a more attractive guy. I deserve a better-looking guy with more status. But I have to feel confident and attractive enough to get the new guy.

E: Yes, who you attract is a reflection of your self-image. What will happen if you don't get this weight problem resolved soon?

S: I'll feel like a total loser, sad and miserable. I would eat myself to death and be stuck in the house for the rest of my life because I'd be too embarrassed to go out. And be stuck with my loser husband.

E: So are you saying that if you don't get this weight problem resolved, you will be lonely and shut out from the world? You would also not be fulfilling your full potential and your dreams because you don't have the courage to finish your Ph.D. and go after the bigger position; and you don't feel good enough about yourself to have the confidence to be on your own and eventually attract another mate. Sounds like the reason why you really want this is to be with someone who's as hot as you can become. And to have status in the educational community so you're no longer defined as the girl with the rich daddy, not identified by the money you inherited; that you are your own independent person, that you *are* somebody important, all in the name of showing daddy that you are good enough. Losing weight is all about showing the world that you are *good enough.*

S: Yes, you're absolutely right.

E: What is it worth to you to solve the problem?

S: It will mean everything to me.

E: On a scale of 1-10, how important is the weight problem to solve, right now?

S: 9.

E: You know, Sarah, I can definitely help you with shedding the weight. But the bigger issue that needs to be addressed is your lack of confidence and self-esteem because of how you grew up.

S: I've gone through years of therapy around this. I know it's my daddy issues. I just want you to help me with the weight problem.

E: I'll take you on, but you have to promise to do the deeper work of understanding the real motivation behind why you do what you do.

* * *

Truth be told, Sarah is going on a diet for the wrong reasons. Losing weight for a special event—reunions, weddings, beach vacations and cruises—is a guaranteed recipe for getting fat again. In order to have lasting transformation, it needs to be done for the right reasons, such as wanting good health in old age so you can play with your grandchildren, or needing the health and energy to do the work that will make a difference in the world.

Unfortunately, most people can't see this far into their future. They want instant gratification. So the diet industry is selling them what they want—the hope of a skinny body that turns heads in a short amount of time. The diet industry knows 95% of dieters are going to fail again and again, so they just cook up another scheme to get you to empty your wallet "one more time," which is often followed by another. So sad.

If you want to stop charging your debt-ridden credit cards with your hard-earned money on diets that don't work, then you need to spend the money on understanding your emotional issues instead. I know you might hate the thought of going inward but it is the right answer if you never want to go on another diet again! Doing the emotional work is not an instant fix like detoxing with green juices for 10 days but it will be the fix you need to enjoy lasting transformation. And yes, you might have to have sessions with a few coaches and/or therapists before you find the person who resonates with you.

Another reason why people can't sustain healthy habits is because their self-image does not match the new skinnier body they want. If you lose 20 pounds, you become happy and you're confident for a while, and then you kind of slide. You lose steam and start drifting back to your old ways. More than likely what happened is you looked in the mirror and saw someone pretty darn hot, and you said to yourself, "Who is that in the mirror? I'm not someone who is supposed to turn heads. My mom always told me I was never going to be as pretty as my sister. She always got the attention. I'm supposed to be a loser. Who do I think I am?" (It's your exiles talking back at you.)

So because your low self-image (of your exiles) does not match the hot body in the mirror, you are guaranteed to sabotage yourself back to your old weight. Until you make the decision to spend the time to discover the exiled parts of you that are stuck in the past when your mother humiliated you (the parts who don't believe you are supposed to be beautiful) and you unburden those exiles of their faulty beliefs, you will be forever emptying your wallet to participate in the next "Drop 30 lbs. in 30 Days" diet gimmick.

So if you want to stop the cycle of yo-yo dieting, I encourage you to do the real work of finding out why you don't unconditionally love yourself enough to prioritize lifelong healthy habits. Spending money on diets is just a Band-Aid, you've got to discover where the bullets are (the exiles)—the wounds that caused your faulty beliefs that keep the pounds on—and get those bullets out so you no longer have to spend all your energy thinking about food and about the body you hate, as Sarah is doing. Instead, you can spend that energy to unlock and unleash your potential.

Sarah is going on a diet with my help so she can be skinny for her reunion. She's doing it for the sake of validation. We all want to know that the opposite sex is attracted to us (or the same sex if you are gay). It's the primitive brain's way of operating on survival and reproduction mode.

Our primitive brain always wants validation that we've still got what it takes to attract a mate to pass down our genes. It's primal. That's why when we are presented with the opportunity for validation (Don, the hot guy at the office that you want to have an affair with or Shelly, the old girlfriend who is going to be at the reunion), we'll do what it takes to get noticed, including exercising like crazy, buying a new wardrobe, and getting plastic surgery or Botox. Sometimes it just becomes an addiction to want that validation fix from the opposite sex— like a hit of cocaine. That's why so many affairs happen. It's that part of you that craves the excitement of love that you did not receive as a child, and it has you going crazy for love and validation anywhere you can get it.

* * *

In Sarah's case, the quest for validation started early. She grew up in a wealthy family; her father took over her grandfather's manufacturing business. But her dad was never around, he was flying all over the world to check on his suppliers. Mom was there for Sarah and was a loving mother, but she was engulfed in her own misery and resentment, having given up her career as a communications specialist to raise the children. Sarah's mom spends her time participating in charity fundraisers (which she doesn't really enjoy doing, but it gets her out of the house).

Sarah was sad to see her mother depressed for most of her life. Mom kept up the perfectly beautiful house that was decorated to the hilt but she just didn't show any enthusiasm for being a stay-at-home mom married to a rich guy. Sarah felt like she was walking on eggshells around her. The slightest thing might set her off on one of her bad moods.

Sarah was encouraged to seek a profession where it was relatively easy to have a family life and children and have the summers off. Teaching was the perfect fit, so she went to college to become a teacher.

Growing up, it was obvious to Sarah's friends that Sarah was the richest kid on the block. They had the biggest house, the fanciest cars and took the most luxurious vacations. Sarah was able to buy anything she wanted—and she did. She frequently showed up in designer clothing and accessories in junior high and high school. She asked her parents to go to the local public school instead of being sent away to a private boarding school, but acceptance didn't come easy, and the kids talked behind her back. She was singled out for being the spoiled brat because daddy always bought her gifts. He would come home from his overseas trips with expensive trinkets that she didn't need. He didn't have much time to spend *with* her but he sure had enough money to spend *on* her. Daddy essentially bought his love with money, or tried to anyway.

Just as the kids who are poorer than their peers feel the sting of being poor, the kids who are richer than their peers feel the sting and the prejudice of being different. Sarah was lonely growing up. Although she realizes as an adult that mom and dad loved her, she just didn't *feel* loved. She felt neglected because her mom was miserable with her own emotional baggage and Sarah just didn't feel like she enjoyed being a mother—it felt more like the kids were a burden because they held her back from pursuing her dreams. And to make matters worse, when dad would walk in the door from one of his business trips, he would hand the kids their expensive presents and retreat to his office to make phone calls overseas.

Sarah remembers a particularly painful incident when she was five years old. She made a fantastic drawing in kindergarten. She couldn't wait for Daddy to come home and show it to him. She was jumping up and down with her picture. As her dad walked through the door, he took one glance at it, said, "That's nice," nonchalantly, snapped at her mom and slammed the door to his office.

What Sarah didn't know was that Dad had just lost a huge business contract. The stress of it was just too much for him to be present for the family. Mom understood what his bad mood was all about but she didn't bother to explain it to the kids. Mom had no idea children could understand the stresses their parents were experiencing. So Sarah felt rejected because her feelings weren't validated and she retreated to her bedroom and cried.

Given what you have just learned about *exiles*, this five-year-old part of Sarah was frozen with this painful memory of feeling rejected by her father. This five-year-old part took on the belief that "I'm bad" as a result of Daddy's foul mood. Mom was not there to explain and to validate Sarah's feelings when Dad rejected her drawings; to simply say, "I see that you are upset. I would be upset too. Your dad is under a lot of stress." A five year old just absorbs what he did and came to the conclusion that her dad literally didn't love her and that's why he ignored her.

Sarah interpreted her dad's actions literally because of that hypnotic trance we are in from birth to about seven years of age. It's the same trance a hypnotist employs to render a professional body builder unable to lift a pencil. Your brain at this young age interprets every bad thing that happens to you literally—everything that happens gets imprinted as true and these form our programmed belief systems about who we are. Your brain does not have the intellectual capacity to understand how stressful it can be for mom and dad to raise a family and put food on the table. That's why it was so easy for our younger selves to take on faulty beliefs when negative things happen.

When Sarah's dad ignored her, her mom didn't know about this hypnotic state. She didn't take the time to lovingly reassure Sarah that she understood that she was feeling rejected, but that she really is lovable and that Daddy does like the drawing, he's just got a stress boo-boo right now that he has to take care of. Daddy also did not take the time the next day to show his concern for Sarah's feelings and to reassure her that he loved her very much.

When enough of these similar negative situations happen, that *exiled* part that felt neglected by Dad gets frozen solid and relegated to the dungeon to be protected from anyone hurting her again. This belief that Sarah is not lovable gets further reinforced by her friends at school who talk behind her back about her family's wealth. Sarah believes that she must not be good enough and that's why kids gossip about her. In fact, Sarah was very ashamed of her family wealth because it made her feel like she didn't belong. She knows that some of her friends' families struggle to make ends meet (because they are keeping up with the Joneses and living above their means).

Sarah tried so hard to feel like she belonged in school but it just didn't happen because of her family's wealth. Because the need for love and belonging is one of the most important core human needs, if we feel like we are not loved and we don't belong, we might as well stop living and die.

So, the Little Sarah parts of Sarah that don't feel worthy of her Dad's love and the parts of Sarah from school that feel the shame of wealth are the dominant *exiles* hidden in the *dark caves* of her psyche. They are being protected by the part of her—the protective soldiers guarding the entry to the *cave*— that likes to eat cookies and ice cream. It just makes her feel good, it just numbs the feelings of shame and unworthiness.

So when these exiles came into existence from the devaluing experiences at home and school, a part of her that used to be *playful* and *carefree* stopped that role and took on the role of *eating cookies and ice cream*. She developed this sugar habit at five years old. Because she was growing, the sugar habit didn't show up as obesity until later on. The part that likes to indulge in sugar was a *protector* that just needed to do its job of guarding the door to the part of her that feels unworthy and unlovable.

Sarah forced herself to maintain a good, stable weight while she hunted for a husband in her 20's. After marriage, she just didn't feel like working so hard anymore. She'd already nabbed the husband. Now it was time to eat to soothe her emotional pain. It's no wonder the part that likes to eat sugar overtook the part that wanted to exercise and stay fit.

So you see that Sarah's lifelong dieting struggles are rooted deep in her experiences with her parents, especially her dad. She went to years of therapy to address these daddy issues. She's not clinically depressed, she just has this blah feeling about life. She's aware of her issues and has basically put them to rest, consciously. The problem is that part of her is still exiled in her system, feeling neglected and worthless from

Daddy not paying attention to her, running her subconscious and keeping her stuck.

Sarah is very well aware of this part and understands why it has these feelings of unworthiness from years of therapy, but this "frozen" five year old was never thawed out from the past. Her therapist basically told her to break free from it, not think about it, reframe it, go around it, meditate, or just believe it's over—but the therapist was not trained in Internal Family Systems to help her take the exiled five year old out of the cave and unburden its faulty beliefs. That's why her eating issues remain. Because eating sugar was her *protector,* it is still protecting her from getting triggered by the little girl.

Sarah kept saying to me, "This is just who I am, the rich girl who didn't get Daddy's love. Emily, just help me lose the weight and make sure I don't eat sugar." This is her conscious desire—the 10% of her that pushes her to do the work to exercise and eat right. But the 90% in the subconscious—those exiles and protectors—are in mutiny with the part of her that wants to eat healthy and be trim. The parts that believe she's unworthy of her greatness are driving the bus of her life, so she's spending all of her energies on yo-yo dieting instead of on more important feel-good activities, such as doing the work that will make a difference in the world of education.

If Sarah actually healed her exiles, then her protector part that likes to eat sugar wouldn't have to work so hard to keep her numb and safe with sugar. The protector doesn't know that sugar causes diseases and makes her fat. The protector doesn't know that Sarah doesn't have the energy to think about graduate school and taking the next steps because she's so consumed with dieting.

Sarah needs to get to know this part and its positive intentions behind its negative behavior. She needs to show appreciation for how it has kept her safe from feeling unworthy. Then she could ask this part to show her which young part of her it is protecting. Then she could go into the cave where the five year old was hiding and give her the love she never felt from Daddy when he didn't acknowledge her beautiful drawing. She could rescue her out of the darkness of her emotional pain. Then, when the protector part sees that the five year old it has been protecting has been rescued to safety, it wouldn't have to do its job of eating sugar anymore. It could go back to what it was doing before it took on this role at five years old. It could be *carefree* and *happy* again and give Sarah the energy and freedom to explore the next steps of her career.

Note: A protector such as the one that likes to eat sweets can be protecting multiple exiles. So if the five year old is rescued from the "I'm unworthy and unlovable" belief, there could be other exiles formed from other bad experiences hiding in other caves. If there are more exiles that the same protector is protecting then it may take several sessions to work through the story of "the protector that likes to eat sugar." When all of the exiles are unburdened of their faulty beliefs and unstuck from the past, then the protector can finally let go of its job that it has worked so hard doing all of these years—keeping those exiles safe. When there aren't any more exiles in the cave, then it can finally significantly reduce or stop the sugar addiction—or any other undesirable behaviors and feelings such as addiction to alcohol, shopping, gambling, working, and feelings such as sadness, irritability, anger and numbness.

In essence, Sarah wanted to unleash more of "who she is." She knew there was more she could do besides being a teacher. But her identity was always wrapped around being someone who spent all of her energy going on diet after diet and being obsessed with finding the next magical solution to her problems.

She was someone who always thought in terms of, *If I were thinner, prettier and I had the energy . . . I would go for my*

Ph.D. in administration so I could become a principal and then a superintendent. I'm just not utilizing all of my capabilities as a fourth grade teacher. I love being in the classroom but there's a part of me that knows I'm capable of influencing the quality of the educational system in my town. I want to make a bigger difference, but I'm just too lazy, I'm just too fat, I just don't deserve it. So I'll just stay the way I am.

It saddens me to see how Sarah's potential was shut down due to her excuses and the stories she told herself. She is living small. She's shrunken herself to fit in the box that her friends and family expect of her. She has lost opportunities of what could have been—keeping her dreams tucked away in a drawer because she doesn't believe she is someone who deserves to go big. The weight problem is the perfect excuse to hide behind. Deep down inside she knows she's capable of so much more. She just needs the courage to step into the unknown. But she's just too afraid of her greatness.

She's convinced herself that she doesn't deserve to go after the administrator's job by getting her Ph.D. She's too fat and ugly to be considered for such a visible position in the community. She's identified with the protective and exiled parts of her. She's *blended* with her parts and is acting out from her wounded parts. Her true Self that is fearless and unstoppable is buried so deep that she's not consciously aware it even exists. She would rather make excuses, "I'm just the rich kid that Daddy ignored," "I'm just someone who will always have weight problems."

She might even be subconsciously thinking, *If I get thin, and I'm rich with a trust fund, and I doll myself up and I take a position of power in the school system, nobody will like me because I'll be too perfect. I'll lose all my friends.* ("I'll be too perfect and I'll outshine others" are two of the most common fears because it triggers the fear of isolation—that nobody will love me anymore. I'll be too good for them.)

The fear of the loss of love and belonging is keeping Sarah in her current state. She feels like she belongs because all of her friends struggle with weight. Otherwise if she were too thin, too pretty and too confident, she might be on a deserted island all by herself with no friends. (She's already too rich so she's got to make herself humble and dim her light so she doesn't make her friends jealous.)

She toils along with the same activities day in and day out, so boring but so familiar. The devil you know is better than the devil you don't know. It's just sad to see the lost opportunities. She just might be one of those people who dies with regrets - "I shoulda…." "I coulda…." "I woulda…"

Sarah did lose 20 pounds in the four months I coached her. I heard through the grapevine that six months later all the weight came back on and she was off trying a supervised medical weight loss program, eating 1,200 calories worth of pre-packaged meals a day. That is no way to live. It's very likely that Sarah has failed again.

So just imagine if Sarah had the real reasons why she wants to get in shape anchored into her psyche. "I want to get in shape because I have a bigger purpose on this planet. I am here to improve the education system in my town and to make a difference in the next generation of kids. I want my tombstone to say that without Sarah, the kids would not have had the learning opportunities they have."

So with this anchored in, Sarah realizes that in order to go to work, get a Ph.D., have confidence to schmooze and accomplish her life's mission, she needs to have Energizer Bunny energy everyday. That can't happen with all the crap she's eating. She feels tired, irritable, bloated and gross. She has no energy to focus and implement her plan to make a difference in the world. "Wow, that means in order to achieve my goals, I need to have energy and concentration to write and research and take care of my family. I need to keep eating healthy every day and I'll know that if I reach for a cookie, I will eat more than one and then I'm gonna want to take a nap and my productivity will be shot. I'll never accomplish everything. I can't eat this junk, I have a mission and that mission requires me to have energy by taking care of my body every day. I can't eat like this anymore. It's not serving me."

So every day that she eats, she thinks twice about the consequences of eating poorly. It's delaying her mission. She's too excited about this mission to not make it happen. So this will help her to ingrain healthy eating habits (in addition to healing the exiles). This would have been the ideal way that Sarah could have resolved her weight problems for good. This unfortunately was just too scary of a journey for Sarah to fathom.

Sexual Abuse and Health and Weight Issues

A common unspoken problem that explains why some people have weight issues is that they were inappropriately touched as kids. They often use food and excess weight to form a layer of protection around their bodies, to feel safe so that they are not attractive enough to invite unwelcomed assaults. I never asked Sarah about whether or not she experienced sexual abuse. Now I know to ask that question of everyone I work with.

Fear of Failure Can Stop You from Taking the Steps to Get Healthier

Sarah is one type of yo-yo dieter. Another type of yo-yo dieter is *former yo-yo-dieter* who has gotten off the dieting treadmill because they are sick and tired of the humiliation of losing weight and getting fat again.

"Why should I bother to diet? I kept gaining and losing 20 pounds over and over. It was humiliating to have friends and family compliment me and then watch me gain it all back and wear my fat clothes again. So I'll just stay put . . . I'm not going through that humiliation again."

They have decided that they are indeed a *loser*, which just reinforces the original low self-image they had in the first place. "Mom always said I was never going to amount to anything. I'm never going to measure up to my sister, why bother trying again? Even if I lose the weight, I'm never gonna be as pretty as Ann."

So they just give up and resign themselves to a life of miserable failure. They don't even care if they get sick. They'll just blame their genes for their fate and pray that the magic of pharmaceuticals will make it all better. They don't want to hear that genes are only 20% responsible for whether or not they get sick. It would be too sickening to admit there's the possibility that they did this to themselves because diet, lifestyle and mental health determine how disease-free we are.

One too many failures and the feeling of humiliation as friends and family watch them get fat again makes so many people throw up their arms and say, "Forget about it! My genes make me fat. Why should I bother to diet again? I'm just gaining and losing the same 20 pounds over and over again. It's too embarrassing. I'll just stay put. At least I have the satisfaction of eating my donuts and being a couch potato. Besides, everyone else around me is fat. I'm in good company."

So if you feel like you are in good company with friends and family with regard to your struggles, you are. Motivational guru Jim Rohn famously said, "You are the average of the five closest people you spend the most amount of time with." If you struggle with weight, the people you hang out with more than likely struggle as well. That's why you may not feel so bad about yourself. If you want to get slimmer and **stay** slimmer, you will need to find a new tribe of healthier people to socialize with. Ever notice that fit people usually have fit friends?

If you continue to be around others with weight issues, then as you get slimmer you become a threat to this group of friends and family. As you become more confident, they will unconsciously sabotage you to get back to your old weight. "Jane, come on, you're getting too skinny! You don't need to lose weight, you look fine! Come have this delicious cake with us. One piece of cake is not going to hurt you." And you cave in and eat cake and break your so-called "diet."

One of the reasons why your friends say this is because you have triggered a part in them that feels jealous about your journey to your best self. (The part that felt *less than* when she couldn't get a date for the prom.) When your friends sabotage you, it's not about *you*. By doing the work to get healthier, it forces them to examine why *they* are not doing the same things.

They feel bad about themselves when they see you *gain more confidence, get more attractive and get more attention*. It's their primitive brain from the hunter/gatherer days saying to them, "Do something, Jane is getting more attractive. That means she will snag the guy (the caveman) with the bigger resources. You're gonna lose out. Sabotage her!" So they unconsciously do everything they can to undermine Jane because she's making them feel small. Sabotaging her and succeeding in getting her to stop becoming trimmer will make them feel better about themselves.

Jane, on the other hand, feels that her love and belonging is being threatened if she becomes too fit, too pretty and too confident. She just might be kicked out of the tribe and made fun of (just as she was made fun of in high school). If this high school exiled part of her gets triggered—because she has not done the work of examining of her emotional health—then she will fail again at another diet attempt.

In order for Jane to succeed and transform for good, not only does she have to explore her parts and unburden them of faulty beliefs, she must have the courage to take risks to find another "healthier" tribe of people who will accept her.

This part of the journey of leaving one tribe and trying to find a new one is difficult. Floating in "no man's land" is very scary and many people just give up altogether. There are just so many aspects Jane needs support with as she finds her way to a better self image and finally has the confidence to take the next steps (and find new friends). This is why just about all successful people have coaches to support them to unleash their full potential. It can be uncomfortable and lonely at times and that's why you need the support of a trained expert who can get you back on track.

Essentially, when you are ready to change for the better and live your truths, (not living your truths is the #1 regret of dying people), you have three options to choose from with regards to your tribe:

1. Be the *leader* and let your tribe know that this is the journey you are on. Encourage them to come along for the ride and do the same. You will have the support of each other as you climb the ladder of greatness.

2. Decide the current tribe isn't serving you and *leave them discreetly* (by hanging out with them less often). Being the big fish in the small pond is not going to help you grow. You need to look for a pond where you are the small fish in the pond of big fishes. The big fishes will be more than happy to help you

become a big fish. You will rise to their level because you'll be hanging out with them and their levels of excellence will create an environment that propels you to keep up with these exciting new-found peers and go outside of your comfort zone to achieve your goals. The big fishes will support you as you do this.

3. *Stay in the same tribe* and live the same way for the rest of your life.

If the fear of failing again has you stuck in a rut, and you didn't get a chance to feel good about yourself or become more confident, then the dreams of taking your life to the next level get shattered. You just continue on in a life that philosopher Henry David Thoreau calls, "one of quiet desperation." And you lie there on your deathbed wishing you had the guts to live your truth!

Binge Eating, Binge Exercising, Eating Disorders

Do you know anyone who binge eats and then exercises like crazy? There's a few of these people at every gym. Again, these are extreme behaviors that are *protectors*, doing these things in the name of protecting the *exile(s)*. An example is Greg eating a whole loaf of fresh Italian bakery bread and then exercising for two to three hours to burn off the calories.

If you do something similar to this, it probably makes you feel disgusted to binge like this. It's an alien part that took you over. You felt compelled to eat the whole loaf. You couldn't stop yourself. You feel disgusted and then another part gets worried about becoming fat and that part has you working out like crazy. Some of the fittest people are closet binge eaters and they spend all their time and energy at the gym, leaving no time to pursue other interests. Their energy is consumed with their body, and that's sad.

There are other people who have hot bodies who grew up chubby. They were teased when they were overweight, and these humiliated and shamed parts of them are locked up in the dungeon. So they develop *protectors* that have them do everything they can to create awesome physiques. Thus, they get addicted to going to the gym and grab every opportunity they can to show off their bodies— wearing skintight revealing clothes that leave nothing to the imagination and getting fake boobs that are out of proportion with their bodies. They may even be addicted to plastic surgery and tanning beds and wear very provocative clothing to get the validation from the outside world that they are not the shamed fat kid anymore. This addiction to a perfect body is all done to protect the chubby young self.

Those parts that develop the love for exercise contain the positive qualities of trying to keep you fit and healthy. So appreciate them for what they have done. But if working out too much affects other areas of your life, then you need to discover and unburden the exile(s) that are being protected so that they can ease up a bit, not work so hard, and allow yourself do other things instead of working out all the time. Maybe this part just wants to rest and take a nap—and that's okay.

Then there are those people with weird food habits. They need their foods cooked a certain way . . . "Please, everything needs to be steamed." Or "I don't eat vegetables. I only eat meat and potatoes." Or "I control the amount of food I put into my mouth. I could use another five pounds but I like the way I deny myself foods." These are all protective parts, protecting exiles underneath these behaviors.

"You're so skinny! I hate you" or "You're still fat?"

Ever been jealous of someone who seems to have their body in control? "You're so skinny! I hate you!" You may even have said these words to people you know. If you ever feel envy for someone else's "good fortune," just thank that *jealous part* of you for letting you know what you are feeling and how it wants to be condescending to others to put them in their place so you can make yourself feel better. This is a great opportunity to look inward to see why you are jealous. Do you feel "less than adequate?" What situation from the past is this reminding you of? Was it when the cool girls had the latest fashions and you didn't, and they made you feel you didn't belong?

So being jealous of others is a great tool for you to uncover the *exiles* that need your help. If you have been at the receiving end of this kind of jab, then have compassion for the person that is saying it to you. You're just triggering them and making them feel inferior because you are reminding them of how they were rejected growing up. Just let the comment roll of your back. It's not about you, it's about them.

The other scenario is the parent who is always reminding you that you are not good enough. You visit them at Thanksgiving and they make remarks at you, "Looks like you've gained weight," or "Oh you're just as chubby as last Thanksgiving." These remarks are just going to trigger the shame of the *exiles* that were at the receiving end of the criticisms as a child. So you ended up with protectors that like to eat and couldn't give a sh*t about your health. It's a way of forming that layer of protection to keep the *exiles* safe.

Just remember that mom's need to be condescending is her protector. She might feel not good enough as a mom. Maybe she feels she's failed as a mom because you have health and weight issues. It could be embarrassing to her to show the world that you are not perfect. It's a reflection on her and she feels incompetent compared to her friends and that stirs up her *exiles*. The more you understand the relationship of protectors and exiles, the better it will be for both of you. This might be a good conversation to have to explain what is going on and she may have more compassion for you and minimize her criticism. You might even want to give her a copy of this book so she gains an understanding of IFS.

When Your Parts Express Themselves in Disease

Your past can show up in your present reality as disease. It's been interesting to see how most of us are intuitively aware of how our negative thoughts contribute to ill health. I've had a number of clients say to me, "I know my thyroid is shot because of how toxic my childhood was. I think those ugly stories kept circling in my brain and decided to let my thyroid get sick." Or they intuitively know that their gastrointestinal problems, asthma, fibromyalgia, headaches and cancer were due to anger, resentment or other negative thoughts and emotions.

As I explained in the last chapter, your thoughts can literally create an inviting toxic environment to turn on your disease genes. Many studies by mind/body medicine experts have shown that 80% of whether or not the "bad genes" you inherited from your parents—such as cancer, heart disease, auto-immune diseases—are determined by what you eat and what you *think* about day in and day out. Your negative thoughts literally make you sick because those thoughts contain the negative energy that has the power to activate your bad genes. When you heal the negativity of your thoughts, the healing of your body can follow. You can learn more about this by looking up the books written by Lissa Rankin, MD, Andrew Weill, MD, Mark Hyman, MD, Bernie Siegel, MD,

Deepak Chopra, MD. There are many more experts beside these that have the evidence to show you that your thoughts and feelings are very powerful in determining the state of your body and health. These books also provide a lot of the data on the fact that the more unhappy you are, the more likely you are to be sick. Cure your mind (of your exiles) and the curing of your body can follow.

So if you are holding onto anger and resentment from the past, this can accelerate the growth of cancer cells and other ailments. Most diseases don't happen overnight. They silently simmer over 10-30 years before they give you symptoms. Conversely, you can reverse diseases growing silently in their "baby" phases with positive thoughts, concentrating on being happy and not stressing yourself out (and eating a healthy plant-dominant diet, of course).

You can make all the excuses in the world about why you can't forgive those who have hurt you and declare that you will forever be damaged because of the past. But is this justifiable anger really worth your mental and physical health—to hold onto the grudges and the old stories and be stuck in a rut for the rest of your life? You're not hurting the person who has hurt you by doing this, you are only hurting yourself.

Your Thoughts Can Make You Well: The Power of Placebo

Dr. Joe Dispenza, *New York Times* bestselling author of *Breaking the Habit of Being Yourself* and *You Are the Placebo* and bestselling author Lissa Rankin, M.D.'s book *Mind Over Medicine* have personal accounts of the power of healing through positively changing their beliefs, thoughts and feelings. Dr. Dispenza was bedridden for three months with broken bones from an accident. All the orthopedic surgeons he consulted recommended he should have surgery or he would end up in a wheelchair for the rest of his life. He decided against it and refused. For three months, laying in bed, he just concentrated his thoughts on healing the bones. And sure enough, he healed them through positive thoughts alone. Dr. Rankin's book chronicles how her debilitating emotional and physical issues were primarily healed through her lifestyles and positive thoughts emotions. Western medicine of putting Band-Aids of prescription medicines on her symptoms didn't heal her. Changing her thoughts and emotions did.

In 1993, the Institute of Noetic Sciences published *Spontaneous Remission: An Annotated Bibliography*. These are 3500 cases studies of people with incurable diseases and cancer who had a disappearance of their diseases without medical treatment or medical treatment deemed inadequate. Your mind is more powerful than you give it credit for. Heal your mind and you can heal your body.

Toxicity from the Past Causing Cancer

Allow me to share the story of Pattie, a 45-year-old divorced and unemployed woman living with her two small kids in a small house with her mother and her brother. Her wonderful friend cared so much about her that she gifted my services to Pattie when Pattie was diagnosed with cancer.

When I asked her, "How do you think your past has affected your physical health?" Pattie said that her cancer was brought on by her thoughts about the past and her toxic relationship with her ex-husband. And, she added, by eating lots of processed food and fast food and very few fruits and vegetables. Pattie intuitively knew that her lifestyle and negative attitude contributed to her problems. The cancer had probably been brewing inside starting in her 20's.

We all have baby cancer cells (or other chronic lifestyle diseases) growing inside of us every day. If our immune system is healthy—by eating right, managing stress and having a positive outlook—then these baby cancer cells can be killed off as fast as they grow. But if we don't prioritize taking care of our bodies and our minds, then these cancer cells will keep growing and growing, and one day, we get diagnosed because it has gotten big enough to give us symptoms and show up on diagnostic tests.

So Pattie's negative thoughts and her stressful relationship situation contributed to her ill health. By the time Pattie came to me, she had already lost 30 pounds from the cancer so she didn't look like she needed to lose more than 15. She just wanted to know how to eat healthier so the cancer wouldn't come back. So I guided her on a healthy diet and she complied for the most part. Then I asked her to anchor into her psyche the real reason why she was doing this. She said it was for the sake of her young kids. If she died, they would have to go back to being raised by their dad, which wasn't ideal.

Dr. Lissa Rankin states in her book *Mind Over Medicine*: "When your life falls apart, either you grow or you grow a tumor."

During Pattie's follow-up appointments, she would tell me that she still cheated on pizzas, burgers and sugar. If she wanted to heal as fully as she could, she shouldn't be eating the junk that fueled the cancer cells. By the time I took Pattie on as a client, I had already started my training in Internal Family Systems and she was willing to explore the parts of herself that made her eat the junk despite the fact that she knew it fed the cancer cells. "These parts of me just take over, they don't care about the consequences of cancer," she said. The parts started to understand that if they kept eating junk Pattie might not live long enough to see her kids grow up. This fact started to scare these parts.

We did a couple of sessions over Skype but Pattie was always interrupted by the needs of her young kids, or her car broke down, or she was too tired from the chemotherapy. One excuse after another interfered and we never finished what we started. Soon there weren't enough financial resources to continue. (I had already gifted her much more time than we had originally contracted for).

The sad ending to this story is that she died a year after she was diagnosed and left two young kids in the care of her their father, which, according to her, was not what she wished for them.

Keeping Doctors in Business with Your Health Issues

Did you know that without the Standard American Diet (SAD) or our fast-paced money and status-driven society our doctors would be on the unemployment line? Let me share how some of them get scared if you get healthy.

When I was promoting myself as a nutritionist, I had 10 minutes to make a presentation to a group of cardiologists to let them know about my *Recover From Heart Disease* program. So I started out my spiel with, "Imagine if all of your patients took your advice on adopting healthier eating and living habits. How would you feel about coming to work every day?" I didn't even have time to take a breath when one of the doctors blurted out "I wouldn't have a job!"

Wow!! I knew this would happen in a perfect world, but for a doctor to have that as top of mind and admit it front of everyone was pretty shocking to me. But this fear of his would not materialize anytime soon. Our whole economy would tank if everyone prioritized their emotional and physical health. There would be no need to keep spending our hard-earned money on medical bills, the commissions of nicely-dressed drug reps that make your doctors late to their appointments with you, or fattening up the bank accounts of CEOs of pharmaceutical and biotech companies. The fruit and vegetable farmers of America and the IFS therapists (and other types of therapists and healers) don't have the millions of dollars to spend during the Super Bowl to tell you that better living is not all through pills, it's through taking care of your emotional health with coaching and talk therapy first.

There is so much evidence on the power of your mind to heal yourself physically and mentally. So what's stopping many of us from doing it? I think the answer to that we don't love ourselves enough to make it a priority. There are too many parts of us that hold the "I'm not worthy, I'm not lovable, I'm not enough" belief. They drive us to live stressful lives, all in the name of proving something to someone. It's time to get off the treadmill to nowhere. Maybe in the next generation we won't need as many doctors or pharmaceutical companies making a good living off of our bad lifestyles. So if you want to keep your doctors and the drug companies in business, you can keep ignoring your parts and let them wreak havoc on your mind and body.

If you don't have your health, what is really **missing** in your life? What do you **need** to make it all better? Deep down inside, I think you know the answer. (The answer might be: leave the job you hate, leave your abusive partner, let go of the past, do something meaningful with your life, reduce your stress, get off the "keeping up with the Joneses" rat race, stop participating in retail therapy, deal with your mother issues, etc.)

Nagging Your Loved Ones Will Not Change Them

I attended a healthy cooking demo at Whole Foods a while back. During this workshop, samples of green juices and other healthy fare were passed around. I noticed a woman in her 40's in attendance with her aging, obese mother, who was probably around 70 years old. The expression on the mom's face was very sad. It was obvious to me that her daughter dragged her to Whole Foods to learn about healthy eating and she wanted nothing to do with being there. When the healthy orange, red and green juices were passed around, this woman just shook her head. And when the healthy sautéed dishes were distributed, again, she refused. She was as defiant as a two year old.

It just saddens me to watch elderly people like this woman living in a depressed state yet wanting nothing to do with changing for the better. They seem like they are just waiting to die and be buried in their ground to relieve them of emotional and physical pain. You don't have to end up like one of these people when you get old. It's never too late to positively change your life right now.

* * *

You've seen through these stories how people who have the symptoms of weight and health issues are not addressing the problem from the right point of view. They are attacking the symptoms from the outside-in with the Band-Aids of Western medicine and diet books instead of treating the problem emotionally from the inside-out. Weight and health problems are handy excuses for not getting dates, not seeking the promotion, not getting out of the house, not making new friends and not having sex with your partner.

When you feel good about yourself from unburdening your exiles, you will naturally take the *actions* needed to get that slimmer body and sustain your good health. Eating healthy becomes as natural as brushing your teeth. Healthy and positive thoughts promote healing and contribute to a healthy body. This can mean the difference between life and death. Unhealthy thoughts promote disease. Your positive thoughts and feelings will drive you to reach for healthy foods every day instead of junk. This is what happened in Matt's story in Chapter Two. He had 20 pounds to lose. Once his self-image changed, he looked in the mirror and said, "Oh my gosh, who is that guy with the big gut? What I see in the mirror doesn't match how good I feel about myself. I deserve a better body. I'm going to drink my green smoothies, eat my vegetables and cut out the ginormous portions of steak and wine!"

Anti-Aging Benefits from Unburdening Your Parts

The *real* fountain of youth is in your mind, by discarding the skeletons in your emotional closet so to speak. It cannot be bought in a drugstore or in your dermatologist's and plastic surgeon's offices. Sure Botox and a nip and tuck here and there can boost your self-esteem a bit from the outside but it doesn't address the real issues. Exiles left abandoned in your mind can age you real fast. If you do the work to unburden your exiles, the bags under your eyes—a reflection of the emotional scars you've been carrying around—can diminish. The pallor and dullness of your skin can perk up. The sadness and vacancy in your eyes from being fixated on the pain of the past can diminish. The new you has a smile on your face and a glow to your skin that can belie your age. The light in your skin and your eyes comes from the inner radiance of finding and following your life purpose. Your light can catch the eye of similar bright lights inside potential friends, romantic partners and business compatriots and draw them to you and your animated and engaging self.

When your parts are in love with you and you are in love with them, that's when you'll look like you've spent a week resting on the beaches of Bora Bora. It's a radiance you can have for the rest of your life, without baking in the sun. And the anti-aging procedures at the doctor's office can be the icing on the cake of inner beauty and self-love.

* * *

So the bottom line is, if you want to change the state of your health and body and look younger, you need to change your thoughts and beliefs. If you are "sick" despite the fact that you are a health freak, then it's a high likelihood that your emotions are contributing to how lousy you feel despite your healthy diet. You have to look at the negative thoughts that are polluting your mind. A lot of these thoughts are rooted in your past. So to get to the bottom of the problem, you need to address the real issues—the ghosts of the emotional scars. When you unburden your exiles you will love yourself enough to treat your body right, and then your energy can positively shift and you can gain the confidence and self-esteem to dive into the world of delicious possibilities.

So if you don't want to age prematurely, become invisible and forgettable, then please prioritize your emotional health. Everyone has the ability to turn heads. You don't have to win the genetic lottery, you just have to love yourself from the inside-out and the body and health can follow. That self-love energy reflected in your radiant skin and healthy body is what can make you magnetic and unforgettable.

Chapter Eight

Prince Charming and Fairy Princess in Conflict
Free Yourself from Emotional Jail

"You will not attract what you want, you will attract who you are."
—*The Law of Magnetism*

Ever wished your relationship was like a fairy tale? Living *happily ever after* with the person of your dreams, feeling lucky to be with them, and having the ability to express and connect in the most authentic and vulnerable way? We all crave that person who can tell us, "I love you" and we feel it in our bones. It sends shivers up our spines. Life would be perfect if it were like this. But usually one person in the partnership closes off and becomes less emotional, saying, "Everything is fine. Why do I need to share my feelings with you? I don't want to talk."

Maybe you and/or your partner have shut your emotions down and have no interest in "going there." It's just easier to hide behind the responsibilities of parenthood or work. The relationship becomes more distant and you wonder why you don't have as much sex anymore. So sex becomes a chore—like you're making love to a turtle who has its head in the shell— empty mechanical lovemaking and the perfunctory, "Love you!" before you turn over and start snoring. How boring!

Maybe both of you were very emotionally open in the beginning but then Dr. Jekyll turned into Mr. Hyde and you started to wonder, "Who the heck did I fall in love with?" You may end up splitting up and vowing never to fall in love with the same type of person again. And, to your dismay, you end up repeating the very same relationship problems over and over again.

In Dr. Harville Hendrix's audio recording of one of his live seminars, *The Four Essentials of a Dream Relationship and Keeping the Love You Want,* he says that only 10% of couples are truly happy. The other 90% are either divorced or living like roommates—not really emotionally engaged with each other, and actually quite stressed and anxious.

What makes those 10% of marriages mind blowing is . . . drum roll . . . you guessed it . . . emotional intimacy. Here's a message to many men that most women would like to share with you:

> There's nothing sexy about avoiding your
> emotions and keeping your vulnerabilities bottled
> up. If you want women to be crazy for you, you have
> to be brave to show all parts of you, including the
> vulnerable parts. When you don't care about what
> others will think when you open up, that shows real
> confidence. Unfortunately, many men don't even
> know they are faking their confidence. Deep down in

the dungeons of your mind are the parts of you that you've abandoned—the exiled little boy parts that have been shamed, humiliated and rejected. These are the very parts of you that have you denying your real feelings, showing up numb and perhaps even acting out with anger, control and arrogance. These are the very parts of you that hold you back from happiness, real confidence and self-esteem and being able to share your feelings.

You're afraid of being seen as weak. But the truth is when you don't share, you are seen as weak because you're afraid of something. When you do share, that's what makes you more lovable and sexy and has many women crazy for you. We want to know what you are afraid of and what your hopes and dreams are. We want to see you cry. We want to cradle you in our arms as you tell us what caused you to be hurt during childhood and we want you to allow us to do the same when we're with you. We don't want you to freak out when we get emotional and tell us to "Stop crying! You need a therapist." You don't like it when we are raw because *you* have a hard time handling your own emotions when they come out.

Vulnerability creates connection and real love. This is what causes explosive lovemaking. (Isn't this what you want?) The best thing you can do for yourself is to participate in some sort of therapy or coaching. IFS therapy would be ideal. I know it's going take time to find someone who resonates with you but isn't your life worth it to do so? If you are not willing to do that, at least finish reading this book and take yourself through the exercises in Appendix A & B. You'll be eternally grateful if you take the time to get to know your inner landscape. You'll love yourself, be a better parent, be a better boss, be a better friend and be that man who can live a fully charged life so you can take care of the people you love and inspire others.

Dr. Hendrix and many other relationship experts say that most of us end up marrying someone who is most like the negative traits of one or both parents. Essentially, you are marrying your mother or your father. Yikes! Through this love partnership, you are trying to get the connection and validation you never got from the parent who most negatively affected you. He says that to make the marriage and yourself whole, you need to encourage each other to develop the side of you that is lacking. For many men that means cultivating and revealing their emotional side (because that's what usually needs healing) and for women, it might be furthering their intellectual side and challenging themselves on how much they can learn about the world, or having a career that challenges them. Dr. Hendrix supported his wife in her dream of getting a Ph.D. and his wife encouraged him to be more emotional. Now he thinks nothing of showing emotions and he's not ashamed to cry at movies!

For many of us, it's the young version of us that's marrying the young versions of our partner, both stuck in the past and trying to complete childhood with each other. It's unfinished business—we're not even consciously aware that this is happening because the initial attraction is so magical and comfortable that we're floating on air—and we just know this is the right partner for us. But when the honeymoon is over and that dopamine high comes crashing down, we wonder, "Who is this person I'm married to?" And we become increasingly unhappy. The dissatisfaction with the relationship creates stress and anxiety, and we become more emotionally distant.

Or, the attraction may not have come from your exiles seeking validation from a partner who reminds you of the parent that hurt you the most. Your relationship might not be full of conflicts—but it is full of boredom. That's because you're living through your protectors. As the founder of Internal Family Systems, Dr. Richard Schwartz, says in his phenomenal must-read book on relationships, *You are the One You've Been Waiting For: Bringing Courageous Love Into Intimate Relationships:*

> It's not true, however, that all mate-selection choices are made from those needy parts. If your exiles have been hurt repeatedly by intimacy, your protectors will override the exiles' redeemer search and begin looking for a partner who won't trigger your exiles. When you make a protector-based decision like that, you trade passion for safety and settle for a partner who may be boring but is, perhaps, conscientious, steady, loyal, nice, and so on. In other words, you have a partner who doesn't threaten your vulnerability or even want to get near it. In such an arrangement, whenever (they) strays from that safe profile, your protectors will punish (them). To stay with you, (they) will have to lock up any parts that want intimacy or any communication that goes beneath surface façade that initially attracted you.

I encourage you to read Dr. Schwartz's book. (It is only available on the Selfleadership.org website.) The insights in it will blow you away. It goes much more deeply into what I am discussing in this chapter.

After a number of years in your relationship, you may even get to a point where you do everything you can to be with other people so that you don't have to suffer the silence of being with a partner where you don't have much to say anymore except, "What do you want for dinner?" Or, "What are we doing for Ben's birthday?" You fill the emptiness by taking on more projects at work and keeping yourself busy with the children's activities. If you don't manage this emotional stress, the ever-increasing overload can surely lead to disease and weight problems and age you faster than you'd like. You saw how Pattie in the last chapter intuitively knew that the toxicity from her childhood and marriage contributed to her cancer.

Unfortunately, the person you are attracted to is also stuck in the past with their own wounded parts and the two of you end up in conflict, unable to help each other finish childhood. It is possible to give each other what is needed if both of you are willing to do the emotional work in couples therapy.

Because not all partners are willing to participate in therapy, another alternative is to start the healing journey by getting to know your *protectors* and *exiles*. When you heal the exiles, they gain the validation of worthiness from your Self, and then they don't need to seek validation from your partner. You become your primary caregiver. Your partner becomes your secondary caregiver—the icing on the relationship cake.

If you're in the market for love, and you go through IFS therapy, then you'll be able to attract a better partner than the last time and you won't be repeating the same old issues and problems that make you miserable. (The partner you end up attracting is a reflection of your self-worth. If your exiles are still abandoned in the dungeon, they will drive you to attract the same type of losers as before because they are still feeling worthless. So "a worthless you" will attract a partner that is full of unhealed emotional scars and this relationship will be more prone to conflict). Once you heal, your energy will be more positive and you can attract winners instead of losers.

Even if you are the only one willing to work on yourself, understanding your parts through IFS therapy and coming from a more loving place, the Self, can improve how you relate to each other. If you become more Self-led (instead of having your nasty protectors run the show), that can invite your partner to let his or her guard down and treat you better. They may very well soften their edges too and your relationship can improve.

Ideally, the best situation is for both parties to work with an IFS practitioner so that both of you show up as the best of who you can be, treating each other well and living happily ever after. And if it's meant to be that you're not supposed to be together, then at least you can part ways without animosity and your kids won't be as greatly affected by the breakup.

Just know that you are not alone suffering silently with boredom and/or conflict in your love relationship. Most people do a great job of putting on the perfect mask, pretending that "Everything is great!" You might even stir some envy amongst your friends because, "You just look so cute together! You're perfect for each other." If they only knew the truth of what goes on behind closed doors . . .

Well, here's your opportunity to get a peek behind the curtain into a common relationship struggle via the story of Liz and Jim.

The Devil Came Out of the Closet

Liz and Jim are 39 and 40 years old respectively. They were college sweethearts and best friends who couldn't get enough of each other when they were dating. After college, Liz got her MBA and Jim went to law school. They married when Liz was 28 and Jim was 29 and had a daughter three years later.

Liz fondly remembers when Jim showed emotions and vulnerability during courtship. That seemed like ages ago. Like many men, as the years went by Jim gradually started to lock himself in emotional jail. This is how most of my clients typically describe their relationships: *When we were dating, he was open with his feelings. Now he's numb and "dead" and I can't get him to be vulnerable and tell me how he feels.*

Jim was fine with showing feelings during their courtship because a part of him made him *fake it* to be open and trusting so he could win Liz over. But afterwards, that part didn't want to work so hard anymore and he just let his unemotional self come out because that's where he's most comfortable.

Jim is in great company. Men are socially encouraged to "be men" and avoid their emotions, especially crying. When they did cry, they were shamed by mom or dad, "Stop! Boys don't cry over dogs that want to lick them. You're gonna be a sissy if you keep crying." Boys were never validated with words such as, "You must be in a lot of pain. I know that hurts. I want to cry too. That dog wasn't nice to you."

It's no wonder men don't show emotions as adults because when they did express them as children they got shut down. Showing emotions is equated with "I will be criticized." So eventually they erect protectors such as numbness, anger, drinking too much or working too much to avoid the past. Unfortunately, this slowly destroys their relationships and hurts their children in the long run. Their exiled parts that showed emotions took on the burden that "If I show my feelings, I will be criticized and ridiculed, so it's not safe."

Liz and Jim were climbing their respective marketing and law corporate ladders and were the envy of their friends. Life just seemed so perfect—until seven years into the marriage. That's when things started to unravel, until it reached the point of no return and divorce papers were filed. Jim wanted out and Liz couldn't take the emotional abuse anymore. Liz felt like she married the devil.

Liz learned about me through one of my clients. She truly did want to salvage the marriage but thought it wasn't possible, since Jim decided that being married to her was just not what he wanted anymore. She had been going to couples therapy and individual therapy for the past year to deal with the relationship issues but she wasn't finding any relief or answers to explain this turn of events. She was so confused. The therapists mainly encouraged her to move on. "You'll be over it with time. I'll give you tools to deal with the feelings, but your main job is to let it go and move on. It's gonna take at least a year for you to feel better." "A year, are you crazy???!!!! I want to feel better now! I want to start dating sooner rather than later," she told me.

Liz, being analytical, wanted more of an explanation about why she was so triggered by her husband and why her self-esteem became non-existent when Jim would say, "You're not pretty enough for me. I don't know why I married you." Or, "You're just not a good mother. You don't know how to feed our daughter good food or how to discipline her." And this devastating zinger: "Why can't you be sexier in the bedroom? You don't turn me on anymore." Jim would often masturbate while Liz pretended she was asleep, dying to blurt out, "Am I not good enough for you?" She just felt so rejected and repulsed by his behavior.

During couple therapy, the therapist told Jim that his past was affecting his relationship. Jim was in denial. He said he was fine. "It's Liz that's the problem. If she were prettier and sexier, I might want to sleep with her."

Needless to say, this was damaging to Liz's ego and she spiraled downward from there. She always thought she had an ample amount of confidence and self-esteem but now she began to question herself. Self-doubt clouded her thinking every day and she just couldn't concentrate at work.

She also began questioning her ability as a mother and as a wife. The only thing that hadn't been affected yet was her job and her upward trajectory to become VP of Marketing at her company. But now, even her confidence about being able to achieve that seemed shaky since Jim kept lobbing assaults at her. She's so afraid of sabotaging her upward mobility, so afraid of being a statistic—another woman unable to bust through the proverbial corporate glass ceiling because of self-doubt.

When Liz contacted me, I let her know that there was a solution to her angst, because her parts from the past were getting triggered by Jim. Jim's parts were acting up big time too—he just doesn't know it. Since their therapist isn't familiar with the Internal Family Systems model, she's not able to give them the answers they need to move forward.

Liz and Jim's struggles are the classic example of relationship conflicts fueled by their respective *beach balls of the past* that had been pushed down under water by their psyches. The beach balls can no longer be submerged and have bounced back up in the form of verbally belittling and insulting each other.

Both of their exiled parts are causing them to relate to each other from a wounded place, with their protectors running the show, being controlling, demeaning, demanding, angry, irritable, not trusting, full of rage or simply numb.

Their respective pasts are coming back to haunt them because their exiles can't stand hiding in caves and dungeons anymore. The protective soldiers guarding the doors to these dark places are doing their jobs of being controlling, critical and demeaning, especially on Jim's part. They want to make sure his exiles are on lockdown, so these devilish parts of Jim are out in the open, lashing out at Liz, and he thinks there's nothing wrong with him—it's all her.

Liz tells me that during couple's therapy, Jim would say that he's over his past. Sure, he had an alcoholic father whose anger would accelerate into rages and a mother who was severely depressed and often threatened suicide. He knows they are mentally sick, he's accepted it and has *consciously* jumped over this obstacle. But remember what I shared about the subconscious running our lives 90% of the time? The subconscious stores all of these old negative memories, especially all of the exiles. Jim is only 10% over his past—because his *conscious* thinking that he's over it is only 10% responsible for him actually being over it. He hasn't accessed any of his exiled parts to heal them. He has a lot of protectors such as anger, irritability, rigidity, controlling behavior and numbness that he's erected to prevent him from the anguish of his emotional wounds. It's just safer for his psyche to be numb and be in total denial.

* * *

Jim's father would be drunk almost every day and was barely coherent enough to get his two sons ready for school. Mom was in no shape to get them ready either. She had a hard time getting out of bed in the morning because of her depression. So Jim had to fend for himself from a very young age, walking himself down the block where the school bus picked him up, ashamed that he was the only kid without a parent standing at the bus stop with him. On many days, Jim's mom forgot to pick him up from afterschool activities. He had to find a ride home with another parent. On other days, he would come home to an empty house, with no idea where his parents were. Talk about feeling *abandoned!*

Jim never felt like he mattered because his father was so self-absorbed. His father's alcoholism was a cover-up for the pain he suffered from feeling neglected by his own dad. When Jim participated in sports, his dad was always yelling the loudest from the sidelines and embarrassingly criticizing him in front of the other parents and teammates. Jim just felt like he was never going to be *good enough* for his father, no matter how hard he tried. His dad has never told him how proud he is of him or that he loves him.

Jim didn't realize that his dad desperately wanted Jim to be the superstar on the sports team so that he could brag about his accomplishments to his co-workers. Because dad never felt good about himself, he needed to get outside validation through his son that he's important and good enough. "See the son I produced? I must be pretty great if my son is able to shine like a superstar." Jim never felt like his dad was genuinely proud of him, he just felt used by his narcissistic dad.

It's no wonder that Jim feels like there's nothing wrong with him because he has dissociated so much from the traumas he endured. His exiles feel so worthless, and as a result there are layers and layers of protectors to prevent him from ever feeling the pain, shame and humiliation of childhood. All of the negative episodes such as having to fend for himself in the mornings and being forgotten at school have created the exiles that feel rejected, abandoned and unloved. "I must be bad. Why else would Mom and Dad ignore me like this?" (It's that hypnotic brain of our youth that soaks up every damaging event literally.)

Jim's father managed to show up for his manufacturing job and hid his alcoholism from his boss. His mom would work temporary clerical jobs when she wasn't too depressed. By the time he entered the local state university on a scholarship, he wanted nothing to do with his past. He met Liz at a fraternity party during his sophomore year. They were a hot couple from day one.

Liz, in contrast to Jim, grew up in better middle class circumstances—dad was a teacher and mom was a part-time bookkeeper. Her parents were loving toward their five children. Liz was the oldest and had to set the example for the rest for her siblings.

The therapist tells Liz that Jim's going to need years of therapy just to accept his past and realize he's acting out from those harsh conditions he had to withstand. Jim doesn't think there's anything wrong with him. His protectors have him *numb, controlling* and *addicted to work* and there's also a part that make him *drink too much* to bury his emotions. And his *arrogant* protector seems to be on-call most of the time. All of these behaviors and feelings have the job to cover up his lack of self-esteem (which he consciously doesn't know is the root of all of his angst). Jim is the perfect case of the successful person showing up with the mask of the confident exterior, protecting the little boy parts inside of him that feel totally worthless.

* * *

It broke my heart when I heard Jim's story. If Jim would ever come to grips with his past, stop being in denial and show his emotions, his relationship with Liz wouldn't be so toxic.

Liz tells me their therapist would say to him, "Please tell me about your childhood." Jim would answer, "I had a narcissistic dad and a depressed mom. There's nothing to discuss. I'm over it." So no progress could be made because it didn't sound like this therapist knew how to talk to his *protector*, which was the part that was saying, *"There's nothing to discuss."* It might have been more productive to start the discussion with, "Tell me about the role of this *there's nothing to discuss* part of you. What is its job? How does it keep you safe? What is it *afraid* of if it doesn't keep doing its job of never discussing the past?" Jim needs to find another counselor. An Internal Family Systems therapist or coach would be helpful. Hypnosis would also help because it will guide him to bypass the conscious mind and he would be able to access the wounded parts that are living in the subconscious.

Sadly, Jim may never change, just like some alcoholics who need to hit bottom—ending up in jail or losing a job—before they seek help. Something like a DUI or another broken relationship may be the "two by four" that needs to injure him before he realizes he needs to come to terms with his past. This may not happen until he's 70 year old. It's so sad. Since Jim could not progress in couples therapy, Liz was not willing to wait for him to heal, and she agreed to the divorce.

If Jim stays in denial and parents his daughter from this wounded place, she will surely have problems when she grows up. The daughter has already witnessed many fights between her parents and those fights more than likely have created frozen exiled parts in her because no one was there to reassure her that she's not the reason they are fighting. (Jim and Liz didn't think she was old enough to understand the issues and the strained emotions between them.) Because she's too young to understand the stresses of marriage, she probably took on the belief that there must be something inherently wrong with her . . . *Why else would Mommy and Daddy fight like this?* When we heal *our* exiles, we become better parents because we're more conscious of how we speak to our kids, and more aware of the long-term damage it can do to them if what we say comes out the wrong way.

For example, if your daughter Kelsey brings home a B on her report card, instead of saying what we heard in our childhood, "What? Only a B? Where's the A? Dad and I will have to whip you into shape. How do you think you can become anything great with these mediocre grades?" Now you know the right thing to say that would not cause irreparable damage and prevent her from feeling "I'm not good enough" would be "I'm so proud of your B in Math. I know you put a lot of effort into this hard class. Great job! How do *you* feel about your grade?" *"Well, I wish it were an A. I just messed up on the final because I was too rushed. I'm so capable of getting an A."* "So, what can Mom and Dad do to help you get an A the next time?"

Asking how our kids feel in this way will produce a better outcome because they will feel validated that they're good enough and that mom and dad have their best interest at heart.

* * *

Liz had very loving and validating parents but there were many moments when she was smacked across the butt by her mother when she acted out or when her grades weren't perfect. She was compared unfairly to her younger brother who was born two years after her. He had the brains of an engineer and was always praised for his intelligence. He received the doting attention of Mom and Dad pretty quickly. It sure showed Liz who the favorite kid was.

Liz felt *neglected* because of the favored treatment of her brother. She acted out to get their attention. (A little bit of attention is better than no attention, that's why kids act out, even if they know there will be consequences. Again, the need for validation drives this behavior.)

So Liz became an overachiever—always taking on more projects, studying hard to get more A's, participating on the Debate Team, taking piano lessons, active on the cheerleading team, etc. She found that she really loved psychology in high school. She went ahead and studied that in college and then after college was admitted into a prestigious MBA program. Mom and Dad were proud. But they still made backhanded comments about how her brother was doing such phenomenal research in engineering. Ouch! The sting of being compared to her brother just never seemed to stop.

During one of our sessions, Liz wanted to get to know the *insecure* part that Jim activates every time he is verbally abusive to her.

Emily: Where do you feel this *insecure* part?

Liz: My stomach. My stomach gets in knots when I get insecure. It acts up when I'm confronted with situations at work and I think I'm not capable of the challenge, or it acts up when Jim is shouting nasty things to me and I'm thinking, "I'm not good enough or pretty enough."

E: How do you *feel* towards this *insecure* part?

L: I hate it.

E: Would the *I hate it* part be willing to step aside or go into another room while we got to know *insecure* part?

L: (Liz has her eyes closed and thinks for a moment) Okay, it stepped aside.

L: Now how to do you feel towards the *insecure* part?

L: I feel *sad* about it.

[When I ask her about how she *feels towards* a part, I am looking for her to say things such "*I'm curious, I'm compassionate, I feel connected, I want to get to know it.*" This shows me that it's her Self that is now present to get to know the *insecure* part. When all the *protectors* have stepped aside willingly and will allow Liz's Self to get to know *insecure* part, then the Self can do its job of being the agent of healing.]

[If more and more *protectors* keep popping up, we would have had to forget about getting to know *insecure* part right now and get to know some of the other *protectors* that just jumped in, addressing their *fears* and *concerns* before we can finally talk to *insecure* part, because they are *afraid* of something bad is going to happen if *insecure* part starts to talk about the past.]

E: Would *sad* part be willing to step aside?

L: Yes, it would.

E: Now how do you feel towards *insecure* part?

L: I want to get to know it.

[Finally, the Self is showing curiosity towards wanting to get to know *insecure* part.]

E: When did the *insecure* part's job come into existence?

L: When my brother was born when I was two.

E: Invite it to tell you what's its job is.

L: To protect me from being alone. It felt unloved when my brother was born. It didn't want to be alone and have no one. It's worse to be alive and alone when no one cares than to be dead. At least if you're dead you don't feel the pain of loneliness anymore. So if I acted insecure, then people wouldn't reject me, they would feel sorry for me and pay attention to me.

E: If *insecure* didn't have to work so hard to protect you like that, what would it rather be doing?

L: It would like to help Liz know that she's never going to be alone—she's very friendly. Everyone loves her.

[So this *insecure* part is stuck in the past at two years old, thinking that Liz is going to be left alone, since her brother was born and he got all the attention and she felt alone and lonely.]

E: Would you like to update *insecure* part on how old you are now and what your life is like, and show this part how many friends you do have and how much you are loved?

L: Sure, I'll do that. (Liz goes inward and has a dialogue internally to let this part know how much she has accomplished and the large numbers of friends she has.)

188

[This is the beauty of IFS. IFS practitioners don't need to know the details of everything. You can go inward to talk to your parts and process the meaning of the stories yourself. In fact, you can keep anything you want private, unlike traditional therapy.]

> **E:** How is this part taking in the update on your life?
>
> **L:** She had no idea I was 39 years old. She's quite proud of everything I have accomplished.
>
> **E:** Is there anything else *insecure* part would like to share with you?

[For the sake of simplicity, the dialogue of this session is abridged to show you the main points of the story that were uncovered.]

> **L:** No, it feels heard.
>
> **E:** Now would the *insecure* part be willing to show us the little girl (the *exile*) it's been *protecting*?

[This is asking permission of the *insecure* protector to show us the *exiled* Little Liz.]

> **L:** Yes. (Liz has her eyes closed.)
>
> **E:** What image are you seeing of this little girl?
>
> **L:** All I see is a *black dark image*.

[This is another *protector* that just jumped in that doesn't want us to access the exile. The hardest part of doing IFS work is dealing with the *protectors* that continue to leap in. They want to keep things just the way they are. They are *afraid* of someone accessing the little girl that's been safely locked up in the dungeon.]

E: Would the *black image* part be willing to step aside to show us the little girl?

L: No, it's a little hesitant.

[Now we have to address the fears of the *black image* part.]

E: What is black image *afraid* of if we talk to Little Liz?

L: That she's gonna be hurt again and stirred up with painful emotions.

E: What does the *black image* part need to hear from you so that it's assured that nothing bad is going to happen—that you, the Self, is going to visit her?

L: (Still with her eyes closed.) I told *black image* that nothing bad is going to happen. Yeah . . . now the *black image* is lifting and I see light. I see this part of me with a ponytail and white bobby sox and black Mary Jane shoes. I see her at her new school and she doesn't feel like she fits in.

E: How do you feel towards Little Liz?

[I have to double check that her Self is present to want to get to know her and that another protector hasn't jumped in.]

L: I want to get to know her.

[Whew! Her Self is present because she's curious about Little Liz.]

> **E:** So this *exiled* part started at two years old and it just kept growing up with the same negative beliefs and now you are seeing the five-year-old version of this *exile*?
>
> **L:** Yes.

[This is the *exile* that the *insecure* part had been protecting since Liz was two years old. *Protectors* can protect *exiles* as they grow up because if it's the same "injury" over and over again, it's the part with the same negative core belief all rolled into one *exiled* part.]

> **E:** Is this part aware of you? How is she reacting to your presence?
>
> **L:** She's looking up and wondering who I am.

[Oftentimes, the *exile* doesn't recognize the adult Self, it has no idea it's a grownup now.]

> **E:** Update her on how old you are and what you have been up to.
>
> **L:** Hey Lizzie, I'm you, but just the grownup version. I'm 39 now, with a kid and a good job.

E: How is she responding to you?

L: She's amazed. She's letting me hold her hand.

E: Invite her to tell you her story.

L: She's telling me that she didn't feel like she fit in at the school because she's Jewish, just like the way she didn't feel like she fit in at home because she was made to feel inferior to her younger brother. She just imagined that the worst was going to happen at home and at school. She's scared and concerned about the unknown. She's afraid she might be abandoned and forgotten and she's afraid of getting punished at home for not being as good as her brother.

E: What is the *belief* that she took on as a result of feeling ignored at home and feeling different at school?

L: That *I'm not smart enough, I'm not lovable, I'm not normal.* That's why I'm being neglected by mom and dad, why else would they favor my brother like that?

[Again, it's that hypnotic brain that absorbed every negative experience literally as bad things happened because they believe they are inherently bad.]

E: Ask Little Lizzie what she needs from you so that she doesn't feel scared and alone and abandoned.

L: She wants me to hold her on my lap.

E: Go ahead and do that and when you are ready just ask her what she needs from you so that she isn't so frightened anymore.

L: (With tears rolling down her face.) Lizzie, it's okay that you are a different religion than your classmates. Not everyone is from the same background. You are different and you just have to appreciate how great it is to be unique. But in the end, you are not that different. Being alone sometimes is okay. It's not that scary. You're gonna be okay. Look, I turned out okay. I'm proud of you. You are a leader for your siblings. Mom and Dad do love you as much as your brothers and sister. They were too tired to give you as much attention as you used to get for the first two years of your life. After that, four more kids were born and it was exhausting for them to be caring for so many kids. I love you. *You are lovable, you are enough, you are smart, you are normal, you are beautiful.* I will always be here for you. Let me give you a big hug and a big smooch.

[Liz has her eyes closed and has her arms around her chest as she hugs her younger self. Tears are streaming down her face. Liz has just "deleted" the old memory of being all alone and re-created new memories of being loved by her adult Self. It is now filled with new positive core beliefs of *"I'm lovable, I'm enough, I'm smart."* This "Self-led re-parenting" essentially untangles the old wired negative memories and forms new connections with new positive beliefs. This is reprogramming your mind. This "rewiring" will help Liz stop replaying the loops of her old negative experiences. Instead, she will now be replaying this positive experience of hugging and loving her younger self every time she thinks about this part. This will help take away her *insecure* feelings.]

> **E:** Just take as much time as you need to soak in this new memory of being with Little Lizzie.
>
> **L:** Haaaahhhh…. (as she's wiping the happy tears away). That was amazing!!
>
> **E:** Ask Little Lizzie if she's ready to *unburden* the faulty negative beliefs she's been carrying around since she was two years old?

[For some clients, at this point, a *protector* part can jump in and say, "No, we're not ready for you to let go of this burden." This *protector* is afraid that something bad is going to happen if the burden is released, such as Lizzie not being able to stay small and hide behind her excuses. It's another protector that wants to keep things just the way they are. They are afraid of the unknown. If this were the case, then these new protectors' stories and fears would have to be heard before they give permission to the exile to unburden old faulty beliefs. Fortunately, this didn't happen to Liz.]

> **L:** Yeah . . . Let's just put it in a bonfire and burn it away.
>
> **E:** Set that up and let me know when the process is complete.
>
> **L:** (She sets it up and imagines the burden out of her system.)

E: Now invite the *insecure* part back and the other parts that stepped aside and ask how they feel about what just happened.

L: They are so cool with this. They feel so much lighter now that their burden of protecting Little Lizzie has been lifted. They've been exhausted with working so hard to protect me. And my stomach is no longer in a knot.

E: So these other *protector* parts are ready to take on positive roles in your life instead of making you feel insecure?

L: Yes!! They are going to keep me *secure* and *confident* so that anytime Jim needles me, I won't get triggered, especially when Jim tells me I'm not pretty enough, because that little *insecure* part has had its story heard and Little Lizzie has been rescued out of the past, safe with me, with the new memories of me hugging her and being with her.

E: Now do you see the connection? When Jim was saying abusive things to you, he was taking jabs at the Little Liz that was frozen in time with all of her insecurities. Now you and Little Liz can come together and just let his comments roll off you.

L: Yes, definitely. I also have more empathy for Jim, now that I have done this work of knowing and healing my parts that were frozen in the old negative memories. I can just imagine how many frozen and stuck parts Jim has from his past. Now, when Jim acts out, I can just shrink him down to the abandoned and traumatized five year old that's seeking control and attention. It's much easier to feel sorry for him pretending that he's a five year old, than to get mad at him when he abuses me.

E: Thank your parts for letting you get to know them.

L: Thank you parts, I love you, you've done a great job of protecting me all of these years.

* * *

The situation between Jim and Liz are just re-enactments of their childhood dramas. Neither of them acted from their true loving Selves when they fought. Their exiled wounded child parts get triggered and the protector parts (anger, condescension, etc.) take over and do everything they can so to stop their respective *exiles* from feeling shame, rejection and humiliation again. This is a big reason why couples fight—to act out the old childhood dramas and the desire to get control so they feel significant and important.

Liz worked with me for a few more sessions and unburdened more of her *exiles* so she does not repeat the same patterns in future relationships. She was so confused about why things happened the way they did and now everything makes so much rational sense to her.

She's also so grateful that this is going to make her a better parent. Because she understands how negative messages can influence her daughter permanently (like the way Liz's mother caused Liz to have insecurities), she will think twice before saying anything critical. She's realizing that if she's not careful, she could be creating frozen *exiles* in her daughter and give her insecurities, self-esteem and confidence issues when she says or does negative things.

Now that Liz has overcome her self-doubt through healing her exiles, she feels she is perfectly capable of becoming the VP of Marketing and breaking through that glass ceiling of the old boys' network. That's because self-doubt and fear will be absent during the interviews and the corporate schmoozing because all of her little exiled parts have been healed of their insecurities. All of her parts are in alignment, behaving and sitting nicely in the passenger seats of her bus, allowing her Self to show up and drive her behaviors so she can magnetize the success she deserves and attract the perfect Prince Charming.

I have also shown Liz the "reframes" through which she can understand her experiences with Jim. So anytime she has to converse with Jim regarding their daughter, she can think to herself:

> *Thank you, Jim for all the sh*tty things you've said to me. It's given me the gift of reaching out to Emily to do the deep inner healing so I can be the most awesome parent to our daughter. And I won't repeat the same patterns in my next relationship. The Universe knows I deserve better and this is the negative experience I needed to launch me to that next level, including getting me to that VP of Marketing position.*

> *If it weren't for this experience with you and the gift it has given me, I'm not sure if I would have gotten over the self-doubt of whether or not I deserve the next level of my success. Now I know I deserve it because all the little girls inside of me are now in support of me doing this work.*

I am so grateful for you being the catalyst for the next level of my greatness, which I am going to live out as the most beautiful, confident and vibrant version of me (and be a great mom because I'll know the right things to say to our daughter so she isn't damaged when she grows up.)

And all my parts will be in alignment to allow me to unleash the most unstoppable version of me and finally meet the right soul mate. I know you can't come to grips with your past. I feel sorry for you . . . You're showing up as the abandoned and unloved five year old right now. You've taught me so much in this relationship. You came into my life for a reason. Yippee!! I couldn't have asked for a bigger and better GIFT from you. I love you for allowing me the courage to step up to be the real me. I hope you find your own gift from the time we spent together. I wish you well. And I hope one of these days we can be friends again.

When she interacts with Jim in the future through this filter, feeling sorry for what he must be going through and having compassion for him, he will sense an energy of compassion and will less likely to attack.

Liz is doing great now and feeling so good after these IFS sessions. She's no longer confused, she's unstuck, she feels unstoppable and is very happy with the outcome. Her therapist sensed a different energy from her and she couldn't believe she wasn't spiteful towards Jim anymore. She questioned what was going on, almost accusing Liz of being out of touch with the reality that she just became a divorced woman. I told Liz that she better tell her therapist about the work we did unburdening her exiles. Liz told the therapist how the shift came about and that she will no longer need therapy because she's over Jim and she finally feels good about herself. I can't wait to continue watching Liz step take her life to the next level, attract the love of her life and get promoted to VP of Marketing.

Trapped in Emotional Jail

Jim is in denial with his emotions. Here's what might happen to him if he continues this. He might be able to "fake" his emotions for the next relationship just like he did with Liz and he will end up finding another woman who will experience the same thing Liz did—verbal and emotional abuse. He may end up divorced again. This pattern will get repeated over and over again until Jim comes to grips with his past and does the work of getting to know his *protectors*, and then unburdening his *exiles*.

Jim is in denial about how numb he really is. "I don't do emotions" is a *protective* part that is safeguarding the little boy in the dungeon who has been shamed when he cried or showed other emotions. His dad or mom may have said, "Stop it! Boys don't cry" when one of the kids on the on the playground took Jim's truck. Jim may have whined and cried a few more times and Dad and Mom said, "If you want to grow up to be a man, you need to control your feelings."

The reason why many men have a hard time with the thought of ever visiting their past is that their numbness protector is so afraid that if they went back to visit the little boys hiding in the dungeon, that they would start sobbing and wouldn't be able to stop. They would have a massive meltdown and end up in the mental hospital, unable to work and shamed for being emotionally weak. The thought of going back into the "torture" of the past and its consequences is just too painful for most men to even conceive. So they deny there's anything wrong with them and they keep showing up with protectors that are accepted by society for men to have: anger, numbness, arrogance, control, drinking too much, working too much, having affairs and so forth.

Jim's feelings were never validated and he was shamed when he expressed them, so he decides that showing any feelings produces nothing positive and shuts them down altogether. "I don't do emotions because emotions equal criticism." And the subsequent numbness means that Jim (and many other men and some women) silently suffer with loneliness and emptiness in adulthood. They don't feel safe expressing their true Selves. I hear this pain of loneliness from all of the men I work with: *"I don't have any real friends. I have friends I do stuff with but I don't have friends I can share my deepest fears, hopes and dreams with. I don't even know how to begin that conversation. We just keep our masks on and pretend that everything is great!" "I was more emotional when I was courting my wife but I just couldn't keep up with sharing my feelings all the time. I don't know why."*

When some of these men get married, the *numbness* protector kicks in big time because they see how sometimes their partners do not fully support them when they talk about something vulnerable. In a common scenario, maybe their wives brushed off what they were saying from their hearts because the dishes had to get done and they didn't realize how much courage it took for their husbands to start talking about their emotions. Then the *exiles* that hold shame get stirred up because they feel the shame of being ignored by their partner when they talk about feelings, a partner who would rather finish the dishes than listen to them. So the numbness *protector* decides to clamp down with even more pressure to make sure this guy doesn't show his vulnerability again.

Insights alone do not heal. If you had overbearing helicopter parents, you may have had to erect a wall to keep to yourself and feel safe. Therapy may have brought the issues out on the platter for you—but now what? You're still numb, you still don't want to share with your partner. This means the next time the women want men to talk about their feelings, the men say, "What? I'm supposed to have feelings? I feel fine! If you want to talk more about feelings, that's what your girlfriends are for."

As the years go on and this lack of emotional intimacy drives a deeper and deeper wedge between the couple, they begin living like roommates in the bedroom, having sex with a "turtle" with its protective shell on, until one of them says silently, "I don't want to have sex with someone who acts like a roommate. This is not the Prince Charming and Fairly Princess life I dreamed about." So some of them decide to have affairs instead, or get into other destructive behaviors.

The "I Have a Hard Time Trusting" Jail

Just like men, women can be numb too, holding back from the ability to trust and be vulnerable. Much of it can be traced back to early *exiles*. Here's a fascinating example of how someone developed trust issues:

Tracy, 44 years old, introduced herself to me after I gave a talk and shared that she has trouble connecting deeply and trusting new friends. She goes to a lot of Meetup social events (local social networking events based on similar interests) but she can't seem to take the next steps with her new "friends." She's so afraid to get closer. She's lonely and feels like she doesn't belong, and she can't take living like this any longer. I asked her to go back to the first memories of when she decided it was scary to trust people.

Tracy had the answer right away. She recalled three surgeries before the age of three. She was able to recall the events as if they happened yesterday. As her young self was being wheeled on the gurney to the operating room, looking up into the fluorescent hospital lights and into the eyes of the doctors in surgical caps and scrubs, she also saw her father. All of them reassured her that everything was going to be okay. Shortly thereafter, she smelled the anesthesia gas and a mask was descending over her mouth and nose. She got frightened and wanted to scream but couldn't. She felt like she was suffocating, and then everything went dark. As a result of experiencing this traumatic event three times before she was three years old, her *exiles*—frozen in the operating room— took on the belief that "The world is not safe, people can't be trusted . . . bad things will happen . . . like suffocation . . . and you won't even be able to scream!"

I let her know that these traumatic surgery experiences are more than likely the major reasons why she has a hard time trusting and being vulnerable. This insight made so much sense to her. The *protector* part that *doesn't trust* has been protecting the one, two and three-year-old parts of her with the scary surgery memories. The *doesn't trust* part thinks it has been keeping her safe. It thinks that she's still a baby. It is not aware that the job of keeping her safe by holding her back from trusting people is making her lonely and miserable in midlife.

What's the solution to overcome this fear of trust? Tracy needs to update this *doesn't trust* protective part and tell it that she is no longer the one, two and three year old in the operating room . . . she's a 44-year-old woman who is lonely and afraid to make deep connections because she can't trust. This part has no idea that it's affecting her life because it's stuck in the past, in the operating room. She needs this *doesn't trust* part to let go of its job so she can make new friends through being open about her feelings and trusting that she's not going to get hurt or suffocate.

Once this *doesn't trust* part feels the appreciation, understanding and love from her adult Self, it will allow her to talk to her *exiled* toddler parts, healing them of their faulty beliefs that the world is not safe. Tracy will have to take herself back into the scene of the operating room to be one of the adults in scrubs wheeling Little Tracy into the operating room. Little Tracy needs to let big Tracy know how scary it was to be "suffocated" like that. Then, adult Tracy can also let Little Tracy on the operating table know that back in the 1970's, her father and the doctors didn't know that you shouldn't put an anesthesia mask on a child while they are still conscious. They need to sedate the child with a tranquilizer first. Little Tracy's exiles (one, two and three years old) need to know that their intention was not to suffocate her. Tracy can give her exiles the loving reassurance she needed at the time of those traumatic surgery experiences. Then she can take her out of the memories of the operating room and bring Little Tracy and the three exiles to the park, (or anywhere else that feels safe) to be safe with adult Tracy for the rest of their lives.

Now when these *exiled* parts of her unburden from the belief that "The world is not safe" and are no longer engulfed in the frightening memories of the operating room, they will finally believe that people *can* be trusted—that it's okay to be vulnerable. She's an adult now . . . not a toddler. When they release the burden of the faulty belief that people can't be trusted, adult Tracy will have the courage to trust and be vulnerable and know that nothing bad is going to happen. That's because the *doesn't trust* protector can once and for all let go of its job of protecting the exiles in the operating room since they are no longer there, they are at the park, safe with adult Tracy. She will finally be able to form new deep friendships instead of staying stuck with loneliness.

Tracy's story illustrates that every issue that keeps us from the results we want can be traced back to faulty and limiting beliefs we took on when bad things happened to us. Once we are aware that it's related to the past, then we can *decide* if we want to do the work to unburden the faulty beliefs created by our *exiles*. (The first step to change is *awareness*.)

Turned Off by Lack of Emotions and Lack of Confidence

Here's the case study of another couple whose relationship was affected by lack of emotions and lack of confidence.

Debra is a very attractive 43-year-old mother of two. She had been married for 15 years to Steve and they were living like roommates. The relationship had been out of gas for a long time and divorce was imminent. Debra was physically and emotionally abused by her drug-addicted mother, who was also the target of abuse by her own mother. (Victims creating more victims.)

Debra had been through a few months of therapy but the toxic energy of the past has not left her body. The issues had been laid out on a platter but she just didn't know how to clean the platter of the rotten past. This is where *unburdening* the negative feelings and faulty beliefs of the *exiles* is so powerful in order to finally be able to move on. She's ready to rid herself of the empty relationship, file for divorce and move on to a better man.

Just like Liz, Debra and I did something similar with getting to know her parts. She felt much better about herself after unburdening the exiles of their pain created by her mother's treatment of her. Because she had such great results, she suggested that Steve work with me. She indicated that she might hold off on divorce if he overcame his lack of emotion and lack of confidence. As the years went on, Debra got more and more turned off by Steve's lack of confidence. There was no spark left in him or their relationship. So Steve came to see me for a deep-dive four-hour coaching session. (Long sessions make clients feel safe and heard and it provides the trust and safety to unburden something deep because we're not watching the clock.) He was willing to try this to see if he could save his marriage and revitalize his motivation and confidence so he could jumpstart his career.

Steve is a handsome 52-year-old guy in a middle management job for an insurance company. When I met him, I immediately detected a lack of confidence energy—especially through his voice. He consciously wants to move up the ranks to a higher position in the company, he knows he's capable, but he's not sure if he could secure the position.

This negative thought "I'm not sure . . ." already tells me that his subconscious doesn't believe he can get the promotion, that he's convinced himself that he doesn't deserve it, and he doesn't have enough confidence to schmooze with upper management to be considered. Even if it's only a little bit of doubt, the Universe will pick up on that doubting energy and prevent us from getting what we want. In fact, it will make us self-sabotage.

Steve feels that he can be more successful at work but the parts of him that hold him back are: the part that's *too laid back*; the part that wants to *avoid conflict*; and the part that would rather be *passive* instead of aggressive. (Lots of protector parts for sure). Steve knows he's too "vanilla," with no passion or spice. He's terrified of getting too excitable or becoming vulnerable.

I learned that Steve had a father who was like Napoleon, ruling with an iron fist. He would beat Steve and his brothers, never demonstrating that he loved them. This history tells me that he has many, many frozen exiles living in his dungeon, afraid of showing his Self as an adult because those young parts of him still think he's going to be beaten down if he does become vulnerable, just as his father had beaten him. Those exiles have already been reminded that it's not safe, ever since his wife Debra made angry attempts to try to get him to show his emotions. His exiles have been stirred up because the "scoldings" by Debra reminded Steve of his father scolding him.

I took Steve through a couple of exercises to help him forgive his alcoholic father, and to access one of the painful memories by getting to know the *numbness* protector. This is the shell of protection he has built up. A little bit of it was released but there were many other protectors that needed to be addressed in order for him to be more confident and less numb.

After this long coaching session, Steve let me know that he didn't want to take it any further. It was nice that he got to know one of his protectors and one of his exiles was unburdened but he's not ready to confront the rest of his protectors and exiles that keep him stuck. Although his marriage is breaking up, he would rather stay the way he is because that's all that he has ever known, and for right now, that's all he can deal with. It's so unfortunate that fear is running Steve's life, breaking up his marriage and holding him back from his full potential at work. He has no confidence or self-esteem as a result of his father's beatings and lack of validation.

So the fear of unleashing his greatness is what stopped him from continuing with the coaching. Once again, as Marianne Williamson put it so nicely, "It is our light not our darkness that most frightens us." The devil we know is more comfortable than the devil we don't know.

Just like Jim, Steve is running away from his emotions and just like Sarah in the chapter on health, he is running away from his potential. This is similar to the way Sarah used her weight problems to avoid going after her dreams. By not achieving these dreams and being a failure at relationships, this reinforces Steve's original beliefs he took on when he was beaten by his father that he is *worthless and unlovable* and that's why nothing ever goes his way. It's a self-fulfilling prophecy. When things get bad, it just makes him realize that he was right all along, that he is a "loser."

Steve can't even conceive of being any other way (just like Sarah couldn't) because numbness, fear and lack of confidence have been his reality for so long. He is *blended* with his parts and doesn't even know that there is a true Self underneath the rubble of his wounds. His parts are what he is familiar with. This *might* change when something even worse happens, like another divorce with the next wife. It's not bad enough yet for him to change.

Just like some alcoholics have to a wall before they admit there's a problem, Steve might have to hit rock bottom before he does more work to get to know his protectors and unburden his exiles. Steve, like Sarah with her weight problems, wants to hide behind his excuses, so he doesn't have to confront what it takes to realize his true potential. In contrast, Liz was not attached to staying in mediocrity and was ready to go very deep to unburden all of her baggage so she could move on to a better partner and career success.

The Controlling Part that Needs to Feel Important

Sharon is another interesting client that couldn't help being *nasty and controlling* to her boyfriend, George—and he put up with it. (He's a mild-mannered brilliant computer programmer with an abusive upbringing.)

Sharon's *nasty controlling* part was a re-enactment of how her mother treated her father. She knows she's doing this to

George just like her mom used to abuse her dad but she can't help it. Through IFS sessions, Sharon realized that she had to be *nasty and controlling* to feel important and significant over her boyfriend. (One of our core human needs is the need to feel *significant and important.* For some people, the most extreme way to show this is to kill people to claim the notoriety.)

Sharon's mom used to call her "stupid" even though she was one of the smartest kids in her class. Sharon continued to feel stupid all of her adult life (she's 48 now) even though she went to one of the top colleges. She felt *stupid* no matter what she did. She amassed more and more education in the hope that she would finally *feel* smart. But that little girl inside of her just felt *stupid* because she was frozen in time, saddled with the bad memories of her mom's cruel behavior.

Since Sharon didn't feel significant with mom, she took out her feelings of inferiority on her boyfriend. When this *nasty and controlling part* gets activated, she snaps at him when things are out of order in the house. "Can't you put this newspaper in the recycling bin after you're done?" "Why is this laundry on the floor? You are such a slob!" "Can't you do anything right?" Sharon hates it when she has outbursts and feels so bad that her boyfriend is at the receiving end of her rages. Her boyfriend doesn't talk back. He obeys.

I guided Sharon to unburden the *exile* that took on the belief that she was *stupid,* and as a result, her *nasty and controlling* protective part did let go of its role. That little girl in the dungeon who believed she was *stupid* now believes she is *smart.* Now the *nasty and controlling* protector can let go of its job since the *exiled* little girl has been rescued out of the dungeon.

Sharon no longer verbally assaults her boyfriend and their relationship has improved tremendously.

The Need to Have Affairs

A chapter on relationships wouldn't be complete without discussing why we get obsessed with certain people and why some of us cheat on our partners. By now you know that the parts that likes to be *unfaithful* and gets *obsessed* are *protectors*. These parts are just like any other addictions—to food, to work, to alcohol, to shopping, etc. they are protecting *exiles* that got hurt. These parts that need to have affairs or need to be obsessed over someone can let go of these undesirable protective behaviors if they show you which exile(s) created these protectors in the first place. Let me give you an example of the story of someone who worked with one of my IFS therapist colleagues.

Linda is 55 years old, married to an obese husband with congestive heart failure who is in poor health because he doesn't take care of himself. She's afraid he's not going to live too much longer. Their sex life is non-existent because he's impotent and Linda is very turned off by his obesity and lack of self-care. (Her husband probably doesn't care about his health because of his self-loathing.) So she has turned to obsessing over one of her co-workers and having a clandestine affair with him.

Linda feels guilty about this and wants to end it and stop her obsession, but she's having a hard time overcoming this on her own. So her IFS therapist helped her to get to know the *obsessed* protector and why it is so enamored with looking for love in the wrong places.

Linda's *obsessed* part took on its job around one year old, at the time of her mom's death. Linda witnessed the killing of her mom by her dad, in her bedroom, while she was lying in her crib. Dad ended up in jail and Linda was taken in by her aunt and uncle. When Linda entered college, her aunt and uncle died in a plane crash. Needless to say, Linda has experienced her share of loss at a young age.

Linda's *obsessed* part's job is to look for love and validation wherever she can get it since she lost all of the people she thought loved her: her mom and dad, aunt and uncle. *Obsessed* part was afraid that if it didn't do its job of looking for love anywhere it could get it, it was going to be alone. Being alone means no one wants her and life would not be worth living. It was also afraid that the imminent loss of her cardiac-impaired and crippled husband would mean she would be alone again, like when mom, dad, aunt and uncle vanished. So it had to find someone to love *now* (thus the obsession with the co-worker) so that she wouldn't be left alone when hubby died.

Being alone is scary for this *obsessed* part. This part was protecting Linda from taking her own life, which might have happened if she kept thinking that she was not lovable. During an IFS session, *obsessed* was updated that married people are not supposed to have affairs and that marriages can break up as a result.

Obsessed finally agreed to show Linda the *exile* it had been protecting all of these years—the one year old in the bedroom that witnessed her father killing her mother. As a result of losing her parents, this exile took on the belief that, "I'm not lovable, that's why Mom and Dad abandoned me and shipped me to aunty and uncle's house." This exile then got triggered again very badly when uncle and auntie died in the plane crash.

And now, those abandonment feelings are rising up again with her husband's refusal to take care of himself. His death is imminent and the exile will get triggered again when hubby dies. So the *obsessed* protector has sprung into action. It wants love anywhere it can get it, and a co-worker will work just fine. This co-worker makes her feel she is worthy of love.

It's the one year old part of Linda that is madly in love. The one year old doesn't know that Linda is not supposed to have sex with a man who is not her husband. She's very obsessed with this relationship and doesn't want to lose it even though she knows she shouldn't be in it in the first place. (Protectors don't care about the consequences of their behaviors. This is a *manager* protector, it's proactively managing the *exile* from getting stirred up when her husband dies.)

So how did her obsessed part finally let go of the need to have affairs? *Obsessed* part gave Linda permission to go back into the scene of the bedroom when her one-year-old part witnessed the murder of her mother. It was extremely emotional. Linda imagined scooping this one year old out of the crib (and out of the murder scene with cops all around her) ushering her into her car and droving her to the beach, where she could be safe with Linda. Rescuing the baby and loving her and keeping her safe was what this exile needed. She had been forgotten and left in that bedroom all by herself for 54 years. Now she is finally safe in the arms of 55-year-old Linda. After witnessing and re-parenting her young part, the burden of "I must be bad and unlovable, that's why mom and dad are gone" was finally released. (Because the memories of many exiles are loaded with emotional pain, please do NOT access exiles on your own. A trained IFS therapist can safely guide you to rescue exiles out of the past. It's okay to start the process of getting to your protectors but it's NOT safe to complete the exile work on your own. Please find an IFS practitioner on the Selfleadership.org website.)

Now that this *exile* is safe, the *obsessed* protector no longer needs to perform its extreme role of looking for love in the wrong places. As a result, Linda's obsession with the co-worker stopped, she came to her senses and ended the affair. Now she realizes she will be okay alone if and when her husband dies because this one-year-old part will have 55-year-old Linda taking care of her. Linda has become the primary caretaker of this part, not the man she was having an affair with.

Can't Get Over Obsessing About an Ex

I've had several clients still obsessed with lovers after a broken relationship; they just couldn't get these people out of their minds. Similar to Linda's story, the reasons for obsessing can always be traced back to bad childhood memories. An example of this is John.

John was still obsessed over the girlfriend that broke up with him a year ago. Janet beat the emotional crap out of him. She was pretty narcissistic and she ran the show.

John was not assertive at all and Janet was just like his narcissistic mother, who was very controlling with his father. So when Janet was treating him like dirt, it was very familiar territory. Growing up, John didn't feel like he mattered at home, so he developed obsessions with taking care of some of his high school friends so he could feel that he belonged. He would do one of his buddy's homework for him and was praised for being such a good friend. John's own needs always took second place. So it's no wonder that John develops obsessions with love relationships even though he knows they are not good for him. He can't help it. The *obsessed* protector is protecting the *exile* that didn't feel loved by his narcissistic mom. So in order for John to get over the obsession with the old girlfriend, he needs to go back into the memories where his mom made him feel unloved and unburden the exile of its pain. Then the obsessed part can let go of its extreme destructive feelings.

Can't Ever be Alone: Obsessed with Love

Another example is Tania's desires to sleep with whoever will come to her bedside. Tania was raised without a dad because he was always on military duty overseas. Her lack of a father figure made her obsess over boys, even in elementary school. When she got to high school, she slept with anyone who would have her.

This part of Tania that was obsessed with love and attention dressed provocatively. This part had Tania get breast implants that went from a perfectly fine B cup to a D cup, way out of proportion with her petite 5 foot 1 inch frame. This part liked wearing tight and low-cut clothing to show off her physique. The more she turned heads from the way she dressed and strutted her body, the more Tania felt good about herself. By the time she got to college, she'd so many one-night stands, she stopped counting. It made her feel good to get naked and let men penetrate her body. Tania didn't feel lonely when she was with men. She felt lonely and abandoned if she didn't have men to sleep with. In fact, she has never been alone. She wouldn't know what to do with herself. She went from one boyfriend to the next. So to overcome this bad behavior, it's the same process I've been sharing with you. Get to know the story of this *obsessed* protector and let it reveal the exile(s) underneath the undesirable behaviors.

You probably know people who have affairs and who have a hard time being alone without a romantic partner. It's all rooted in their abandonment issues. The obsessed protector parts are so afraid of being abandoned—after all, being alone means that life is not worth living, and may even mean taking one's own life. (If you peel back the onion deep enough into the core, many protectors fear death.)

An *obsessed* part, along with a *cheating* part doesn't know that sleeping with lots of people can get you hurt and can give you a bad reputation. It can also hurt your career. So the obsessed protector needs to understand the consequences of sleeping around. It doesn't know you can get fired for fooling around with your boss. This part still thinks you are three years old when daddy abandoned you. You can change these looking-for-love and obsessive behaviors when you understand who the exile(s) are and unburden them of their faulty beliefs such as "I'm not lovable" and "I'm abandoned."

Improve Your Self-Image, Attract Your Dream Soul Mate

Caroline is a 44-year-old sales rep for a biotech company who has repeated the same abusive relationships over and over again. When she became aware of the pattern—each person becoming dependent on the other to make them feel worthy— she realized how this created plenty of drama, with repeated breakups and makeups.

Caroline had been through years of therapy, read many self-help books and completed several transformational programs by well-respected leaders in their fields, but still found herself insecure, procrastinating and full of fears. She was sick and tired of being in this state and didn't know where to turn next to move forward. That's when she saw me at a talk and knew that she had to work with me to unburden her negative feelings. She told me she feels like she "can't get her act together" and she blames herself for the suicide of her husband, who was severely depressed.

She always felt abandoned, unworthy and unloved because her mother left her alone as a child and would emotionally and physically abuse her—it got so bad that she would pull her up the stairs by the hair. Caroline's room was her special place where she could escape the mistreatment—until the day her mom entered her room in a rage and messed up her doll house with the little furniture and the tiny people. She pulled her pictures off the wall and scattered her stuffed animals, shattering her sanctuary and her sense of safety and security. Her father never attended important events such as her music recitals and high school and college graduations making her feel as if she didn't matter. Therefore, Caroline she took on the belief that she was unworthy of love and attention. Her parents were unpredictable and fought a lot, and her mother had symptoms of Asperger's Syndrome that made it difficult to communicate with her. So Caroline was basically raised by her two older brothers.

Caroline's past affected how she showed up at work, letting others insult her, lacking the spine to stand up for herself. Feeling *abandoned, unworthy* and *unloved* is what also attracted her to needy men who had their own issues. Caroline told me she was very stressed about her embarrassing past as if she had something "dirty" to hide. She felt this contributed to allowing others to take advantage of her, and held her back from moving forward. For her entire life, she has always been overly concerned with what others thought of her.

The image of the exile that came to Caroline during her session was that of a young part of her that was soiled in the crib. She wasn't sure if this *dirty* part was inappropriately touched or just neglected and that's why she was "dirty." She went through the ritual in her mind of "cleaning up" this dirty baby and caressing her in her arms. She rescued this baby out of the past and brought her to the beach where she was safe with her and loved by her. Whatever negative thing was going on with that little infant part, it shifted that day. This was the *part* that was keeping Caroline stuck from moving forward in her relationships, career and happiness.

After a couple of days of processing what I took her through, Caroline felt *happier* and *"cleaner."* Others who noticed the shift told her, "You look happier and lighter, Caroline." It felt like a heavy weight had been lifted off her shoulders.

Caroline felt like "The real sparkling me finally got turned on. I'm more self-assured, more relaxed, freer and more animated to express my feelings, and I'm much more confident. I stopped focusing on others first and I'm prioritizing me. I'm not allowing my bosses, peers or family victimize me anymore. The need for approval from others is gone now since now I know my parts were looking for me to validate them, not someone outside of me. I don't care what others think anymore. I believe in myself and I'm attracting better men because I'm comfortable showing my vulnerabilities. I'm so grateful for the breakthroughs I was able to achieve. This was the unburdening I needed after years of working on myself."

Caroline was able to get such a dramatic shift in one concentrated three-hour session because she had been consciously working on herself for a long time. Working with me was just that the last step (IFS "clean up duty" so to speak) she needed to unleash the best of who she is. This positive shift in her self-image was a result of releasing the old energies of shame, guilt, and fear, from this soiled exile that was in the crib. The new self-image has allowed her to manifest better and better relationships.

Later on, Caroline sent me an update three months after her session. "I am discovering all these new amazing aspects about myself that I never knew I had. I thought only other people were gifted with them. I've met the man of my dreams and I know it's all because of the work I did with you. This awesome man is an extreme reflection of what is going on inside of me as I grow and love myself unconditionally. Thank you! Thank you! You saved my life from doom and gloom!"

(Getting feedback like this is why I get up in the morning to do the work of my soul's calling. ☺)

* * *

Caroline's manifestation of her dream relationship and the positive results from the other stories I've shared are possible for your own romantic relationships when you break free from the shackles of the past. The unresolved baggage is what has you repeating the same relationship conflicts and patterns over and over again. Instead of moving right into another relationship, it's best to work on yourself first. When you rescue your exiles out of the past and unconditionally love all parts of you, your self-image will improve and you'll be able to finally attract the right loving partner that will allow you to live the Prince Charming and Fairy Princess life that never needs to break up.

And men (and some women) listen up—stop being so numb. There's nothing sexy about not sharing your feelings! You are alienating your friends, family and loved ones and you are not being true to yourself when you bottle up your emotions. The women want to hear from your true Self so you can create a lively relationship full of laughter, spontaneity, with true admiration and acceptance of one other.

When you understand who you are and unburden your emotional scars, then the turtle can finally peek its head out from under the shell of protection and make love like you really mean it from your heart and soul. Just imagine feeling the validation and empathy from your partner as both of you are vulnerable with each other and really listening and reflecting back what the other person is feeling— just what you've always wanted to feel from your caregivers that you weren't given enough of.

So if you want to live happily ever after as Prince Charming and Fairy Princess, both of you need to get out of emotional jail, be in touch with your inner worlds and understand why you are the way you are. You must unburden some of these exiles so that you don't attract the wrong frog for your mate. When you positively change your inner landscape, you will believe you are "hot" and a great catch because you have become the primary caretaker of your exiles, you don't need someone else to complete you, *you* will make *you* feel whole. Your partner becomes the secondary caretaker of your parts.

Sophia Loren famously said, "Nothing makes a woman more beautiful than the *belief* that she is beautiful." Let me take that one step further for the guys, "Nothing makes a man more attractive than the *belief* that he is attractive." And you will believe you are attractive when your exiles are unstuck from the past and finally believe they are beautiful, worthy, and enough." And you'll never be alone again because you have the company of your Self. If your partner has also explored their inner world and they are the primary caretakers of their exiles, then being with each other is the icing on the "happily ever after" life. The intimacy you will experience will be mind-blowing and you will feel like you died and went to heaven. Haaahhhhh... Bliss!

Chapter Nine

Ghosts of the Past Haunting Your Bank Account
Happiness First Manifests Financial Abundance

*"Money may not buy you happiness
but happiness can help you get rich."*
-Jim Loehr

There is nothing wrong with the drive for success and financial freedom. We all want to live comfortably and not have to worry about becoming a "bag lady" or a "hobo" going to the soup kitchen for meals, standing in line at the food pantry or the local shelter for the homeless. Studies have shown that if you are making at least $75,000 and fulfilling the basic needs for food, clothing, shelter and money tucked away for retirement, then making more money doesn't necessarily bring additional happiness from the inside-out. (This figure is much higher for expensive major cities, of course.)

I mentioned the Law of Paradoxical Intent in an earlier chapter. It bears repeating here. "You must have goals but your happiness *cannot* be tied to those goals, you must be happy *first* before you reach your goals." If you are happy *first*, then making more and more money becomes the icing on the happiness cake, as long as you are not also sacrificing your emotional and physical health or your relationships as well.

Some people set higher and higher arbitrary goals to try to reach that state of elusive internal joy, but reaching these goals may only bring temporary joy. They have a good car already and they want a better more luxurious model, or their house is big enough but they want to buy a bigger one or they want to join an exclusive country club. (There's nothing wrong with acquiring nice things—but if we are doing it to get "high" or to unconsciously show someone that we've made it, then we are never going to be fulfilled.) These people get that high when new things are acquired but shortly thereafter go back to their old way of being. As they climb this social ladder, living expenses get higher and they might have to put on a "mask" to convince their new social group that they belong. God forbid their new friends find out they were raised by an alcoholic father in a trailer park!

"Oh honey, I'm so happy about your promotion. Let's buy a bigger house in a fancier neighborhood and upgrade our cars. Boy, I'll finally be really happy then. My dreams will come true. I'll be the wife of the V.P. of Marketing of a Fortune 500 company! I'll bet my sister will be green with envy. Hah!!" (Many times, the drive to be better is driven by the demon of the sibling or the bully who made fun of us growing up. *I'll show you who's got their act together!*)

A roomier house or better education for the kids in a tonier suburb is great, but at what point is it enough with the social climbing? Unfortunately for some, the relationships with the new peer group are about keeping up with these new "Joneses" and faking it. Faking it for what? They may feel like they can't let their hair down and share their vulnerabilities as they mask their inner Selves to prove something to somebody.

So what's the solution to stop this madness of always wanting more and more? Get to know your protectors and exiles—the demons that are driving you. Heal and unburden them of their pain and you will become happy when you are loving your parts unconditionally. Then you can enjoy the fruits of your labor and go after your goals for the right reasons.

Protectors such as *overachievement* and *perfectionism* don't have to completely let go of their jobs 100%, they have helped you to achieve a lot. However, if working too much has affected your physical and/or your emotional health and/or your relationships, then you can let these protectors know that other areas of your life are being negatively affected (they are unaware of this) and you can ask these protectors to dial it down and relax a little bit (maybe 25-50%) so that you have the energy to take care of other parts of your life that are not at 100%.

You may even get to a spiritual point where you say, "I've had enough with keeping up with the Joneses. Being on the treadmill of status and more stuff is for the birds! I want to simplify. Why do I need all of this stuff?! Life is about so much more than the accumulation of things. I feel so good about myself that I want to be more humble."

There are many stories of well-known wealthy people who lead simple lives, the most famous of whom is Warren Buffet. He doesn't care if he's driving a 10- year-old car, it's just transportation to get from point A to point B.

And, if you have done the work of seeing how your past affects the present, and you love yourself and are not ashamed of the ghosts that were in the closet, you can be the leader to start the deeper more soul-satisfying conversations with your friends who still have their masks on. Letting your hair down gives others permission to do the same so you don't have to keep living like a fraud. Your relationships will be more authentic and more satisfying to your soul.

Brene Brown, PhD, LMFT, the world's leading expert on shame and vulnerability and worthiness (Google her talks on YouTube), says that when you are comfortable sharing a little bit of your old shame (everyone has it), that's when you form deep human connections. These kinds of connections satisfy your soul. When you unburden your exiles, you'll be comfortable sharing the old shame. When you embrace your imperfections and shed the mask, you'll be free. Even telling your employees vulnerable stories that help them understand what made you who you are will connect them deeply to you like no pie chart or Excel spreadsheet ever can. If you show you are more similar than different from them, they will be a part of that rare breed of people who love to come to work and produce for their boss. They will make you look really good.

I hear quite a bit about the lives of "rich people" who insist on going to exclusive $1000/night resorts when their kids are young (kids don't care about exclusive resorts). They do this so they can brag to their friends that they went to such-and-such resort. It's all to show off and perhaps to one-up one another. *If you can go to this resort, I'll show you I can do it too!* $400/night hotel rooms are no longer good enough because who wants to want to be in the company of people who can only afford a $400/night room? (I'm not saying there aren't legitimate amenities that the higher-priced hotel room provides, but if they're going for the wrong reasons, such as bragging rights and snob appeal, it's ultimately an empty reason for a vacation.) Unfortunately, through the stories I hear, many of these people are miserable, going through the grind, with shaky and abusive marriages and messed-up kids. But they sure have lots of "toys" —houses, cars, jewels, drivers, etc. If you don't have to worry about money, then the most important question is: "Are you happy with the state of your health, relationships and emotional well-being?"

There have been more than a few occasions where I have either coached a client or have gotten to know strangers well enough on the first meeting that they reveal to me their deepest pain. (Okay . . . it's just my natural ability as someone who was in sales for 27 years combined with my skills as a coach that I am able to make people feel safe enough to tell me everything. The conversations are never about me. I always focus on the other person and make them feel heard and important. If you simply follow the techniques outlined in the classic best-selling book *How to Win Friends and Influence People* by Dale Carnegie, you'll make more new friends in two hours instead of two years by getting interested in them first and making them feel important versus talking about yourself.)

Exiles Sabotage Your Financial Success and Happiness

I was eating lunch at the bar of a fancy New York City restaurant when my friend had to leave and go back to work. I had not finished my lunch and was leisurely enjoying my salad when I struck up a conversation with two men seated to the left of me. (There goes my *fearless* part of striking up conversations with strangers, again.)

It turns out that these two people were in town for a major league sporting event—in fact, they were famous athletes with special backstage passes to the game. Their names didn't ring a bell since I didn't follow this particular sport. After they left though, I Googled them and it turns out one of them was a

Hall of Famer. I told one of my male friends about this man I had lunch with and he said, "Holy moly, you met one of the most famous people in this sport." I had no idea he was this multi-million dollar a year athlete because he exhibited a lot of humility when we chatted. (Maybe because he sensed that I had no idea how famous he was in the sporting world.)

Within a matter of half an hour, this Hall of Famer—let's call him David— told me how he should have retired a few years back with all of the money he made but his financial situation didn't allow him to do so. He had a lot of "expenses" and "a lot of people to take care of." (Mind you, he's only in his early 30's, he's not married and he makes over $5 million per year. His salary contract is on the Internet.) It was obvious that he was living the lifestyle of the rich and famous and didn't have as much money saved as he should have.

David is the oldest of seven kids. His father was a firefighter and his mother stayed home to take care of the children. David remembers how he was constantly told that he couldn't have something—a toy, a videogame, clothes, athletic shoes and so on. He passed on his own needs to let his younger siblings have what they desired. He remembers wanting another serving of chicken because he was still hungry but he gave the last piece to his brother instead and went to bed hungry. It was the same story with not being able to have the sneakers he wanted.

He remembers a very painful incident in 6ᵗʰ grade. Gym class was on Fridays. His only pair of sneakers fell apart three days prior when he flipped over on his bike. His father didn't have the money to buy another pair before Friday so he had to wear his ratty, ugly work boots to gym. He remembers the shame and humiliation of showing up and being teased for not wearing sneakers. The teasing went on for weeks. (The *exile* that this incident created is heartbreaking.)

David feels that he has to say "yes" to every person in his lower middle class family who asks for a handout. His lavish lifestyle of drivers and entourages and multiple homes with service people to take care of them has left him broke. I shared with him that he is probably afraid of saying "no" to his family's requests for fear of losing their love. He didn't realize this but he agreed with my assessment. Unfortunately, he doesn't have the spine to put limits on them since they know he makes over $5 million a year.

David's self-image is that of someone who grew up poor on the streets and was humiliated at school because of his inability to keep up with his peers, as witnessed in the gym incident. Now he has achieved all of this fame and fortune but he can't seem to keep the money he makes and can't seem to find happiness. *If I just got financially secure . . . I would be happier.*

By now you know that that's not the key to happiness. His exiled parts living in the dark dungeon of his mind make him believe that he is still the worthless little boy who didn't have enough food to eat. These exiles are frozen in the bad memories and have no idea what his life is like now. His faulty beliefs that he's unloved and worthless makes him bow to his family's requests for financial handouts. Add to that the part of him that needs to keep up with the lifestyle of other famous athletes and the result is living above his means and sacrificing his financial security. His exiles don't believe that he deserves financial security. Pretty soon, he'll be too old to keep playing this sport and then what is he going to do to replace all of the money he was making? He may end up as one of the statistics of a penniless famous athlete.

David's image of himself now (in the limelight of being a famous sports superstar) does not match the self-image of the little boys inside of him who are still identifying with being the poor, abandoned, rejected and humiliated. The two images are not congruent because the little boys in the dungeon don't believe he deserves success. These exiles are unknowingly helping him make bad decisions that keep him stuck from ever achieving financial freedom and happiness.

Unfortunately, after my half-hour conversation with him, I had to leave and catch a train, and his entourage of young beautiful women started to enter the restaurant and shower him with attention. So I never had a chance to explain the *protector* and *exile* concepts to him so he could at least understand what was driving his feelings of angst.

* * *

Stories are legion of many other famous athletes who went broke after making millions—and many of them grew up on the streets in poverty. Several other stories detail actors' battles with depression, and even committing suicide. Suicide is the ultimate protector that acts out in response to acutely feeling the hopelessness and the bottomless pit of worthlessness. If their parts can't escape from being stuck in the painful past, it makes sense that they sabotage their fame and wealth (and commit suicide because the emotional pain is so bad) because the exiles in the subconscious (which drive 90% of our feelings and actions) have overruled them and made them self-destruct (or even kill themselves).

Some people who've achieved success feel like imposters. The Imposter Syndrome goes something like this: "Who, me? You're saying I deserve success, happiness and a hot-looking partner? You must be talking about the wrong person!" As an imposter, you're excited when you first overhear someone describe how great you are, but then you get this uncomfortable feeling that they are confused, describing someone else. You think it's only a matter of time before they find out who you *really* are.

You are not alone in feeling this way. This Imposter Syndrome (feeling like a fraud) is a psychological phenomenon that was originally coined back in the 70's. You are beautiful/handsome and successful, but you can't believe it's true. It must be a mistake. You feel like you're living in a dream because you haven't been able to internalize the accomplishments that make you insanely attractive. So this incongruence drives you to sabotage your success in health, career and relationships. Some more examples of Imposter Syndrome are:

- "I got into Yale. Really? I'm not supposed to be that smart . . . they must have made a mistake . . . it's only a matter of time before they revoke my acceptance letter."

- "I got the VP position. Wow! I wonder when they are going to find out that I'm not as smart as they think I am?"

- "I can't believe I just overheard someone describe me as beautiful. I'm not supposed to be beautiful. They must me talking about someone else."

- "I just won an Oscar? Really? I've always felt like a fraud . . . I'm not in the same league as the other Oscar winners."

Now you know it's the *exiles* that are responsible for making you feel like an imposter when you achieve anything great. They make you self-sabotage and self-destruct.

Money Legacy Burdens Keep a Lid on Your Financial Ceiling

David the superstar athlete is a case of someone who earns an extreme income that 99% of us will never be able to duplicate. Here's an example of a more "normal" case of a client who just couldn't keep hold of the money that came in.

Cliff owns an architectural firm that specializes in luxury homes. He makes roughly $200,000 a year but finds himself spending all of his profits buying whatever his wife and kids need and giving the rest away to charity. Like many women, his wife's closet is bursting with clothing with the tags still on them. (Sound like emotional shopping to fill the emptiness. They live paycheck to paycheck despite their high income. After they bought their upgraded house, they had to take out loans to fill it up with furniture.)

Cliff and his wife don't fight about money. They just avoid the subject. But here's the tragedy, his retirement savings has only $75,000 in it and he's in his late 40's with two kids in high school. With college tuition looming, there's no way he's going to have enough saved for retirement. He's going to be working for the rest of his life and that thought does not sit well with him.

Cliff wanted to figure out why he isn't more prudent with his savings (he thinks nothing of ordering a $80 bottle of wine at dinner) and why he doesn't have the courage to get more client referrals from his existing wealthy clients so he can make more money. Well, it turns out he is stuck because of one of his exiles that took on a belief around money that doesn't belong to him.

Cliff grew up in a very loving home where his parents granted him every wish for every toy. He felt very loved and he didn't seem to have too many bad memories of his childhood.

So I asked him about the *energy* around money growing up. Cliff's dad was a well-known trial attorney. His mother stayed home to take care of Cliff and his sister. What he remembered was that his parents always fought about money. As soon as dad deposited his paycheck, mom was ferociously spending it all on the kids, her clothes, the house, and so on. So mom and dad would always be arguing about money, especially after Cliff went to bed. He heard everything that was discussed because the yelling was pretty loud.

This part of Cliff that witnessed and soaked up the conflict around money is an *exile* that took on the belief that having money is equated with tension, conflict and fighting. Mom and dad were often threatening divorce. It can be a burden to make money. It can destroy relationships. So this *exile* took on the burden that having *lots* of money meant conflict—a burden that didn't belong to him. This is called a "legacy burden" because it doesn't belong to Cliff, it belongs to his parents. (Making $200K now does not make him feel like he's making too much, it's just enough for his upper middle-class lifestyle. It's the next level of wealth that is scaring him.)

Cliff uncovered that if he did make a lot more money, then it might cause more tension in the house because his wife would spend more and he didn't want to escalate the conflict to the level that he witnessed with his parents. This issue was holding him back from having the courage to get more clients. I helped him access the part of him that witnessed his parents' fights and had him unburden the belief that achieving the next of level income would cause major conflict and destroy his family. With this burden gone, Cliff felt he deserved to acquire more wealth and that he can handle whatever arguments over money might come up between he and his wife.

Feeling Guilty Because You're Not Suffering Financially with Everyone Else

Christine, 42 years old, is a former Wall Street money manager, who helps entrepreneurs manifest financial abundance. When she made the decision to help others erase their money blocks, that's when she started experiencing her own. She couldn't unburden herself from the money story she kept telling herself—that she needed to suffer financially along with her clients. So she's been hiding behind the shame of not attracting financial abundance herself. A part of her was feeling that she didn't deserve the abundance she was trying to help her clients achieve. How could she possibly be this kind of mentor to women when she was financially stuck herself?

Christine told me about a dream she had that revealed that her money drama didn't belong to her. She'd taken it on because of the love for her family. She knows she's a powerful, wealthy woman with more than enough abundance, but she's been hiding for the past two years under other people's stuff. She knew it was time to let herself shine. That's when she reached out to me to get unstuck.

Christine had an *unrealized* part that took on this sabotaging role at nine years old. Its job was to fix everyone else's problems. If it didn't do its job, it was afraid that others would suffer, and they wouldn't like her because of their suffering. If others didn't like Christine, she'd be alone and sad. But this part was now tired of carrying this burden of suffering. It would rather play like a normal nine year old. This *unrealized* part represented all the times Christine said, "I get 'three feet from gold' and then everything falls apart." This part would rather do the fun job of being the *power surge* that gives her the final boost when she's close to the goalpost to push past the finish line and get the results she craves.

So I asked if this protector would be willing to show us the *exiled* little nine-year-old Chrissy that it had been protecting. At first this protector wouldn't show us the little girl. Christine saw a *black image* part (another protector that jumped in). *Black image* was afraid we were going to get mad at little Chrissy. But Christine reassured her it wasn't going to happen. Then she finally saw the image of her young self: an image of her with her arms across her face, hiding in a cave. Christine stroked Chrissy's hair to see if she would respond. She did.

Little Chrissy was stuck in the cave, unsure and confused about why she was taken away from her parents and brought up by her grandparents. She was afraid to ask them what the circumstances were because she felt silly to be curious. Plus she didn't want to sound like she was complaining—after all, she was still being taken care of. She wasn't suffering like her brother and sister— they were still in an abusive household with mom and her boyfriend. She felt guilty for not suffering like her brother and sister. She was worried that her grandparents wouldn't love her if she asked them why mom gave her away. She was afraid if she asked that her grandparents might think Chrissy didn't love them. So Chrissy took on the belief that she must suffer in order to be loved and accepted by others. (You see how protectors and exiles take on irrational beliefs and fears because they are kids, without the intellectual capacity to understand adult problems.)

So after Christine updated the *exile* Chrissy on how old she is now, what she has accomplished and what is going on in her life to keep her stuck, Chrissy finally got an explanation from Christine of why she was given to her grandparents. It was because Mom didn't have the financial resources to raise three kids. And it made Chrissy feel guilty about not suffering along with her siblings.

This nine-year-old part had Christine believing that if she were not suffering financially along with her clients, then "I'm not helping them because I'm not empathizing with their plight." This part of her took on suffering with those around her at the age of nine due to her guilt that her mother sent her to live with her grandparents while her sister and brother were still in an abusive household. "I chose to silently suffer and took on the idea that in order to belong and have a sense of community, I must suffer with those around me because my sister and brother were suffering."

This supposition was acted out in her life in this way: Every time she made good money in her business, it would magically disappear through spending on frivolous things or by making bad investments. If she amassed wealth, it was not congruent with the belief the eight-year-old part of her took on—that she must suffer with others in order to be accepted. It also believed that if she wasn't suffering with money problems like her friends, she was not helping them by being "superior" to them.

So Christine reassured Chrissy that there is plenty of goodness to go around. She doesn't have to suffer with others. She can be the fairy godmother that gives others goodness to achieve financial stability. She will still be loved by others despite her wealth. Now she understands where the seeds of her financial career came from. When her dad lost his job when she was 17 years old, that's when it was cemented that she had to help others gain financial stability. ("Your deepest wound is your truest niche.") Taking care of herself and being financially stable was the lesson she needed to learn, and in turn, she is helping others do the same.

So in her inner world, her burden of "needing to suffer with others to be loved" was taken away by the ocean. Now the *unrealized* protector could take on the new role of being the *power surge* to take her to the next level of her career. Christine's takeaway from this was that "I don't need to suffer with my clients or anyone else around me. I'm still going to belong and be loved when I let go of the need to suffer with others."

In my latest follow up with Christine two months after our session, the energy around money is much better, and she's clearing up some real estate financial blocks that had been in the way. Once that is taken care of, a heavy load will be lifted off her back. She's closer and closer to the finish line and feeling like she is finally getting ahead. This positive energy is what is going to propel her forward. The negative energy from the past has been released and she's on her way to receiving abundance.

So now you see as some people achieve financial success they end up losing it all because of their exiles. They don't even know that this is happening because they chalk it up to bad luck or the economy.

"F *** the Money and the Fame, I Just Want to be Happy!"

George is a well-known artist who amassed an enormous fortune from selling his work. He became a client after I was introduced to him at a Christmas party. George was a silent partner in his friend Stan's real estate business. Unfortunately, the partnership broke up and he is still not over it. After the dissolution, the business soared to new heights without him and George is angry about the press coverage and notoriety his old partner is getting. He feels shut out and ignored.

George certainly isn't hurting for money—he just hates to see his old partner get the attention and make even more money. He can't understand why this person is driving him to be so obsessed. George says what many wealthy and famous people say "F*** the money and the fame, I just want to be happy!" His confusion over this obsession, angst and unhappiness were what drove him to want to work with me.

Just like the "obsessed" stories I shared in the chapter on relationships, his partner was reminding him of his mother. He felt abandoned because his mother was never around— he was raised by nannies. She was a socialite who was often highlighted in the society section of the newspapers. George knew this was important to her and he felt that he wasn't, that he didn't really matter. The way his partner treated him was just like the way his mother would treat him and make him feel invisible, and the way Stan ended the business agreement and ignored him afterwards stung just as much as his mother's indifference.

He wanted Stan to show some appreciation for the ideas he'd given to his business. He just wanted to be validated, just as he wanted his mom to validate him. The two of them were like oil and water and this created conflict. (People who push our buttons are a gift from heaven. They help us trace the breadcrumbs back to our deepest wounds.)

George was also obsessed with trying to accomplish more and more just so he could show Stan that he's better than he is. Through my guidance, George finally realized that the harder he worked, the more miserable he was becoming, because garnering more fame for himself was not necessarily noticed by Stan. And even if Stan did notice, he would probably ignore George's notoriety anyway. George was never going to get the validation he wanted from Stan to feel that he's good enough, just as he's never going to get the validation from his mom that he's good enough. George was going to have to give himself the validation he's been looking for all of his life.

George did unburden several exiles that were causing him angst and keeping him unhappy despite his money and fame. We worked together for about four months and he finally arrived at a good place where he understands and loves his parts and is now much happier as a result.

Career and Potential Stalled by Sexual Abuse History

Sexual abuse is one of the most shameful and humiliating acts that can be inflicted on someone. This frozen exile holds an enormous amount of shame, "I must be so bad that I deserved to be sexually abused." Every client who works with me is asked whether or not they have been inappropriately touched. In attempting to coach them to bust through their fears to achieve greatness, nothing good is going to happen until the exile that suffered the abuse is taken out of the past. Sure, they may be able to achieve fame and fortune, but perhaps that happened with the enablers of addictions and emotional misery (like many cases in Hollywood). This shame can hold one back in just about all areas of your life—health, wealth, relationships and happiness. Here's the story of how Mary was held back from her potential because of her sexual abuse history.

Mary is 34, married with a two year old. She has been laid off for six months from her last staff attorney job at a medium-sized firm. She knows she doesn't want to stay in law anymore. She went to law school because it was her way of rebelling against her parent's messages that she was never going to amount to anything. "I'll prove them wrong." She realizes she would rather do life-changing work with non-profits that makes lives better for inner city children. She's been trying to find her next steps but she wakes up most days with an overwhelming feeling of anxiety and heaviness in her chest. So she ends up feeling lost and just wants to lie on the couch all day. She's been spinning in circles with unproductive days for the last six months. She contacted me because she was confused and paralyzed.

Mary, like many of my clients, had many devaluing moments in her life, with her parents putting their lower middle class values on her, making fun of people with college and graduate school education, and not validating her uniqueness and intelligence. That's why Mary rebelled against their beliefs and went to law school, to prove them wrong. One of the most painful parts of her past was being molested by a cousin on repeated occasions between two to five years old. (She had been through many years of therapy for this and has talked about it ad nauseam but never felt a complete resolution. That's because she has not "visited" her exile locked in the dark basement to help her unload this sexual abuse burden.)

I knew that this was a major exile that was keeping her stuck. Recall from Chapter Six when I showed you the "States of Being" diagram and how the energy of *shame* is the lowest of them all. Shame wreaks havoc on everything. Mary didn't access this sexually abused exile right away. Exiles don't like to come out of hiding so fast, as it may upset the other parts. We first have to get to the exile through the protectors.

I read Mary the Path Visualization I shared with you in Chapter Three during Matt's session, and her *anxiety* part was the major part that was holding her back from walking freely on the path to expressing her true Self. This *anxiety* part took on its job when Mary was two years old, to keep her safe by not speaking out about the abuse, otherwise bad things might happen if she tattled on her cousin. She might be hurt by the cousin, maybe even strangled and killed. So anxiety is keeping her from death by not speaking up. She wakes up with this heavy feeling on her chest every day and can't seem to shake it. No amount of anti-depressants and anti-anxiety meds make her feel better.

As we worked together, the anxiety protector eventually gave Mary permission to access the young exiled part of her that was molested by her cousin. She saw this part hiding in the closet of her bedroom. At this point Mary went inward to talk to her and update her on what Mary's life is like now, since this part has no idea that she's a grownup. Mary asked this young part to share her story of abuse, since exiles want someone to witness what happened. Mary's Self would be the witness.

Mary was talking to her exile silently. (She was talking to her exile in private. I didn't need to know the details.) She had her eyes closed with tears streaming down her face as I watched her over Skype. When she opened her eyes, I asked if she would like to take her young part to a safe place. She took her to the beach and soaked up this new memory of her adult Self being with this young child. IFS has the power to "rewrite" and "rewire" in a positive way the scene of the horror movie clients have been stuck in for so long. You, like Mary, get to give the exiles what they need to get out of the film of the past. The shame of this sexual abuse memory and the unburdening of the faulty belief that "I am bad" to "I am lovable" released Mary's sexual abuse story for good.

Mary woke up the next day with just about all of the heaviness in her chest gone. It seemed like the *anxiety* part was only protecting this lone exile. (A protector can be protecting multiple exiles.) So if Mary remained anxious after this unburdening, then we would have to find out the rest of *anxiety's* story of what other exiles it is protecting.

After *anxiety* was addressed, other protectors popped up in subsequent sessions that needed attention. The part that *procrastinated,* the part that *afraid of rejection*, the *frozen* part, the *impatient* part, etc. After about three months of coaching with me, Mary finally landed a job in a startup non-profit she believes in. She feels really good about herself, her self-esteem has risen (from a 4 out of 10 scale in the beginning of our coaching to an 8 out of 10), her disturbed sleep from anxiety is gone, she has more energy, she's more present and patient with her toddler, is communicating better with her husband, and is happier overall. Mary continues to coach with me as she navigates the new career landscape, getting the courage to do scary things at work, such as speaking in front of large groups of people. (She has exiles that were humiliated when she spoke in front of classmates in elementary school and high school.)

Mary is on the journey to doing big things. After the initial sessions working mostly with protectors and exiles, the IFS coaching relationships move more into the coaching arena of holding clients' hands as they move outside of their comfort zones. And going outside of the comfort will reveal even more fears of the exiles. Now, whenever fears come up or when they are stuck, the conversation starts with "Tell me about the part of you that is afraid to approach your boss to constructively share your thoughts about what went wrong at the board of director's meeting." This fear of approaching someone, again, is some part from the past that fears the worst if you criticize an authority figure. It reminded Mary of a part that was beaten down by her seventh grade teacher when she spoke up. IFS inspired coaching is beneficial for the long term. It keeps you accountable for taking risks and scary actions so you can make your dreams a reality.

Holding onto a Family Secret Can Keep You Stuck

I've encountered a couple of cases where distress and inertia was caused by family secrets young parts had been holding onto. One of them was Lillian, a 45-year-old retail sales manager for a large well-known department store who was stuck because she wanted to leave her current company and seek another position in advocacy for children. She had a happy childhood but there was a part of her that felt confused about her inability to move forward into a position that was more fulfilling. And she wanted to attract a life partner. She also felt stuck caring for her aging parents and just kept telling herself that her parents were her priority. The truth is, her siblings could help out and her parents were not as needy as she made them out to be. She just needed to let go and delegate. She was hiding behind her excuses.

When I asked how she was feeling about stretching her boundaries, she just felt this heaviness, the heaviness of keeping a deep dark secret—that her dad had an affair and fathered another child. She discovered the pictures of this other family hidden in a drawer that was supposed to be locked. Lillian found it when she was 10 years old.

She decided to keep this a secret from mom and her younger brother since her brother was so happy and carefree at eight years old. She chose to be the shield to take the consequences if mom ever found out. (It's interesting that she took up fencing in college, representing that shield of hers.) So the protector that was erected to protect the 10 year old was an *anxiety* part—always on the lookout to make sure the world was safe. This part proactively protected her mom and little brother, and it kept her safe in adulthood by always taking the safe route with things so nothing bad would happen—such as playing it safe staying in the same job even though she was unhappy. It doesn't know that this results in being afraid to explore new opportunities. Instead of working so hard to keep Lillian safe, this part that is *anxious* would much rather be the *guardian angel* that watches over everything.

So when *anxiety* part showed us the 10-year-old *exile* that discovered the family secret, she had been aware of adult Lillian. She had kept her company all of these years carrying the backpack of this heavy burden of the family secret. Lillian updated her that she doesn't have to keep the secret anymore, her mom and her brother know about dad's affair. Everything is good now. Dad is sick with cancer and is not expected to live much longer. As she was processing this memory, another young part of Lillian appeared, the part that was happy and carefree before she discovered the pictures of the affair. This happy part took the hands of this exile to run and play outside. Lillian released the burden of the secret of her father's affair by imagining that burden and the pictures getting burned up in the fireplace.

Anxiety protector was now ready to take on the role of *guardian angel*. Now Lillian was imagining herself walking on the path to her true Self and her greatness while her other two parts were happily playing outside. And all of a sudden, an image of M&M candy characters flashed through her mind, and the boots that the M&M character wore were thrown into the air. Freedom and lightness were liberated by taking off the heavy boots. She can now skip along on the path to unleash her full potential. (I'm not making these images up, this is what happens in the IFS process. Clients get all sorts of interesting downloads and images when they have their eyes closed.)

Now Lillian feels so much better since this heavy burden has been lifted off of her—the backpack she's been carrying around is gone. She consciously knew she should be over these yucky feelings but her exile that was still stuck in the 10 year old's memories was taking up so much energy. That's why she just didn't have the courage to take the next steps in her life. And now that she feels better, she's not afraid to go out there and meet men too so she can move on with her life.

Overachieving **Protector's Motivations**

Let me give you an example of why someone keeps compiling more degrees and education for the wrong reasons. I know Anna through a mutual friend. She was sharing how it was so important to her that she get her Ph.D. in Economics. She is currently in a Masters program.

Anna was adopted at two years old by her aunt and uncle when her mother was committed to a mental institution due to her uncontrolled bipolar (manic-depressive) episodes. (She sure has the *"I am abandoned"* exile.) She came to me when she just didn't know why she was driving herself crazy with stress finishing her Masters and then trying to get into a Ph.D. program. "What for? Just so that I can be called *Doctor?"* So I helped her to figure out "the why behind the why."

> **E:** What will having a Ph.D. do for you?

> **A:** So I can attract a smart guy with a with a Ph.D. or equivalent amount of success in education or money.

> **E:** What will being married to this successful guy do for you?

> **A:** So I can show my mother and my adoptive mom that I can attract a good enough husband. Because I need to show them that I'm worthy of *something* since I felt ignored ever since I was adopted into their family, and they already had three kids of their own.

> **A:** Sounds like if you collapse what you really want down to its core essence, driving yourself crazy for

all of these advanced degrees is really about showing your mother and adoptive parents that you are not worthless since you felt abandoned and neglected. You are looking for approval from your caregivers. You are taking the scenic route with hairpin turns (that is, the hard work of graduate school) to try to achieve what you really want, which is *approval and validation from mom and your aunt and uncle.* Your motivation for working so hard in graduate school is all for the wrong reasons. If you think about it, there's no guarantee that you are going to get the kind of approval you want from them.

It might be very beneficial for you to consider healing the parts of you that feel *not good enough,* *unloved* and *abandoned* that came into existence from feeling abandoned by your mom and not feeling as loved because you weren't your aunt and uncle's biological child. You don't need to seek the love from any of them, they are not able to give it to you. Please do the IFS work to get in touch with and loving and unburdening your parts . You don't need to go through a rigorous Ph.D. program for something you are probably not going to get in the end — which is love and validation you crave. After you heal, then you can discover if a Ph.D. is something you really want. And it's not necessary to have a Ph.D. to attract a successful and attractive guy if you love yourself first.

Anna was confused about her motivations for wanting a Ph.D. She thought she was doing it for the right reasons but as I've just shown you, she was not. She was afraid of losing validation and love from her caregivers because her *exiles* believed that that's what they needed to do to get approval.

* * *

John is another example of an overachiever who doesn't know how to stop. He had loving parents but they were strict and expected a lot from him. His mom never went to college and his dad dropped out, and is now a kitchen cabinet salesman at the local big box home improvement store. They were so neurotic about making sure he had a better life that they went into a lot of debt to have him tutored and got him into every extracurricular activity they could fit into his schedule—all to pad his college applications.

They visited 30 colleges to make sure they had 10 to pick from. They knew that if he got into an Ivy League school, college would be a free ride. (If parents make less than $60,000/year, and you get in, you are essentially going for free with all the grants you are entitled to.) So John got into the Brown University and graduated with honors. He worked for a financial services firm, and then, after 10 years, he decided to open up a marketing agency that helps financial services firms market their services.

So he's been working like crazy, has 10 employees and isn't quite managing them the right way. He gets angry when projects aren't completed perfectly, he is often short with his employees, and employee morale is not where he wants it to be. He realizes he is stuck with the decisions he's made in the past.

He nitpicks his wife and obsesses over his meals. He's very persnickety. His food needs to be cooked and presented in a certain way. It drives servers crazy and it's embarrassing to watch him berate waiters in restaurants. He knows it's irrational but he can't help it. He also detests his nail biting and drinking habits, and can't live a day without popping one of his acid-blocking reflux pills. These behaviors are all protectors running the show, and they are showing up in his digestive problems. He's working like the Energizer Bunny because there are so many fears underneath his nitpicky conduct.

I took John through the IFS protocol for his protectors and exiles. He recognized the overachieving parts that had him rundown with health problems and relationship challenges at work and at home, and he finally realized that he's got to slow down, that nothing bad will happen if he does. In the end, the *overachieving* part let some of its roles go and relaxed a bit so that he could show up for his employees and his family from a loving and compassionate space. The *overachieving* protector is not eliminated completely since that helps him be successful. He's just asked it to unwind somewhat so he can have the energy to take care of other areas of his life.

Living Out the Expectations of One's Culture

Many of us our living out the expectations of our parents and our cultural legacies. In Jane Hyun's book *Breaking Through the Bamboo Ceiling: Career Strategies for Asians*, she talks about how the cultural legacies and expectations of Asians can be detrimental to career advancement and fulfillment. They study like crazy so they can get into the best schools and make their parents proud. They are often steered into professions that make the parents look good and feel proud, such as medicine, law or engineering. It's usually not about asking the kids what they want to do, it's about getting a good job so mom and dad can be proud and show the rest of the family how accomplished their children are. As the kids go along this expected trajectory, pushing themselves, they are oftentimes quite miserable on the journey. If one Ivy League degree wasn't enough, they go after one or two more, thinking that acceptance, love and happiness will result after they tack more initials onto their names. They don't want to be shamed by mom and dad for not living out the dreams their parents had for them, but God forbid they actually have thoughts about what *they* want to do.

Cultural burdens include such admonitions as *never talking back to your elders* and *not speaking up for yourself.* Yet these are the very things that often stop Asians from reaching the boardroom. Many Asians are not outspoken for fear of disrespecting authority figures (because their *exiles* carry the legacy that they will be punished if they speak out). So being obedient to their parents' rules means they sabotage their upward climb on the corporate ladder.

I've experienced this energy of "unhappiness" when I meet Asians in the networking groups I belong to. They get very interested in what I do as a *Be More Extraordinary Magician* and they want to know more about protectors and exiles, especially the protector that has them overachieving to please their parents but not themselves. I sense that some of these Asians are just nowhere near happy, that there's that dark cloud over them. They speak with uncertainty, as if they just don't know how great they are because their exiles have overtaken their psyches. They believe they are never going to be good enough in the eyes of their parents. Their parents have been criticizing them for years. First it was for not getting A's in every subject, now it's for not making it big in their careers or not approving of their career choices, ashamed that their kid is not a doctor, lawyer or engineer. Many Asians have memories of parents wincing when their kids brought home anything less than an "A." There's the formation of the *I'm not good enough* exile that will haunt them into adulthood until it's accessed and given validation by their Selves.

What's interesting is the look on their faces when I describe how our need for approval is what drives some of us to go after more and more academic and career success. They "get it," but they don't want to hear the explanation anymore because it starts to trigger them. It hurts so much to hear the truth. (Hey, I'm only sharing information they ask about.)

So just like these Asians, you may hold cultural beliefs from your ancestors about being a certain way. If these ways are not true to your Self, you should not have to go on living a lie. You can overcome this by unburdening the cultural beliefs you hold that don't serve you.

Being Driven to Succeed No Matter What

So in essence, the motivation to work your butt off is to prove your worth to people who have told you that you're not *good enough* (even if that person is dead or you'll never see them again). "See? Look at the company I've built." This motivation does have positive qualities—but at what expense? Your health, emotional well-being and your relationships. You've been locked up in the prison of hard work and you have the key to unlock yourself and move on to freedom.

If you choose to stay on the hamster wheel there will be no end in sight. "If I just make this much money so I can buy the bigger house and better car and better clothes, I can show them I've finally arrived." You might be miserable on the journey because you're working so hard. You're just not enjoying the journey at all. You might get the promotion and more money to buy the bigger house, then you go into more debt to decorate the house because God forbid the neighbors and your family see that you're house rich and cash poor.

How embarrassing would that be? That'll just stir up the "I'm not enough" exiles again and you'll start the process of accumulation all over again.

Now you need to get the next promotion so that you can buy your partner the right jewelry to keep up with the new Joneses, going deeper into debt. Then the financial pressures are on again because as the kids get older, you've gotta send them to private schools and fancy summer camps. Yikes! When is this exhausting lifestyle going to end? In the meantime, your health has become secondary and your wrinkles are showing up faster than you would like. Forget about trying to look like a cougar or Don Juan. Then the "I'm not enough" exiles kick in and you get the urge to spend money on Botox and liposuction and plastic surgery and "Lose 30 lbs. in 30 Days" gimmicks. You're exhausted and it shows. Get off of this hamster wheel and take care of your emotional health first. Even if you say, "I don't do emotions," you will probably regret this because the #1 regret of dying people in hospice nurse according to Bronnie Ware's book *Top 5 Regrets of the Dying* are:

1. "I wish I had the courage to live a life true to myself, not the life others expected of me."

2. "I wish I hadn't worked so hard."

3. "I wish I had the courage to express my feelings."

4. "I wish I had stayed in touch with my friends."

5. "I wish I had let myself be happier."

Do you want to die with these regrets?

Wannabe Millionaires Buying Hope: Their Fear of Success

Many entrepreneurs like myself invest in business mentors and programs to learn the tactics of how to market ourselves. What I have seen in these programs are a lot of wannabes—wannabes who will never make it because underneath their fake confident exteriors are fears of stepping up into the greatest version of themselves. Some of them just think that spending more money on another program and following the steps to a T will give them the six and seven figure income they desperately crave. What often happens is that they are in their own way, the "movie" that keeps looping in their heads from the past is tripping them up with excuses. "If I just buy this next program and learn more about this tactic . . . I'll finally be rich."

There are many business mentors who talk about the mindset you need to have for success. Unfortunately for many entrepreneurs, addressing it at the surface level as recommended by these "experts" and doing an exercise to scream out loud with your peers or punching out the anger onto pillows at a training session to say you are not your story anymore is not going to produce lasting change. That's because these exercises are not addressing the needs of the protectors and exiles that have kept them stuck. This is similar to when you just talk about your feelings in many therapy modalities and you feel that you've wasted your money because you're going in circles and haven't made any progress.

There is a saying that your business and your love relationships (and how well your kids turn out) will only grow to the extent of your personal growth. To put it bluntly, if you don't empty the suitcase full of your emotional baggage you can forget about ever overcoming your struggles and achieving lasting transformation.

Statistics show that 80-90% of first-time businesses fail. People who are making it big are the business mentors that are selling HOPE—just to be fair, they do teach some useful things—but they become the millionaires by selling you on the fact that their fairy dust is going to make you wildly successful if you invest thousands of dollars with them. (It's no different than the expensive wrinkle cream that promises to erase 10 years off your face.) That's wishful thinking. If you want the biggest bang for your buck, spend your money working on yourself *first* and making peace with the past so you can believe in yourself 110%. Then the tactics that in these programs will work because you'll be fearless about trying different things, and others will be attracted to your belief in yourself.

* * *

Let me give you an example of a coach who has spent over $55,000 on business mentors and she's still far from success. It's actually her *fear of success* that is keeping her in poverty. Kim is 35-year-old life coach I met at a personal development conference in Mexico. We developed a friendship, and on the last day we took a walk on the beach. She was lamenting that she's so broke from investing in program after program and she only has two clients to show for it. As I peeled back the layers of the onion for her, here's what we uncovered:

Kim has the vision of becoming a big personal development guru, inspiring the masses. She has great speaking voice with lots of energy. I asked her what she is afraid of if she becomes successful. (Yes, *fear of success* is a big contributing factor to failure.) Kim is afraid that if she becomes a big guru millionaire she might be attracted to another millionaire and break up her marriage. There is a part that is obsessed with staying with her husband because that's her life plan. She needs to tell this part that life is full of surprises. It's not a guarantee that her marriage is going to break up if she becomes wildly successful. But if she should fall in love with someone down the road, she'll deal with it when she comes to that bridge.

There was another part of her that was worried about criticism. The bigger and more famous we all get, the more criticism we may endure, because not everyone is going to agree with us. But there's a little girl inside Kim that is frightened of criticism because she was humiliated by her mother when she sang out loud at age seven during a large family Thanksgiving gathering. She was told sternly to be quiet because "Little girls should be seen, not heard." She needs to access this exile and tell her that criticism is a part of life. Nothing bad is going to happen to her if she gets criticized since she has the adult resources now to bounce back. Kim also has blocks around the idea that she doesn't deserve to be a coach earning multiple six figures. No one in her family makes this much money. If she did, she might get criticized by her jealous relatives.

Kim understood all of this intellectually as we finished our walk on the beach. There are many other parts that are afraid to let her shine her spotlight on her greatness. As spiritual life coach Marianne Williamson's famous quote says:

Our deepest fear is not that we are inadequate.
Our deepest fear is that we are powerful beyond measure.
It is our light, not our darkness that most frightens
us. *We ask ourselves, who am I to be brilliant, gorgeous, talented, fabulous? Actually, who are you not to be?*

You are a child of God. Your playing small does not serve the world. ***There is nothing enlightened about shrinking so that other people won't feel insecure*** *around you. We are all meant to shine, as children do. We were born to manifest the glory of God that is within us. It is not just in some of us; it is in everyone. **And as we let our own light shine, we unconsciously give other people permission to do the same.** As we are liberated from our own fear, our presence automatically liberates others.*

-*Excerpted from* A Return to Love: Reflections on the Principles of a Course in Miracles, *by Marianne Williamson.*

Yes, that's right . . . it's is our **light**, not our darkness that most frightens us. Many people are so used to living in their darkness. The devil they know— the struggles—are more comfortable than the devil they don't know.

I've kept tabs on Kim since that walk on the beach and she is still stuck— afraid to get out of her own way. It's easier just to hide behind investing in another program and convince herself that she needs to learn more tactics before stepping out. There is a part of her that is afraid to go into the past. And that is exactly the part that needs to be addressed first. She's not ready to change, she *doesn't want* to change. It's sad, but she'll probably remain broke for a long time unless she decides to jump in with both feet and work on her mindset by letting herself out of the old "movie" she's been stuck in for years.

What is Your Money Story?

Money blocks and ceilings have arbitrarily been placed on us due to messages we received as kids. *Look at those rich people, they are nothing but greedy S.O.B.'s.* This may be the very belief that holds you back from making above $100,000. You might end up sabotaging yourself from the next promotion because a) you may not believe you deserve it or b) you fear loss of approval from your parents or your friends if you become one of these "rich people." Ask yourself how much some of these statements apply to you:

- Money will bring a lot of responsibilities.
- Money is the root of all the evil.
- I'm never going to get rich.
- If I get rich, people will be jealous of me.
- I'm not smart enough to get rich.
- If I make more money than my husband, he might leave me.
- I'm not sure if I would be comfortable hanging out with other rich people.
- I'm afraid of the visibility I'll get when I achieve my wildest financial dreams.

The stronger you believe in any of the statements above, the more unlikely it is that you will achieve financial freedom. All of these beliefs were acquired growing up. To overcome these blocks, it's imperative that you get to know these parts through the IFS protocol (Appendix B) and unburden them of their limiting beliefs so that you can become as rich as you want to become.

Making Sense of Why You Like to Do What You Do

When you can connect the dots of your life looking backwards and figure out that the negative experiences of your life were given to you purposely so you could find your soul's calling, that can be liberating and make you jump out of bed with joy every morning because your life makes sense now. You can thank God (or whatever you believe in) for giving you the negative experiences.

I shared how I realized I had to go through every single painful wounding so that at 50 years old, I could finally find my life purpose that has me joyously working seven days a week. To me, it's not work, it's my soul's calling. If I had not gone through childhood rejection and discrimination, having a sick husband, the depression and anxiety, and getting laid off, I would have no business being a B*e More Extraordinary Magician.* Tad Hargrave, a business coach, coined the phrase I've mentioned before, "Your deepest wound is your truest niche." Let me share a few more stories that illustrate this.

* * *

Edward is a client whose father basically ignored him, except when they were restoring old houses. His fondest memories between the ages of 8 to 12 were getting his hands dirty and tearing down sheetrock. As they were working, his dad would open up to him about his childhood and talk about his love of baseball. No wonder Edward loves baseball. After college, Edward went into investment banking where he was miserable for a long time. Fifteen years later, he quit and hired a career coach. After going through an assessment, Edward realized that he needed to go into real estate. It's hard work but he loves it. It's his calling. Although many of his exiles had to do with his dad, after he healed with IFS, it made so much sense for him as to why he is so drawn to real estate. He equates real estate with love.

* * *

Rebecca is a health coach who is good at what she does, but she doesn't love it. What she really loves is organizing people's closets and pantries. She's always been a neat freak. I asked her to go back to childhood memories of organizing. She said that she followed in her father's footsteps. He was in the army and was always organized. She was crazy for him and did everything he did. As we unburdened some of her exiles, she realized that she loved organizing because it is equated with love of her father, just like Edward. I told her she had a beautiful story to tell about why she loves what she does. She became so excited about how her life experiences connected that she is on her way to putting the marketing pieces into place to market herself as an organizer, not a health coach.

* * *

Jennifer is another example. She couldn't figure out why she was so interested in science. She was always asking "why?" and it drove her to get a doctorate in physics. Jennifer came to me with relationship problems. After discovering that the fights with her husband were triggering her exiles that felt worthless, she figured out why she was always on a quest to answer the "whys" of life. She would ask her mom lots of questions, and because her mom was busy with work and her younger brother had special needs, she wouldn't have the patience to answer Jennifer.

One of her exiles was in the middle of the kitchen while mom was cooking dinner. Jennifer was repeatedly ignored and told to go watch TV, but she kept asking, "Why do I need to watch TV? Why can't you play with me? Why does the pasta need to boil for so long? Why is it that I can only ride a tricycle now and not a bicycle?" So the light bulb moment went off and

Jennifer finally realized that the exile that felt ignored when she asked "Why?" is the very reason she became a scientist. She was jumping for joy now. Her life made sense. Now she understands her soul's purpose. She's connected the dots of her life looking backwards and is excited about knowing why she is the way she is and why she chose her career.

Have you connected the dots of your life looking backwards and figured out what you are supposed to be doing with this one very precious life you are fortunate to have?

Understanding Your Motivations and Drivers

Please re-evaluate why you want to be successful (beside the obvious goal of financial freedom). Happiness is not at the end of the success rainbow, it is in the present, by making peace with the parts of you that are stuck in the past. Being happy first will allow success to happen. As bestselling author and leadership coach Jim Loehr put it so nicely, "Money may not buy you happiness, but happiness can make you rich."

Are you chasing success at the expense of not eating right and not taking care of your body, not feeling good about yourself, ignoring your relationships and sacrificing joy? You might run out of gas one day and wake up and realize how crappy you look and how old and wrinkly you've become. Some people in their later years end up spending all the money they've earned trying to get their health back, all caused by the negative thoughts and feelings and the stress they inflicted on themselves because their demons were driving them to work to death. No magic "pill" is going to solve emotional pain. *Deciding* to become the happiest version of you and clearing the ghosts out of the emotional closet is the key that will take you out of that rat race to nowhere.

There is nothing wrong with achieving more and more to feel good about reaching your potential, as long as you are happy on the journey and you are not sacrificing the other parts of your life. Keeping up with the Joneses makes us feel like we belong, like we've arrived. But unfortunately many are "keeping up" by faking it—faking it that we have money when some of us are barely keeping our heads above water, despite making lots of it. It goes out as soon as it comes in, with monstrous credit card debt and very little saved for retirement. When one house isn't good enough anymore, a beach house becomes necessary. Sure, it's an investment, but is it worth the struggle just to keep up by working 70 hours a week to pay the mortgages? Is it worth it living above your means to hold onto appearances and avoid the shame of what others will think of you if you can't keep up with them?

The good news is that you can stop this madness. After you heal your parts, you are not going to care about impressing the Joneses. You'll figure out that you were on this treadmill for the wrong reasons.

Few wish on their deathbed that they made more money (unless you live in poverty). They wish they had taken better care of themselves and they were true to themselves. But in the end, some have a hard time looking in the mirror and admitting that they were the cause of their own misery. Unconditional self-love through rescuing your exiles from the past will give you the space to envision freedom, success and manifesting financial abundance. The next chapter will go deeper into the excuses and fears that keep you stuck. If you are already financially secure (through hard work or inheritance), then the follow-up question is: Are you happy? If the answer is "No," then what is the #1 thing that is keeping you from happiness? What is keeping you awake at 2:00 a.m.?

Chapter Ten

Escape the Jail of Your Insecurities
How Fears Are Gifts to Find What Needs to Be Healed

*"The more scared we are of a work or calling,
the more sure we can be that we have to do it."*
-Steven Pressfield

When you resist and make excuses about changing for the better, it's your fears that are stopping you. When you criticize others who are doing something meaningful with their lives and who are going big, it's because they are triggering the parts of you that are afraid and insecure. You know your spiritual, authentic and unstoppable Self is hidden behind the fears and limiting beliefs of your exiles. Your fears stop you from *wanting* to change. You end up at war with yourself, locking yourself up in that imaginary jail that wrecks self-esteem, confidence, and the health of your body and mind.

Research has shown that pain motivates us to change four times greater than pleasure. We all want to move away from pain and towards pleasure. Just as if you stepped on glass and your foot is bleeding, you're going to do everything you can to stop the pain, you are not going to be thinking about the pleasure of going to Italy until your toe stops bleeding and heals. Or, if you were diagnosed with cancer, you are not going to be thinking about shopping for a new luxury car. It's the same with emotional health. You are not going to think about the pleasure of making a significant mark on the world until you release the critical voices and the old emotional scars that keep you awake at 2:00 a.m. Because these discomforts are taking up space in your mind, there's little room to think about leaving a legacy. So once you are *aware* that the ghosts in the emotional closet are the source of pain (or just feeling stuck without feeling "pain" per se) and that they are the reasons behind your lack of forward movement, you need to spring clean the emotional closet first—ideally through Internal Family Systems therapy. And then you can finally think about what is possible for your life.

So now that you are *aware*, you still may not be ready to change because the nail you've been sitting on for too long has made you numb to its existence, it's a mild ache you can live with that is not in your consciousness. The nail has to be driven deeper to cause excruciating pain, which means something really bad has to happen before you take action, such as losing custody of your kids because you drink too much, getting lung cancer from smoking, or having a toe amputated because you won't keep your diabetes under control.

Some people know they *should* change for the better but they don't. You can't make Mom stop eating cake, she has to *want* to do it. There's always an excuse, there's always tomorrow. (Perhaps their exiles make them believe that they are not worthy of good health.) Others may not be aware or are in total denial because admitting they need to change or that they need help is essentially admitting failure, and that admission would stir up the shame of their exiles—that who they are is not good enough.

I know some men who will never change the way they treat their wives. They are in control. They even threaten divorce if their wives ever get fat. How sick is that? Not only is the man sick but the wife is sick for putting up with it. Maybe the man was humiliated as a kid when one of his friends made fun of his obese mom and that's the reason why he needs to control his wife and make sure she stays thin. And the wife is emotionally unbalanced for allowing her husband to control her because she equates being controlled with love. Perhaps listening to her controlling daddy and doing what she was told was the only time she felt validated by him. So her little exile feels she needs to be controlled by a love partner to feel worthy. Thus she ends up marrying someone who is just like her father. They may live this way for the rest of their lives, losing friends and the respect of their peers because this is what they are comfortable with, based on their upbringing.

In order for people to change, they have to be *aware* that there is a problem in the first place. (They don't know what they don't know.) Then once they are aware of it, a *decision* has to be made to do the work to change, then *action* has to be taken. Unfortunately, *action* may never happen because of the fears they don't even know they have. This chapter will help you recognize those fears so you can understand why they keep you stuck. Before I address the fears, let me share the Six Stages of Change, elucidated by psychologists James Prochaska, Ph.D. and Carlo DiClementi, Ph.D.

Drs. Prochaska and DiClementi originally developed this model to explain why some people suffering from addictions were ready to change and some were not. Now this model has been applied to many areas of business and coaching. The most important question to ask yourself is: *Do you really **WANT** to change?* See if you can identify where you are on the change continuum.

Stage 1: Pre-contemplation

In this stage, you're in total denial that you have a problem. For example, you may be unaware that failure to manage your stress, living with relationships full of conflicts and not eating enough healthy foods can cause cancer cells to silently grow larger and larger. They could be growing for 20 years and eventually the cancer rears its ugly head in an MRI when you are 50 years old. Or you may be unaware or in denial (because you would rather blame your partner) that the emotional baggage you've swept under the rug is the very reason why your marriage broke up. Or maybe you're unaware that the parts of you that are stuck in the past with limiting beliefs about money are holding you back from believing that you deserve to earn more than your family members and your peers.

Being dissociated from childhood pain is very common. The traumas can be seemingly benign—like getting sent away to sleep-away camp for eight weeks when you were seven years old. (Your seven-year old brain's hypnotic state interpreted the event as, *"I must be bad, I must be unlovable, I've been abandoned,* why else would I be sent away for so long?" because no one reassured you that you did nothing wrong to get sent away.) I'm not saying all kids who go to camp at seven years old experience this, but I've heard enough stories from people who are married to narcissistic control freaks with abandonment issues to see a pattern here. Their controlling spouse erects a *need to control* protector so that no one will ever hurt them again.

Stage 2: Contemplation

You realize there is a problem. You want to do something and now you're *contemplating.* "Hmm . . . I'm *thinking* about doing something about my waistline. The doctor said my blood pressure is creeping up. But let me finish these cookies first. Waiting a few more days is not going to hurt me." But you can be *thinking* about changing for a long time without ever getting beyond this stage.

Stage 3: Preparation

You're getting ready to change, you're *preparing* and *doing research*— surfing the internet, buying books and programs, attending lectures, getting others' opinions, etc. Many people stay stuck at this stage for a long time and *never* move beyond research. Their nightstands are full of self-help books *preparing* them to change. "Let me just read one more book on how to quit smoking and lose weight." But they are *not acting* on any of the information. "I'll start tomorrow . . . let me polish off this cake first . . . can't let it go to waste . . . I won't have a heart attack tonight." They know all about how to quit smoking or how to lose weight but it can wait until tomorrow—and tomorrow may never come. Again, fear is behind this lack of moving forward.

Stage 4: Action

You finally get the courage to take *action* and it's scary. "Oh my God! This is not easy, but here I go!" "Yikes! I have to dig up the past to get to the roots of why I overeat. Okay, I'm in—it's scary but I'm doing it."

This is where having a coach/mentor/therapist to hold your hand every step of the way is important so you don't revert back to your old ways. Taking action does get uncomfortable because you're stepping outside of your comfort zone. You *will* eventually arrive at a new and improved comfort zone, but you must go through the uncomfortable phase first. Yes, this is hard work . . . no pain, no gain. This is no different than trying to get to the other side of the river when there's no bridge. There's two feet of water and jagged rocks that are not visible underneath. By putting one foot in front of the other, through the fears and the possible speed bumps (the rocks you can't see underneath) you will make it to the other side.

Stage 5: Maintenance

Maintaining this new way of living is becoming more and more natural for you. You are keeping up with the good new behaviors, but relapse is common at this stage. Since you're now familiar with Internal Family Systems—getting to know your protectors and exiles and unburdening their limiting beliefs—the chances of relapse becomes smaller and smaller, especially since you are conscious of the emotions underpinning your undesirable feelings and behaviors.

Once in awhile, some exiles can get retriggered and are tempted to go back to the old behaviors and feelings but now you know how to talk to those exiles and give them what they need so they don't sabotage you back to your old ways. You're also tuned into the fact that new exiles can pop up that you weren't aware of before. This is when going through the IFS protocol for these parts can be beneficial. (Appendix B)

Stage 6: Termination/Transcendence

In this last stage, your new behaviors and new way of being has become effortless. Eating healthy is the new normal. Treating your partner with love and compassion is the new normal. Being confident and fearless instead of being a manager with no spine is now your new leadership style at work. There is no more temptation to go back to the old ways because you feel so good about leading yourself and showing up as the best version of who you are. You have come home to your true Self and all of your protectors and exiles are supporting you in driving the bus of your life forward.

When Fear Runs Your Life

The most important thing to address are the fears that were taken on by exiles living in your subconscious. They have been 90% responsible for putting the brakes on the bus of your life that's been stalled or spinning in circles. The more fears there are, the harder it is to allow the gas pedal to move the bus forward. No matter how much blood, sweat and tears you use to push the gas pedal down, the protectors and exiles on the brakes will overrule you. Push to desperately lose the last 20 pounds and the weight will come back. Push to climb the corporate ladder, only to be stopped at the proverbial "glass ceiling." Push to learn the tactics of building a successful business and fail because your parts don't believe you deserve to be in the spotlight of success.

When the fears of your parts are erased, they will ease off the brakes and let the Self, full of confidence and self-esteem, go full throttle on the gas pedal. You'll have the courage to speak in front of 100 potential clients and you'll have the courage to go up to that cutie pie at the bar who could be your dream life partner.

Let's explore the common fears (some you didn't even know existed) that ruin your potential and happiness and keep you stuck in self-doubt, low confidence and low self-esteem.

Fear of Change

We all fear change because our egos want things to remain steadily the same. So even "good" changes like a promotion or a marriage proposal can feel stressful because we still have to adjust to something different. Not knowing what is on the other side of change is scary: The devil you know can be easier to live with than the devil you don't know because it's familiar. "I have no idea what it's like to live life as a thin person and get all that attention. I don't want attention . . . I'm okay with staying fat. Besides, all my fat friends will kick me out of the tribe and I'll end up alone . . . that's too painful to fathom." Or, "I don't know what it's like to live with a husband who doesn't control and abuse me. That's all I know from childhood, I'm used to it." Or, "I don't know if my tribe will accept me if I become wildly successful."

When you don't want to change, the first step is *not* to try to force yourself to change. The first step is to get to know the fears of the *afraid to change* protector. Listen to how it's kept you safe all of these years. And let this part know that it is not positively serving your life right now. When you get to know this *afraid to change* part, it will more than likely relax a bit and let you take small steps towards change, such as letting you to get to know your parts so they can give you the courage to take baby steps.

Fear of Failure

The road to success is paved with lots of speed bumps and failures. If you have failed in the past, such as trying to lose weight and then being embarrassed about gaining it all back, or starting a business and then failing while everyone took notice of the shame of your failure, then you might be traumatized from these failures and decide that it's less humiliating to stand still and not try again. But you know that standing still is not what you want either.

Not having the strength to pick yourself back up again to get over this speed bump reminds you of the humiliation of failing when you were young. Maybe you didn't make the varsity baseball team and dad was disappointed instead of supportive. When you unburden the exiles that felt *not good enough* or *smart enough* or any other burdens, you will be able to pick yourself back up and try again.

Fear of Success and Being in the Spotlight of Your Greatness

Yes, there is such a thing as fear of your greatness. In fact, it's the BIGGEST fear of all and that's why many people don't "go big." It's bigger than the fear of dying or living in darkness. Some people are so used to living in darkness, in a "quietly desperate and empty state" that it's just easier and safer to stay mired in misery. At one end of the spectrum is the fear of greatness and at the other end is fear of death. So because we want to avoid the pain of these fears at either end of the spectrum, it's way more manageable to stay stuck and in the middle, going around in circles, living an unspectacular life.

Being in the success spotlight is scary, like being in the spotlight when you were the class president and you were criticized and knocked down a few times by naysayers. The fear of that exile gets stirred up and overwhelms you when you are steps away from the finish line and it makes you self-sabotage or self-destruct. As Oprah said, "You will never rise above how you see yourself."

I shared one of the most famous quotes of all on fear already, "Our Deepest Fear," and the most important line from that bears repeating here:

> *Our deepest fear is that we are powerful beyond measure.*
> *It is our light, not our darkness that most frightens us.*

You won't even be able to conceive of your greatness until your exiles are unfrozen from the old painful memories that have them believing that they are not worth anything. I've had quite a few clients who procrastinated all the time (a protector) because if they didn't procrastinate, then they would actually get things done and move forward, and that's something that they didn't believe they deserved. It bears mentioning again that the exile can be as "benign" as the one that took on the belief that "I'm not lovable" at two years old when your baby brother born.

How afraid are you to express your light? Who might unknowingly make rude and unkind comments when you are shining brightly in the spotlight . . . your sister, best friend or mother? Who might feel even smaller if you succeeded? (You are unknowingly protecting this person from being hurt through dimming your light.) Who might be envious of your courage to unapologetically be you?

Fear of Being Seen

It's very common for people to build up a *shyness* protector as a result of toxic experiences. You may have grown up in an "embarrassing" environment where the neighbors knew that your house was full of fighting and conflicts. This young part of you is scared and wants to dissociate from the "noise" of childhood and shut out the chaos. So the job of this shy protector is to keep people away, stay out of the limelight, retreat into the corner so no one can discover your secrets and hurt you. After all, when you are not shy anymore, others will engage more deeply and want to know more about your background. But no . . . this is too embarrassing to reveal. So you stay shy to prevent this from happening. But shy part has no idea that you need to get over this to achieve anything great in life. The positive intention of *shy* part has been to keep you safe—safe from others finding out about your embarrassing past. But this *shy* part doesn't know that you are an adult now. If you are trying to climb the corporate ladder or be a successful entrepreneur, shyness will be a detriment to your earnings potential. You may be left out of important meetings or not be invited to all the fun parties because the shy part holds others back from inviting you into their circles. Being shy and not speaking up looks to others as if you lack confidence. (Lack of confidence and self-esteem oftentimes go hand in hand with shyness.)

Shy part will let go of its protective role and give you the confidence to be seen when the exile it's protecting that's still stuck in the scary noise and chaos of childhood is unburdened and brought into the present. You may end up taking this exile into the woods or to the beach with you where it's quiet and peaceful. When the shy protector sees that the exile feels safe with you, it will stop working so hard, take a rest and allow you to be lively and animated. That's when your fears about being seen will dissipate and you'll look forward to schmoozing and engaging with others instead of being nervous and retreating into the corner, clutching your coffee and phone for dear life to make it look like you've got it all together.

Fear of Public Speaking

This is one of life's greatest fears. What happened to you when you spoke out—either in song at Christmas dinner when you were five years old or when you were in eighth grade and you had to give a book report? If any of these experiences produced negative feedback, "Be quiet, stop singing already!" or "Your speech was so boring!" that's why you are afraid to speak in public. These memories can scar you for life and minimize your potential unless you access the exiles and unburden them by going back and witnessing the old events together and reassuring the exile with your love. When they finally believe that you performed well in front of people, that's when you'll be less nervous to speak in public—and you won't be devastated when someone gives you constructive criticism.

What is it costing you to be afraid to speak in front of others? How much money are you losing out on if you don't take the next steps in your career that require public speaking? What will that mean for your future financial security? What will that mean for taking care of your loved ones? The protector part that is afraid to let you speak in front of others needs to know that your financial future is at stake so that it can show you the exile it's protecting and then release its fears after the exile is unstuck from the past.

So if getting over the fear of speaking in public is one of your fears that prevents you from reaching your next level of greatness, then please uncover the exile(s) that are holding you back and relieve them of their burdens.

Fear of Happiness and Pleasure

I know this sounds odd but being afraid of happiness and pleasure is a real fear. That's because there's an exile or two that associates happiness with pain, not pleasure. Some people had experiences where they were giddy and carefree, jumping on the bed or the couch and wrestling with their siblings, and every time they had fun they were scolded and told to be quiet, or reminded that children ought to behave. Maybe they even fell off the bed and knocked their front teeth out when their mouth hit the footboard and they had to undergo emergency dental surgery. Their parents kept reminding them that their rowdy behavior caused the pain instead of soothing them with love. When these "happy" moments turn negative, an exile is formed. After being reprimanded, they take on the belief that happiness or rowdy exuberance is equated with pain. As a result, wanting to be happy in adulthood is not synonymous with pleasure, it's now in the "pain" category. And so a part is created that believes you don't deserve happiness.

Here's an example where a *sad* protector had a positive intention of keeping Benjamin safe from criticism. *Sad* part believed that if it no longer did its job and became happy instead, then it was afraid that people would criticize Ben. If it remained sad, then others would feel sorry for him instead and would not dare to be critical because of his fragile state. When he was happy as a child, mom would always be criticizing Benjamin by calling him "hopeless," despite the fact that he was one of the brightest kids at school. He realized that mom had to say negative things to make herself feel significant because she was never validated by her parents. He believed whatever happy moments there were in life would inevitably turn to into sadness. So that's why *sad* protector took on its role to protect the exile that had to absorb mom's verbal assaults and negative attitude. But *sad* part has no idea how much it negatively affects his adult life. It still thinks he's an eight year old whose mom is ready to insult him at any moment. Benjamin was healed from his sad feelings when the exile was unburdened of the trauma. This incident very much contributed to his fear of happiness.

You may even feel guilty about feeling happy if everyone around you is struggling and unhappy. If you feel too happy, your friends and family might get jealous and say hurtful things so you can suffer along with them. This part is afraid of happiness and the possible consequences of being stranded on an island with no friends if you were to become happy.

So you see from these examples how some people equate joy with pain. They believe if they are alive and charged, it could mean punishment and danger, liking breaking a leg from being rambunctious on the trampoline. And they end up taking on the belief that "I must not be worthy of joy." When the exiles associated with these faulty beliefs are unburdened, they will finally believe that it's safe to be happy.

Fear of Abandonment and Loneliness

This fear can be traced back to something as simple as when you woke up in the hospital after getting your tonsils out at four years old and Mommy was nowhere to be found. This little part of you felt rejected, abandoned and lonely because it had no idea that your mom was not allowed to sleep in the hospital and that the nurses are your temporary caretakers.

It's just too painful to admit that "I want my Mommy" is what drives you to neediness. You must have a new partner as soon as you break up with the old one, or get you paranoid when your girlfriend is out drinking with her friends and you need to text her every 15 minutes to see what's going on. It's too painful to be alone because you are *blended* with the traumatized parts of you that were rejected and abandoned.

This fear can also be the driver for some older people to become physically ill so their adult children will visit them more often. If they are healthy and well, they won't get as much attention. This is one of the reasons why it's hard to get some of our loved ones to eat better and take care of themselves. They are full of exiles just like the rest of us. Also, they may feel worthless because some of these exiles make them believe they're not worthy of health and happiness, so they stay trapped in their poor lifestyle habits. They may be waiting to die because they are not happy and they are unknowingly using their illnesses to get attention. If you haven't done the emotional healing, then the older you get, the worse off you will be physically and emotionally, and it's possible that you'll drive your friends and family away.

For only children, the fear of abandonment can cause them to be extra needy and have a hard time being alone without a partner. They may have longed for a sibling but all they had were their dolls. They remember playing on the sandy beach by themselves while their parents were busy reading books. All they wanted was a brother or sister to collect shells with and bury each other in the sand. So this loneliness plays out in school, and has them clinging to anyone who will let them take care of them—always putting their own needs second. (This may show up in their adult life as becoming someone who is always pleasing and caretaking others, neglecting their own self-care and suffering the consequences of health, weight and emotional issues.)

This may also show up as being attracted to people who manipulate and abuse them because they are so in need of their attention, because they wanted a brother or sister so badly. In order to feel less needy and not as acutely abandoned, it's necessary to rescue the exile(s). When they do that and can be with the exile (whether it's in the hospital room after surgery or at the beach building a sandcastle with that exiled part) that's when they will no longer feel alone, because now their adult Self is with their exile(s) and they don't feel abandoned anymore.

Fear of Being in Touch with the Pain of the Past

If you weren't so consumed with work or whatever else you do to keep yourself busy, what would you uncover? More free time could reveal certain destructive patterns of behavior, and then your little exiles will eventually surface.

The part of you that is addicted to keeping yourself busy is afraid that you might start crying and have a total meltdown as you think about the bottomless pit of shame and the worthless exiles that have been ignored for a long time. The fear of not being able to stop and ending up with the shame of a "nervous breakdown" and unable to pull it together is too painful to confront. So it's just easier to bury your head in work and keep busy with other activities to avoid the real issues.

So let that part that is afraid to slow down know that IFS therapy can be gentle. You have the ability to ask your parts to go slowly and not flood you with painful emotions or leave you raw with open wounds. You have the right to ask for a freeing and satisfying resolution.

Fear of Rejection

Something as simple as being afraid to ask for a coffee date with someone after a networking meeting or asking your boss for permission to turn in a report late is rooted in the exile that was rejected by the boys you had a crush on at the high school dance. This part is afraid of the hurt that would be triggered if the new acquaintance you just met rejects you or the boss says no. So this part has you making all sorts of excuses.

However, this is true for everyone: if we all don't risk the possibility of rejection, nothing in our lives will change. You won't receive new career opportunities and you won't find dates. The only sure route to success is having the guts to weather the failures and rejections. And you may have to kiss enough frogs and get rejected before you find the right fairy princess or prince charming. You'll get the courage to endure the rejections when you access the exile that was shamed and humiliated when she was rejected at the high school dance.

Fear of Getting Kicked Out of the Tribe

Much of American culture is wrapped around keeping up appearances and buying more stuff because Madison Avenue's images of happiness revolve around what you look like and the company you keep. Just look at any ad in a magazine or commercials on TV. We all crave to feel connected, to feel validated and to feel that we belong. Motivational guru Jim Rohn famously said, "You are the average of the five people you spend the most time with." Through education and hard work, you can make something of yourself—you don't have to be born into wealth. However, in some social tribes, there is a steep price to pay to belong to a certain group of "Joneses."

If you don't keep up with them, you might get kicked out and have no friends left. Let me give you an example of a "sick" case of a shopping addiction.

Nathan and Betsy are legion in their small, exclusive community for their atrocious treatment of each other and the horrible example they are giving to their children.

Nathan is an Executive Vice President of a very successful biotech company in New York City. They live in a $7 million Park Avenue apartment. Betsy was a former publishing executive who was laid off right before she got pregnant. Word has it that she was not liked at work because of her narcissism. Every conversation was always about her, with no any empathy for anyone else. (Her narcissism is already a big clue that she is broken. The more wounded someone is, the more self-absorbed they become. The extreme form of narcissism is a sociopath, where they have not a care in the world, even if they have to kill and steal money from people—never taking any responsibility for their actions, always blaming others. Unfortunately, some executive suites are littered with white-collar sociopaths.)

Betsy is addicted to shopping. She doesn't think twice about buying 20 pairs of designer shoes and 30 pairs of underwear for her eight and four-year-old daughters. Betsy fights with Nathan all the time and he has no spine to stand up to her. Betsy hasn't talked to her father in 10 years and she's been estranged from her brother for five years. (Her mother died from cancer a year before she got married.) No one from her family was invited to her wedding. Betsy has never talked about her family or her past. She is obviously very scarred and relies on shopping to soothe her emotional pain.

Despite the fact that Betsy doesn't work, they have three nannies taking care of the children seven days a week and the nannies travel with them. Many of these nannies quit a few months after they are hired (forgoing $100,000-per-year jobs) because Betsy treats them like dirt. In particular, Betsy was quite threatened by one of these college-educated nannies, Leanne, because she was very smart and pretty and on the ball (she only took that job on her way to finding a better one).

Leanne was someone that Betsy wished she could be. Betsy felt inferior because she graduated by the skin of her teeth from a New York State school and this nanny went to Duke University and graduated with honors. So Betsy took every opportunity to show Leanne how "superior" she was. She made Leanne go on shopping trips with her to Bergdorf Goodman where she bought $50,000 worth of designer clothing, shoes and sheets for the house in one trip. She just had to rub it in that she could afford the things that Leanne could not. And she just had to get Leanne's opinion on the $4 million ski chalet they were buying in Colorado.

It wasn't long before Leanne couldn't take Betsy's narcissistic behavior, especially the way she was damaging her children and the way the kids acted out in front of their mother. The children were fine when they were alone with Leanne. After enduring a few more of these shopping trips where Betsy continued throwing her wealth in Leanne's face (because she was so threatened by her beauty and brains) Leanne called it quits. It wasn't worth the money to put up with the abuse.

Part of Betsy's shopping addiction is linked to her need to feel like she belongs with the other rich people she and her husband hang out with. All they do is brag about their latest accomplishments, their newest purchases, the fancy vacations they take and how great their kids are doing.

In all likelihood, Betsy was probably abandoned, rejected and neglected growing up, and in order to keep the feelings of those exiles locked away, shopping is her way of showing her peers that she does belong and that she's no longer the little girl who came from humble beginnings. These exiles keep her locked in extreme protector behaviors (shopping, overspending and one-upmanship) all enacted to soothe the pain and shame of her exiles. I would not be surprised if Betsy had other self-destructive protector behaviors besides shopping, including depression and anxiety protectors.

Many of us get the urge to buy something because we're thinking, "I just have to have this. I'll really feel like I've arrived with this fancy pocketbook. I'll show Suzy I've got taste, it'll make her jealous." The unfortunate thing is when Suzy sees you with your new bright and shiny object, she gets a pang of envy, and she goes out in search for something that will one-up you because her little exiled part got triggered with you showing off your acquisition. Then that shame part gets triggered and the shopping protector makes you go and spend even more money you don't have just so you can keep up with your peers and not feel left out.

If you want to stop this cycle of emptying out your bank account and living above your means so you don't feel left out, you need to heal and unburden your exile(s), get off the overspending treadmill and stop climbing the social ladder. Betsy was shopping to relieve boredom and her inferiority complex. She may be in denial of her wounds for a long time. It might take a nervous breakdown before she realizes she needs help. Betsy is very much "running on empty" and is in "quiet desperation" because she is afraid that someone will find out the real truth about how broken she is (because of her likely abusive upbringing) and kick her out of the "rich peoples' tribe." The reality is, when you are faking it because you are so afraid of getting kicked out of the tribe, you are only hurting yourself.

Fear of Losing Freedom

When you have excuses, you don't have to be accountable. That means you have the freedom to avoid stepping up to the plate. If you are battling something like depression or fibromyalgia and you don't feel good, maybe that's an excuse to drag your feet through life. Or you may not want to lose the freedom you have of not being responsible for a demanding yet rewarding career. You would rather keep taking care of the kids (even though they are in high school) and be a housewife. You don't want to have to polish up your resume again and gain the confidence to land a job, or be on the board of a non-profit. Excuses will prevent you from ever becoming anything great.

"My spouse won't feel good if he isn't in control of the finances anymore." "Why should I bother? Who's gonna hire a 50-year-old woman?" "I'm not as smart or as sharp as I used to be." "If I succeed, then I'll have even more responsibilities."

Do you really think life is over at 50? Life begins at 50! In some ways you are more unflappable and can be bolder than ever because of what you've endured, and you come to realize that many of the things you've feared would happen never materialized. You have life experiences, vast stores of wisdom, and your own special authentic take on life. And you may have another 50 years to live. How are you going to make the second half of your life better than the first? As poet Mary Oliver famously said, "Tell me, what is that you plan on doing with your one wild and precious life?" (Now that the kids no longer need you?) It doesn't have to necessarily be a paid job!

Fear of Death

If you keep peeling back the layers of the onion of your protectors, many of them have the fear of death at its core. *Shopping* part had you keep up with the Joneses so you could feel you were part of their tribe. Otherwise you would be ostracized, with no friends. Being alone would make life not worth living and then you might even take your own life. And there's the same type of protection with the *overachievement* part. It had to keep achieving a lot of goals to get validated that you are good enough, so you'd get attention and not be ignored. If you were ignored by your parents because you didn't achieve, then you might lose their love and be abandoned. Abandonment means you'll be alone and life might not be worth living.

In our older years, fear of abandonment looms large. We come to realize it's at the root of why grandma's sick part won't allow her to clean up her diet and lose weight. If she is sick, then her adult children will show up to take her the doctor, and she will feel loved. If she feels loved, she won't feel abandoned. If no one visits because there's no excuse like illness to keep them visiting, then she might find out they are not interested in being with her and then life will not be worth living. So the *sick* part has a very important job to keep grandma from taking her own life or from getting a super serious wallop from something like cancer that will "take her out."

The motivation behind some of these protectors may sound ludicrous to you, but I assure you they are true. After all, most fears are irrational. That's why it's important to update these parts and tell them that having these fears do not serve you in any way except to keep you stuck and unhappy.

Fear of Being Too Perfect and Outshining Others

Shaun is a handsome 33 year old who feels like he's only living up to 95% of his potential. He feels really good about what he has accomplished so far but he knows he's capable of more. I asked him, "What's holding you back from showing up 100%?" He replied without any hesitation, "That I'll make a few of my friends jealous and intimidate other people. I know I'm already a 'triple threat'— cute, successful and humble— and I don't want to become even more intimidating."

"Triple threat" is a common term used in entertainment. It's where someone can sing, act and dance. It's a threat to be perfect at everything. It's no different from the blond, beautiful woman with the Ivy League degree, beautiful body, great income and perfect husband (that's more of a "quadruple threat"). It's easy to hate these "perfect people." We're tempted to find a flaw about them so that we can feel better about ourselves. "She's not supposed to be a bombshell and have brains. It's not fair! Hey, I heard her husband was having an affair with one of his direct reports and he got fired. Hee, hee, she's not so perfect after all."

Shaun wants to prevent these jealous criticisms from happening. He's afraid of losing his friends if he's too perfect. He dims his light so as not to threaten others. This part of him is afraid of abandonment. This part needs to know that if he shows up 100% he can make a significant contribution to the world, that as long as he is showing up 100% with humility, then he will inspire others to achieve their own personal best.

Fear of Judgment:
"What Will Others Think of Me?"

Some people are mortified by the thought of buying a five-year-old used car. Others would be aghast if they stayed at the Ramada Inn instead of the Ritz Carlton. "What will they think of me?" They won't think any less of you unless *you* are ashamed of it. The energy of shame will be picked up (it's your exile that's feeling the shame) and only then will others judge you and think less of you.

Others are not thinking about you, they are spending most of their time thinking about themselves. When you care about what others think, it means that you are blended with the parts of you that had shaming and humiliating experiences. Perhaps you were criticized for being too chubby, too ugly, too short, too poor, too rich, too dumb, too smart—too whatever. These parts are still stuck in the past and that's why they are afraid to let you improve your life. When you love all of your parts unconditionally and they are relieved of their burdens, you will not care what others think. Your family of *parts* will be your cheerleaders. They'll think you are the best thing since sliced bread. If others want to judge you, they are the losers. You don't need to hang out with them. You will hang out in a tribe that accepts you for who you are and not have negative opinions of you. They will love you for *you* and they will have your back.

By the way, it's easy to judge people but it's not always wise because we have no idea what their story is and why they are the way they are. Now that you understand what protectors and exiles are, you are better able to see that people who annoy you are doing so through the filter of their parts. Now you can have compassion for them instead of disdain. They are annoying because they are showing up as one of their protectors or exiles, and they may not have enough Self energy present to be filled with love and compassion and a desire to care about you. When you look upon them with compassion, you're running more loving energy through yourself than being critical and negative. And it's then that it's possible to even bypass their parts and see a glimpse of their true Self.

I had an in-law family member judge me as a stuck-up snob, "too good" to show up to important family functions. I had excuses. I didn't tell my family the real reason why I wasn't showing up: I was overwhelmed with my career and I was caretaking a new baby and a sick husband who had been having major cardiac and gastrointestinal issues. We were constantly in and out of the hospital. I didn't want to worry the extended family so I never let on how sick my husband was.

So for 20 years, this family member avoided all gatherings with me. Until . . . January of 2014, when I published the short version of my painful childhood story on my blog. I posted it on Facebook and she read it and reached out to me through email. She let me know she had no idea of the depths of the pain and stress I was going through and she was sorry for shutting herself out of my life, all because she thought I was stuck-up. I may have come across as stuck-up because of the numbness protector I erected as a result of all the stress I was going through. It was the only way I knew how to deal with it—otherwise I was going to have a nervous breakdown.

I accepted her apology and now she is attending all the family functions. I sensed that she was judging me but I didn't care. It wasn't going to stop me from being true to myself. If I triggered her in some way because I showed up "stuck-up" in her eyes, then it was her problem, not mine. I wasn't going to waste my energy to try to change her mind.

The point is, the more vulnerable you are (such as sharing my story on the internet), the less you will be judged because you are not hiding anything, your mask has been removed. When you live through your mask—making everything seem perfect to the outside world—the more you will be judged. Just like Betsy's shopping addiction, we are all judging her and trying to explain her crazy and ludicrous behavior. I've explained the concept of protectors and exiles to the people I know who have to deal with Betsy. As I hear the story of Betsy, all I can do is to feel is sorry for her because I understand why she is the way she is. She doesn't understand it. She's under the spell of her *denial* protector. If she got help and shared her painful story, there wouldn't be so much gossip and judgment behind her back.

Be proud of the adversities you have gone through to get to where you are today. Your adversities are what make you strong. If people judge you, it's not your problem, you deserve better friends. If you think you are awesome despite your humble beginnings, others will think highly of you too.

Fear of Vulnerability

There is nothing to be afraid of by being vulnerable. Oprah openly shares her humble beginnings growing up poor, being sexually abused by her cousin, getting pregnant at 14 and losing the baby. Does anyone think any less of her because of her "shameful" story? Probably not. More than likely you love her even more and are inspired by her. Her vulnerability contributed to her success. So what's holding you back from sharing the things you've been ashamed of? If Oprah can share it, why not openly share your story? Vulnerability is sexy, it makes you human, it makes you relatable and it gives others permission to do the same. When there is reciprocal sharing, that's when the masks come off and you develop much deeper connections than you would have otherwise.

Do you have the courage to be vulnerable and be authentically *you* when you are dating someone new? Did you ever not trust being yourself because you were afraid that the other person would run away when they found something they didn't like about you? This is simply your fears running amuck. But they will not like something about you if *you* don't like a part of you. You don't like this part of you because you haven't done the work of getting to know it and releasing its limiting beliefs and burdens. You're afraid because you're ashamed of these parts. When you heal your parts, there will be no more shame and you will love yourself enough to be confident and speak your truth! If the person can't handle you, then they are not the right match. Move on and find a better person who is more evolved.

For several years, I've been attending a personal development conference called AwesomenessFest (awesomenessfest.com). Three hundred strangers come together for five days of fun, learning and personal growth in a beautiful tropical location. On the first day we meet, we are taken through an exercise to share with the stranger sitting next to us, "What I don't want you to know about me is . . ." and "What I am most ashamed of is . . ." Would you be comfortable in answering these questions honestly with total strangers? Most of us shared our vulnerabilities at this conference. It created instant connections. The masks came off and copious tears were shed. We are all going through the same human experience!

If you are afraid to show your vulnerabilities, you need to reassure the parts of you that are afraid that nothing bad is going to happen. In fact, good things will happen and new, deeper friendships will result. It's easier to share the painful moments of your life if you are not still living in your old "movie." If you are still living in the movie, please seek the help of a therapist or coach, especially one who is trained in

Internal Family Systems like myself. If you are still living in the old story, it could make others uncomfortable because they feel like they need to rescue you out of the deep end of the water.

However, if you have unburdened your exiles and they are safe and loved by you, and you can talk about your story freely with an energy that shows that you are no longer in it (the way Oprah tells her secrets nonchalantly), that's when people will fall in love with you. You have inspired them to get out of their own stories. This tactic can work very well when you are looking for new love relationships, too. You don't want to hide the past. If you can show that you are no longer in it and have overcome adversity, that's when vulnerability is sexy. The more confidence and self-esteem you have, the less ashamed you will be to reveal your weaknesses and your past.

Fear of Criticism

I met Regina at a money mindset conference. She shared during one of the exercises that she was ashamed of going $50,000 into debt when she hired an interior designer—madly decorating her house to get it ready for Christmas dinner five years ago. She is still paying it off today. She regrets caving into the part of her consumed with showing others that she and her husband had the means to both buy the dream house and decorate it extravagantly.

I asked why it was so important to her that the house be decorated to the hilt. (She could have spent half as much and had a fine house.) She answered, "So I won't be embarrassed to have my family over and so I can host the neighborhood Christmas party since it's my turn this year."

Emily: Why was it so important that you spend over-the-top money to get it done?

Regina: So that I can show my sister and my next door neighbor that I've got great taste and that my husband is successful enough to allow me to do this.

E: What happened between you and your sister growing up?

R: She teased me relentlessly—saying I wasn't as smart and as pretty as she was.

E: Is your neighbor anything like your sister?

R: Yes.

E: So you are spending lavishly to get the house decorated so you can prevent that little girl that was humiliated by your sister from getting triggered by your sister when she visits. You are trying very hard to make sure there's nothing for your sister (or your neighbor) to criticize. You want to show them that you are good enough, in fact that you are better than they are. You just had to do it to prevent the shame of the old memories from surfacing.

R: Yes. (She tears up with this realization.)

E: You are doing this because you are afraid of criticism. You are willing to go into massive debt to do this. When you get in touch with that little girl that's stuck in the past, you will not need to keep spending beyond your means. When you show you don't care anymore about the opinion of your sister, you will not feel the sting when she criticizes you. You'll just feel sorry for her because she's acting out from her wounded parts.

Fear of Loss of Approval From Parents

Cultural expectation and burdens contribute to our fears as well. As I mentioned previously, in Jane Hyun's bestselling book on *Breaking Through the Bamboo Ceiling: Career Strategies for Asians*, our parents' messages can stop us from reaching the pinnacle of success. The concepts she discusses apply to many cultures that are different from "American culture." Many Asians are taught to respect their elders and authority figures and never talk back, which basically means not speaking up. If you were brought up this way and are in corporate America, where you are expected to be vocal and influential in order to move up to the top, then these burdens can be a detriment to your success. This is an exile that took on the faulty belief that they will be criticized for speaking up. If you are prone to this, you need to tell this exile that you are living in America and that nothing bad is going to happen to you when you speak up, in fact, it's what you must do to move ahead. This part needs to know that your parents will understand, you will not be disowned by them, and you need to let this part give you the confidence to do so.

Just as Japanese, Korean and Chinese cultures bow to their elders, the dark side of American culture is being bowled over by the cult of youth and beauty. (Studies show younger and better-looking people receive more career opportunities and greater salaries than not-so-great looking people. Many of the pharmaceutical reps I worked with were as beautiful and handsome as TV stars). Younger Americans are also striving to buy the latest gadget, big screen TV or indulge in costly hobbies or pastimes. They quickly get themselves into credit card debt and spend years trying to dig themselves out of it. Many Americans work hard at the expense of time with their families and skimp on their health to meet their money and success goals. In contrast, several European and South American countries prize spending time with their families rather than spending time at work. They are happy not to be "in the rat race."

So another area where your fears may be driving the show is the need to keep achieving more and more in order to get validated. And you do this despite the fact that your parents are probably not capable of validating you. They are a product of this rat race culture too, and they may want you to go into a profession because that is what is expected of you— they don't care what you're passionate about. It's all about not shaming the family name should you decide to become an artist or be "bohemian." All your parents say is to keep going. If you got your M.D. or JD, now they expect you to become head of the department or become a partner (and not in a small firm but in a big-name famous law firm). So you feel like you're never going to be good enough.

This fear of being disowned by your family if you don't achieve more and more is driving you to work your butt off and sacrifice all the other areas of your life. Many kids who graduate from college spend years unknowingly and unconsciously trying to please their parents in jobs they detest until one day they finally have the guts to pursue their own passions no matter what anyone says. You won't be fulfilled, in fact, you can get emotionally or physically ill from being in the rat race for the wrong reasons. So again, I know I'm sounding like a broken record . . . you need to access the exiles that took on these negative beliefs about what love is so that the fear of loss of approval does not drive you to literally work yourself into spiritual numbness or actual death or disease.

Common Excuses that Keep You Stuck

Here are some excuses we hide behind:

- I don't have time.
- I don't deserve it.
- I can't afford it.
- I'm too scared.
- I'm a loser, I'll never be good enough and attractive enough.
- I'm too tired, I don't have the energy to change.
- I'm not smart enough.
- I've always been this way.
- My partner won't like it if I change.
- I don't have the confidence to do it.
- I'm afraid of the humiliation of failing.
- I'll end up alone and scared if I change.
- I'll never be enough no matter what I achieve.
- I'm too old to start.
- I've never committed to anything before.
- It's gonna be too hard, I don't even know where to begin. There are so many steps. It's too overwhelming.
- I'm afraid of what others will think if I do change.

- I've never accomplished it before so what makes me think I will be able to do it now?
- I've never had good luck. Others are granted their wishes, not me.
- It's too risky to spend money to change.
- I don't deserve happiness and success.
- I can't live my life the same small way if I achieve something big.
- I don't want to be accountable if I achieve more.
- I'm afraid of who I might become.

Trying to move forward without examining your inner world, your thoughts and feelings, is futile. Do you *want* to change? If you can't even imagine moving forward and you're making these excuses, it means there are plenty of fears underneath the fear of change.

What are your afraid of? What do you need to do to move the needle just a little bit? Whatever your answer is, it points back to exiles that are keeping you stuck.

Raise Confidence and Self-Esteem by Overcoming Your Fears

Lack of confidence and self-esteem are rooted in the fears that protectors and exiles hold because they think you are still stuck in the past. If you unburden the past, you'll significant improve your self-image and your confidence and your self-esteem will soar through the roof. It's that simple and that deep.

Marilyn, a success-driven biologist, has a *lack of confidence* protector that shows up in the form of deflated shoulders holding self-doubt. It's been protecting her from feeling inferior because if she doesn't take a risk to try something new, then she won't attract disappointment or failure. If there's no failure, then she won't feel bad about herself. If she feels bad about herself, then that means she's a nobody. If she's a nobody, then there's no point in existing, which means she may end her life. Now this lack of confidence part is very sorry that it held her back. Who made her this way? All her family members.

This *lack of confidence* protector has been protecting the exiled two-year-old Marilyn. This part has a big job in keeping Marilyn from taking her life. The new role it would rather have is to give her the confidence to move forward. The image of the exiled little Marilyn that the *lack of confidence* part revealed was Marilyn hiding in the corner of her closet. Her story was that she never knew what to expect. She wanted to grow into a confident woman but it was not possible because she was belittled, teased, made fun of and compared unfavorably to others by her mom, siblings and teachers. This exile felt that life was not worth living. The burdens of faulty beliefs she had been carrying are: "I'm inferior, I'm not good enough, I'm bad, I'm not as smart as others, I'm an underachiever." (This exile also drove Marilyn to keep going to school. Her overachieving protector made sure she earned a Ph.D. and she still feels stupid and continues to loath herself.)

Marilyn's loving Self gave this exile what she needed to believe—that she is smart and good enough. She explained to her exile that Mom had five other kids and Mom was broken herself and just didn't know how to parent. "You are smart. You have a Ph.D. now. You have a very important job in the community. I will always be with you. You will never be alone again." With the burden released, Marilyn's self-image improved and her confidence and self-esteem were boosted tremendously.

There are countless books on confidence and self-esteem that give you tips on how to address the problem at the surface level. These tactics will not work for you to really believe that you are great until you do the deep inner work with the protectors and exiles. After you do this, then the tips in these books can work for you.

* * *

If you want to change for the better, you have to address the fears that are lurking beneath the surface that hold you back from taking action. American mythologist Joseph Campbell sums it up what you need to do so beautifully, "The cave you fear to enter holds the treasure you seek."

Unconscious fear at the most primitive levels is actually your protector's fear of death, as you have seen in the client case studies. These are running your life 90% of the time because these fears are in the subconscious. The subconscious is the ruler of your kingdom, not your conscious mind. When you get the subconscious healed and in alignment with your conscious desires, that's when you'll be able to release the brakes on your life. This means your fears will be erased and you can easily get unstuck and unleashed: Attracting more friends, more business opportunities, getting noticed by your bosses so you become the obvious choice to get promoted, attracting your ideal mate, eliminating conflicts, fattening your bank account, and feeling really happy about your life.

As Sheryl Sandberg, COO of Facebook and author of *Lean In* famously said, "What would you do if you weren't afraid?"

Chapter Eleven

Unstuck. Unleashed. Unstoppable.

Living Happily Ever After and Making a Difference

"Tell me what is it you plan to do with your one wild and precious life?"
– Mary Oliver

I hope the message of this book is ringing loud and clear now. Everyone has demons. If you avoid them long enough, they will show up in some way in the state of your emotional, physical and spiritual well-being. If you want to live a happy and fully charged life with great outcomes, you have to do the work to clean the skeletons out of your emotional closet first— no ifs ands or buts. You can't become an awesome leader and make your business wildly successful until you go back into the past and discard those skeletons.

Your present realities are a reflection of those skeletons. Just about every challenge can be traced back to some limiting belief that got programmed into you when you were younger. The irony is, you **have to** go backwards *first* to release the pain and suffering in order to move forward. And this can be done gently with IFS therapy because you can ask your exiles not to overwhelm you. Your vision of what you should be doing with your life will crystallize when these skeletons are cleared out. If you don't have a vision, then the bus of your life can't start moving because you haven't plugged the destination into the "life GPS."

A "happily ever after" life boils down to five main things for most people: a healthy and attractive waistline, never having to worry about money again, Prince Charming/Fairy Princess relationship, doing work you love/living up to your potential and jumping out of bed every morning with joy. You may have achieved fulfillment in some of these areas but very few of us have achieved success in all areas (that's why we're always "a work in progress"). Your professional and personal life will only grow and leap to the next level in proportion to the time and energy you spend on your personal growth. Confidence, self-esteem, success, happiness and living your truth are an inside-out job.

So, if you feel drained after years of toiling in the trenches doing what is expected of you: going to college (perhaps study something you're not that passionate about), landing a good job, getting married, buying a house with the "white picket fence," having kids, and spending hard-earned money on "stuff," only to say, "Is that all there is? I know I'm supposed to happy looking like I've got it all, but I'm not. I've lost my spirit in the journey." Or, "How come I can't get out of my own way to take it to the next level?" Or, "I've made all of this money but I've got drug and alcohol problems and miserable conflict-ridden relationships where I'm being taken to the cleaners. I just feel like I have lost everything I've worked so hard for." Or, even if nothing seems to be wrong and you still don't feel awesome, it's the past showing up to haunt you. The people who are aware they are "broken" are in therapy. For the rest of us who think "everything is fine," and "I don't need therapy," I must tell you that it's not about needing therapy per se, it's about getting unstuck from the energies of the past. Even if you had a loving and fun childhood, even something as seemingly innocuous as mom spending more time with your special needs brother could very well be the part that holds you back in midlife.

The best gift you can give yourself is exploring your inner world sooner rather than later, because waiting until you get hit by the "two by four," of cancer, getting fired, getting a divorce, going bankrupt or losing custody of your kids can be too little too late.

So you can get started on your journey to self-awareness by thinking about the behaviors, feelings and thoughts you don't like. Also think about who pushes your buttons. These are the "gifts" to you help trace the breadcrumbs back to find the exiles that are screaming for attention. Ask these protector parts:

- How long have you been in my life? What's your job?

- What are you afraid of if you don't keep doing your job?

- What do you need from me so you can feel safe and relax and let go of these extreme thoughts, behaviors and feelings?

(More details of these steps are covered in Appendix B.)

A Love Letter to Yourself and Your Children

If you want to be the best parent possible and stop the cycle of "victims creating more victims" ceasing to nag and "torture" your kids the way your mother did to you, then you should know that the bestselling authors of *Parenting From the Inside Out*—Daniel Siegel, M.D. and Mary Hartzell— recommend that you *work on yourself first,* just like the message of this book.

When you know about protectors and exiles and you do your inner work, you'll naturally know how to parent your kids so you minimize the number of exiles you create in their psyches. They won't feel worthless when they grow up and they'll be able to live up to their potential. The number one thing we all want for our kids is for them to be happy. The best gift we can give them is to clean those skeletons out *first.* When kids see us happy, they will be happy. Many kids who "act out" are not doing so because they are bad kids, it's because their parents don't know how to parent them from a better place, it's usually a reflection of the parents' unresolved traumas. That's why parenting books advise you to take the first step in great parenting: becoming whole first. When you are whole, your kids will more than likely not act out and become happy and unstoppable.

If you don't explore your inner world, when the kids grow into teenagers and young adults, they have less and less desire to be around nagging, negativity and criticism. They might see visiting you more as a "chore" than something they want to proactively do because being around you triggers the exiles that were created by you in the first place. Some of my clients are "that parent" who wishes their kids would call and come visit them more often. It's a parent's worst nightmare— being abandoned by your own children and wondering what you did wrong.

Doing your own work to become whole can bring you closer to your kids. It's never too late to apologize to your kids and explain how bad you feel about the way they were treated. Your kids just want to know that you love them. It's not too late to repair these "broken" relationships. If the relationships are not "broken" but can use some improvement, it's never too late to voice how proud you are of who they have become. Then your adult children will want to spend time with you instead of considering it an obligation: "I *have* to visit my parents now. Ugh . . . I need a drink!"

Let me share one of the most awesome opportunities I had to tell my son Jason how much I love him and how much I treasure who he is.

* * *

Two months before Jason was leaving for his junior semester abroad (October, 2012) in Hong Kong, he asked me, "Mom, would you like to come to Hong Kong with me and spend time sightseeing before my classes start?" I was shocked that he even asked. I did not expect a 19 year old to ask his mother to take a 16-hour flight to spend time alone with him halfway around the world. The thought of asking him if I could come along didn't even cross my mind, so when he asked, I was flattered. I thought, *Wow, I must have done something right as a parent to have a teenager want to be alone with his mother 8000 miles away from home.*

Of course I accepted this invitation, rearranged my schedule and shelled out the hefty airfare to create some wonderful travel memories with him. (He didn't bother to ask Dad since dad doesn't fly anymore because of the health traumas he experienced on airplanes.) And the trip was fantastic. Jason and I had a great time exploring Hong Kong together, one of the cleanest cities I've ever been to.

On the last night at the hotel, Jason was lugging his shopping bags of dorm stuff back to his room and I accompanied him to the taxi queue. As I said goodbye to him, I could feel this ugly cry coming on. It was very emotional for me to leave my baby so far away for six months, with no way of getting here quickly should anything bad happen to him. (I didn't feel this level of emotion when we dropped him off at Tufts in Boston since it was just a two-hour drive from our house.)

So the ugly cry came and we hugged, and he reassured me that everything was going to be okay. When I got back to the hotel room, I took this opportunity to write a letter to my son that I had always wanted to write. Here's what it said:

My Dearest Jason,

I never thought leaving you here in Hong Kong was going to be so much harder than leaving you at Tufts. I just wanted to tell you that I LOVE you with all my heart . . . I am SOOOO proud of all that you have accomplished and I am honored to have the privilege to be your mother.

You are going to accomplish great things in your life . . . I have all the faith in the world that you can do whatever you want and be really successful at it. You are SOOOO bright in so many ways that it amazes me how dad and I produced such a kid like you. :-))) You're good with "right" brain stuff and "left" brain stuff . . . that's a rarity and you should take advantage of it as much as you can.

I have been so proud watching you mature over the years. You have grown up to be quite the young man. Everyone who meets you is impressed by you.

*Please forgive me when I nag you with certain things...
it's out of love and it's all because I don't want you to
have to go through the heartache of the consequences if
you don't do certain things, such as backing up your
computer.*

Five minutes after sending this email, I got this response from
Jason:

*Thanks mom, this really means a lot and I hope you won't
miss me too much. Love, Jason.*

This letter is an illustration of the kind of validation
some of us wished we heard from our parents growing up.
This is what our kids need to hear from us in order to unleash
their potential, to become emotionally healthy adults who care
about other people instead of being self-absorbed or seeking
empty approval from others.

If you haven't sent this kind of loving message to your
kids lately (or ever), it's not too late. Validation is the most
important human need. They are waiting for you to express to
them that they are worthy, lovable and enough.

If your parents are unaware of how important it is to
validate you, you can validate yourself by accessing your
exiles, witnessing their stories and giving them the love and
reassurance they needed that they never received from Mom
and Dad. (You can write a letter to yourself like this one.) **You**
have the power to heal yourself.

I've become a better parent as a result of overcoming my
past because I am so aware that what I say to Jason can have
irrevocable damage—damage that could require him to have
therapy 20 years later because of the frozen *exiled* parts I may
be creating in him. I wish I knew about all of this before he was
born 22 years ago. Sure I want him to succeed, but if I'm more

concerned about my agenda and my image as a parent instead of his well-being, he will detect that. Kids are not stupid.

So if you have adult children who seem a little annoyed at you and don't call you as often as you'd like because it just seems like such a chore to talk to you, then I would encourage you to look inward and do some inner work. Otherwise, your children might do as many of my clients have done—alienate their parents because they have a hard time being around their negative energy.

We can stop the cycle of victims creating more victims, and it all starts with us. Encourage your partner to do the same. In turn, when the kids are born, you will know how important it is to validate them, not just tell them to "Stop crying," but really validate their feelings. Then they can grow up happy and healthy and be able to unleash all of their desires, gifts and capabilities without fear because they have fewer *exiles* that hold them back from realizing their potential.

You will get to live a life of retirement where your kids can't wait to visit you. They won't neglect you. They'll take your calls. Family gathering won't be tense. They'll be full of love and laughter because you'll have the courage to show your vulnerability—because you are a family that talks about their feelings. Since nothing is bottled up—no anger and resentment—you'll avoid becoming lonely and shriveled up physically and emotionally and be able to remain vital, healthy and energetic to the end.

You are Allowed to "Cheat" on Your Partner for the Right Reasons

My entrepreneurial journey the last three years has been nothing but working all day and all night, seven days a week. It's so hard for me to turn it off because I have so many ideas and I have so much to do to make a difference in peoples' lives. I'm on a mission. This mission is the lightning rod that gets me out of bed with joy every morning. I have made sense of my life looking backwards and made lemonade out of the lemons. I knew I wasn't living up to my potential with my pharmaceutical sales job but I got too comfortable having a steady paycheck—until I got zapped out of my coma and got laid off. Failure wasn't an option when it came to starting my own business, so I charged full speed ahead to do anything and everything I could to get it right. It sure has been a wild and bumpy journey but my parts have been supporting me in this adventure. They are not afraid, so I am not afraid.

Let me share the story of how I got this book deal and the lessons of how important it is to be fearless, to know the vision of what you want, and what it will look and feel like when you get it. It's the only way the Universe is going to answer your desires. Yes, you have to be clear on what you want. You don't have to know *how* you are going to get there, you just have to *feel* it in your bones and taste it as if you already have it—and most importantly, all your parts have to truly *believe* that you deserve to make your dreams come true. So if you have any parts that say, "Who do you think you are to want _____? You don't deserve that!" you will be guaranteeing that you will *not* achieve your goals.

I tasted and I felt success in my mind. (The brain doesn't know the difference between real or imagined.) But the road to success is paved with speed bumps (and what seem like failures) as we get out of our comfort zones. Sometimes getting out there with your vision and your true Self is like putting on a pair of tight fat striped pants that make you look like a clown, and not be embarrassed by it. But this is only possible if you address all of those protectors and exiles that are holding you back from confidently walking down Fifth Avenue with those ridiculous pants on. (Okay, in New York City, you can get away with looking like a clown and no one will blink an eye, except maybe the tourists.)

So let me tell you the gutsy things I have done to manifest a publisher appearing out of thin air to declare that he wants to publish my book. As you read the story, be mindful of the little steps out of your own comfort zone you would take to drive the bus of your life just 10 feet further than the day before. If the bus doesn't start moving, you won't go anywhere. It just has to start, even slowly. As Neal Donald Walsh says, "Life begins at the end of your comfort zone."

My own bus started driving loaded with all my parts that used to afraid. But they were afraid no longer. These parts were now well-behaved young children seated in the passenger seats, all buckled in and happy. "Go for it! We are rooting for you! Just jump in and start the nutrition business." I did a ton of lectures and learned so much about marketing through business mentors and online programs. I got traction and I kept driving, but I was hitting speed bumps. People would say no to working with me. (Unrealistic to expect a 100% closing rate.) I kept meeting more and more people through networking groups I joined but I was joining the wrong ones locally. (I felt like the big fish in a small pond.) It just wasn't where people were looking for individual coaching services. They were barely surviving themselves and the thought of shelling out more money than the cost of a $15 diet book was just too indulgent for them.

So I started going to New York City and Boston and joined a couple of high-level networking groups with very accomplished people. (Mind you, I live between Boston and NYC and it's a two-hour drive each way from my house to either city.) In these groups, there were plenty of times I felt like the "small fish in the big pond" because of the caliber of people I was meeting. *How intimidated would you be if you were the small fish in the big pond? I wasn't. If you are afraid to be the small fish in the pond with the biggies, it will be difficult to move forward. (By now you know these fears are rooted in an exile.)*

I was dedicated to making real in-person connections and helping others solve their problems personally or by connecting them to people in my network who could help them. Most people who have become successful did not do it through close friends or family. Their second and third level loose connections are responsible for the turning points in their careers because the people these "acquaintances" know have the connections to put them on the path to success. However, they will not connect someone to their network until they know, like and trust them first. And that is done by asking people deep questions about their hopes, fears and dreams.

There are a couple of great books to get you started feeling comfortable walking into a roomful of strangers. This may be the first step out of your comfort zone. *How to Win Friends and Influence People* by Dale Carnegie. *Never Eat Alone* by Keith Ferrazzi. *Give and Take* by Adam Grant. *How to be a Power Connector* by Judy Robinett. You may need to find a group where you know no one and give yourself the challenge of doing something out of the box. The more you see that nothing bad is going to happen, the more risks you will take. Implement these strategies and they will start moving your bus. When you hit speed bumps, they are just telling you to re-think your strategy and try something else.

At my first NYC networking group meeting, the crowd was thinning out at end of the evening and I noticed an attractive man I had not met yet. So I went up to him (yes, ladies, you can approach guys, even if you're married). My parts were okay with approaching strangers. They were not stopping me because they were not afraid of rejection. They knew that if I got rejected, it was not because I was a loser, it was because *the other person* was uncomfortable with strangers.

(See how parts allow you to reframe your negative experiences positively?)

So I had a productive conversation with "Dave," no more than 15 minutes. We exchanged cards and I connected with him on LinkedIn. Sometimes these initial conversations uncover something that tells me the person needs to solve one of their challenges, and sometimes they don't. If I can help by connecting them to someone else or with an article or website I know about, I follow up with them right away. That's why it's important to keep going to these gatherings and become a fixture.

A couple of months later, I was traveling into New York again. I reached out to Dave to see if he wanted to have coffee and get to know each other better, and he did. *See I'm the gal who is "asking the guy out first." Would you have the guts to do this? You might feel like you're cheating on your spouse but this is "business."*

Dave and I got to know each other better during coffee. The next month I was in the city I asked Dave if he wanted to get together again before going to the networking meeting. He said "Sure," and we had dinner. *Yes, you can have dinner alone with someone of the opposite sex even if you're married.* At this dinner, he started to share with me the places where he felt stuck. I had no idea he was feeling all of this prior to this dinner. So I gave him my insights and I followed up by sending him some videos. *Solve other people's problems without expecting anything in return, even if that means spending time on the Internet to find the resources for them. The Universe will reward you later.*

Then he started to share some more of his struggles over email and I realized that he was asking for big-time help. I had already started my training in Internal Family Systems and I offered him the opportunity to be my "guinea pig." I told him, "I'm more than happy to coach you to get unstuck. "Yeah right, Emily . . . you're gonna help me get out of my misery?

I've been depressed all my life and 20 years worth of therapy barely did any good. I doubt you can get me happy but I've got nothing to lose and everything to gain." Talk about pressure to produce results!

So here I am giving value to others for free without expectation of anything in return. He was actually helping me out, giving me confidence coaching clients with the IFS method. The more you show you care, the more people will open up to you with their problems.

Who is the one person you can reach out to today to help make his or her life better? Do they need advice on how to better market their business? Do they need a connection to help with their job search? Just start giving. The rewards will come later.

Dave experienced significant positive shifts after the very first long session of unburdening faulty beliefs. His confidence, self-esteem and happiness soared and remained there for good (he spent about 15 hours total coaching with me), and that's when I knew I had landed on my life's calling. Dave is the reason why I shifted from being a nutritionist to becoming a Success and Happiness Catalyst and then rebranding to a *Be More Extraordinary Magician*. (Of course I can help clients with their nutrition issues, but only after they address their skeletons in the closet.)

So lo and behold I coached more and more people with IFS therapy, and I knew I had to spread the message about how powerful IFS is to get people unstuck from anything and everything. Quite a number of times Dave said to me, "You've got to write a book . . . You've got to write a book . . . You've got to write a book! I've read lots of self-help books but none about the kind of powerful healing that you do." And I said, "Yeah . . . yeah . . . I know, I know, I know! One of these days . . . " The thought of writing a book was daunting, even self-publishing it, let alone getting a traditional publisher to give me a book deal. "Ugh! It's going to take forever. But I know it has to be done . . . eventually. Besides, I'm too busy with marketing and taking care of my clients."

Then, in February of 2013, I schlepped to NYC again to the networking meeting where Dave and I originally met. I got there early and I went up to the bar and introduced myself to three men clustered together. (There I go again, a married woman picking up more married men at bars!)

How brave are you to pick up married strangers at bars? Would your parts be okay with it? If not, there are some exiles that need attention so you can eventually acquire the guts to do this. If you don't take risks, nothing good will happen for you. The Universe rewards those who take risks and go out of their comfort zones.

I had a 10-minute conversation with one of these guys who was fascinated with what I do to help people become successful and happy. Ben asked me to come by his office the next time I was in the city. He was the CEO of a well-known marketing company.

Would you be intimidated continuing a conversation with a CEO who is well-known in his industry with boatloads of connections? Your fears might stop you from following through, they may kick in and say, "I'm nothing compared to what this guy has accomplished. Why would he want to talk to me?"

So I followed up with Ben the next day to say I'd be back in NYC three weeks later. *Most people just shove business cards in the drawer after a networking meeting and never follow up. How likely are you to reach out to people first? If you don't, there's an exile that's afraid of taking risks. It's afraid something bad is going to happen, like when you asked the boy in junior high school to dance and he rejected you. This is the exile that needs to be unburdened in order to become fearless with approaching strangers.*

This meeting with Ben led me to an opportunity to give my signature happiness talk to his employees three weeks later. After that speech, Ben invited me to come back to New York in two weeks to a reception he was having with his inner circle of friends and business associates. I accepted. Since I've been in sales all of my life, I wasn't afraid to walk into a roomful of strangers. It's not about me, it's about me taking interest in other people. It's always about being genuinely curious about the other person and getting to know them. Once you make them feel comfortable, they will be interested in getting to know you.

Okay, so now would you have the courage to show up at a reception where everyone knew each other and where you barely knew the host, let alone anyone else in the room? Many people would say, "No way! What am I going to talk about? I don't know anyone! I'll look like a fool." If you feel this way, the negative energy of those thoughts will be emitted. Others will pick up on how uncomfortable you are and they won't want to talk to you. (Just follow the tips in How to Win Friends and Influence People. *If you are afraid, it's your parts acting up to stop you. That part that's frozen in the Fifth Grade memory when you tried to approach a group of cool kids and they gave you a dirty look to let you know you didn't belong. This is the exile you need to address in order to get the courage to get out of the house and meet new people so your life can be exciting. You can make more friends in two hours by getting interested in others than in two years of talking about yourself.*

So I showed up at Ben's office for this reception two weeks later. I just started yacking with whomever was there. I'd smile and say "Hi!" Since I've used *How to Win Friends and Influence People* concepts all my life (all those years in sales), I just applied it here and to every social situation I was in.

I was talking to Ben one moment and then another man, Randy, arrived. I said hello. Randy was curious about how I knew Ben and what I did for a living. Question after question kept coming about my work, and I just kept answering. I had no idea who I was talking to because I didn't have a chance to ask him what he did. He asked if I did speaking. I said yes. He asked if I planned on writing a book about what I do, and

I said, "In fact, *two weeks ago* I wrote in my journal that writing a book has become priority number one on my to-do list. (It was Dave's message that was haunting me: "You have to write a book Emily!") I told Randy I had to figure out how to self-publish a Kindle book.

"You don't have to self-publish," he said, "I'm a publisher. I love your platform and your message. I would be happy to publish your book for you. I'll take on all the risk." I was thinking, *This can't be happening, this is not how it's supposed to happen. People spend years trying to find a literary agent and a publisher. I don't have an agent, I don't have a book proposal, I've never written a book, only e-books and blog posts!*

Randy received the energy of my life's calling. Putting that goal down on paper was the clincher. The goal of this book was to talk about how Internal Family Systems can help you become the most extraordinary version of you. You can overcome your fears, erase negative self-talk and gain the courage and confidence to step out of your comfort zone and go BIG. When you go BIG, you can feel alive and be really happy on the journey to living to your full potential. I wanted to share my life's lessons with the masses about how loving my parts changed my self-image and my life. I wanted to inspired people to take action, to get out of the past and get unstuck and unleashed.

Randy said, "Just send me a rudimentary book proposal in the next week and I'll send you a contract. Can you have the manuscript ready in six months?" "I guess I will," I said, "This is an opportunity of a lifetime!" So I spent the weekend writing a book proposal and sent the 30-page document to him within a few days. A week later I had a contract and voila, you are reading this book, all thanks to Randy's trust in me.

Miracles Can Happen When You Believe in Yourself

My journey is an illustration that miracles can happen to you when you just start driving that bus and making stops at places you've never been before. Get out and enjoy the scenery and "pick up" men and women along the way (even if they're married). Just show your authentic enthusiasm for life and your mission. This magnetic energy is possible when your parts are no longer stuck in the past with their limiting beliefs of what you *can't* do. When they have left the past behind, nothing is off limits. They will let you take as many trips as you need on the bus ride to living to your full potential. Others will pick up on your unstoppable energy and will help you get what you want. Every new connection leads you to the next. That can only happen if you take the time to get to know new friends and transcend the fear of talking to strangers. The unknown is exciting and you can taste this excitement too if you get out of your own way.

This book deal came about because I took initiative in approaching strangers first, saying "Hi!" and not fearing rejection. So the Universe rewarded me with opportunities. This might look like "luck" and being at the right place at the right time, especially meeting the publisher. But it's not luck. If you go back to the "State of Being" chart in Chapter Six, everything was synchronistic, these were not coincidences. Because I have released the bottom-feeder energies of shame, guilt and fear and am now vibrating from the sky-high energies of gratitude, love and joy, the Universe picks up on these higher energies and I end up manifesting what I want. I couldn't have specifically mapped out my journey if I had tried. I just showed up everywhere. All I did was let my Self step on the gas pedal of my bus, unhampered by the protectors and exiles stuck in the past. My parts are now in the passenger seats of the bus of my life, they are the cheerleading squad telling me to keep gunning it and propel my life forward. My parts cheered me on to say hello to strangers. I kept moving and moving and moving, and great opportunities manifested. You too can have this happen when you release the past and the shame and show up as your most confident Self who loves who you are—quirks and all—giving to others first and trusting that you will get what you need later.

The lessons of my journey has been expressed by many blog posts and books on networking your way to success. That is, if you want to take big leaps in your professional life (and personal life too, like finding dates), you can't do it alone. You need the help of others people to introduce you to their network. It is your loose connections that will eventually get you to the people you need to connect with to make things happen. Oftentimes, it is the 3rd or 4th degree connections that are the magic (the friend of a friend of a friend). Your close family and friends are for the most part not the ones contributing to the awesome outcomes per se.

In order for you to make contact with new acquaintances, you have to feel good about yourself, get out of the house and out of your comfort zone to attend meetings or conferences where you don't know anyone. In order for strangers to be attracted to your energy and want to help you, you have to radiate that upbeat energy of confidence. That means it's very important to get rid of the inner chatter and critical voices from the past and work on yourself first. Internal Family Systems has the ability to help you to permanently erase your negative self-talk so you can soar.

It's Never Too Late to Start Today to Reinvent Yourself

Even if you're 50 or 60 years old, (I was laid off at 49 and started my reinvention then), it's never too late to give yourself the gift of inside-out transformation so that the final chapter of your life will be happy and fulfilling. Life has just begun for me, as if I were in a coma for the first 50 years. The Universe had bigger plans for me. It woke me up when my financial security was pulled out from under me in 2011 and I was laid off. If you think you are too old, you *will* be too old. If you think you are younger, you will show up with "young" energy and be that "senior citizen" all the young ones want to hang out with you because you're so much fun!

So what kind of zap do you need to get out of your coma of settling and just going through the motions? How much is negative self-talk (from your parts) holding you back from unleashing the most extraordinary version of You? What is that one thing you can do today to move your bus forward? For many people, it's more than likely making the *decision* to do the inside-out makeover, perhaps through the IFS process, following the steps I have outlined for you in the Appendices. You can take yourself through getting to know your protectors. However, it is very important that you seek the help of an IFS therapist (go to Selfleadership.org) to finish the process of unburdening your exiles. Exile work is NOT safe to do on your own because the memories can be very vulnerable. If you would like to work with me, I work with a specific clientele. You can go to my website BeMoreExtraordinary.com to learn more.

What do you love about yourself that you would like to unblushingly show the world? How badly do you *not* want to live a life of regret? How desperately will you avoid feeling like you've lived your life as a failure, disappointing yourself and others? Are you ready for this journey or would you rather stay small in your box hiding behind your excuses?

* * *

Unconditional self-love can erase the negative self-talk for good and gives you wings to fly out of the small box you have settled into. You can live fearlessly and on your own terms. You can be a better friend to yourself and everyone else around you. And you can be a better parent. If you want to buy more "stuff" and join exclusive clubs after your emotional scars are healed, then you'll be doing it for the right reasons instead of being driven by your demons and unconsciously doing it to show the chorus of the people that have shamed and rejected you that you are "good enough."

The vision of how to live out the rest of your life can be so much clearer once you empty your mind of the old energies and rewire it for good with new beliefs about what the real you is capable of. You will be in for a wild and vibrant life with endless possibilities. You'll awaken your joy, passion and purpose, fully charged and alive, letting out all the songs that have been bottled up inside of you. I know it sounds scary not to know what your next step is, but as long as you are moving forward with fearless action, showing up as your most extraordinary self, that's when the Universe will take care of the details and you will magically be shown *how* you are going to achieve success and happiness. You will be at the right place at the right time and magic will happen.

I didn't call myself a *Be More Extraordinary Magician* when I started my IFS coaching practice. I called myself a *Success and Happiness Catalyst*. As more and more of my high functioning, psychologically stable clients transformed into their best selves, they started to say: "Emily, You should not be calling yourself a *Success and Happiness Catalyst*. This does not do justice for the magic you possess. Sure, you were the catalyst for my success and happiness but what you transformed me into was so magical. You are the *Magician* that transformed me into the most extraordinary version of myself. I don't even recognize myself after working with you. You've helped me overcome my limiting beliefs. I've erased my negative self-talk. You are truly a *Magician!* I came home to my true self and as a result many wonderful things are happening. I couldn't have imagined all of this just a few short months ago. I am on the path to realizing my full potential. I'm just in awe!" So I just let my clients brand me and that's how I became the *Be More Extraordinary Magician.*

Giving yourself permission to be in the spotlight and owning your gifts and showing you are lovable, worthy and enough, gives others permission to do the same. That is one of the greatest legacies you can bestow on your kids and others. Nothing is more magnetic, charismatic and attractive than someone who *believes* in themselves. You are a winner and you'll be attractive to winners.

When you take your dreams out of the drawer, your parts who are being cared for you now, will give you the courage to do scary things. They will happily sit in the passenger seats instead of holding down the brakes to get your attention. Now that you have given them all the attention they needed, they'll let you—the magnificent and sparkling Self—take the leadership role. Then the spirit and soul of who you are that had been hidden for so long will come out and drive the bus of your life to somewhere really awesome. A great bonus is when you release the weight of the past, you will look younger and feel younger and you'll have that sparkle in your eyes that attracts others.

When you hit the speed bumps of failures and rejections, your parts will support you. They'll pick you right back up so you can keep going as you play out the Super Bowl of your one big precious life. Many areas of your life can positively shift —your relationships, your finances, your career and your health. The critical voices, shame, embarrassment, loneliness and emptiness will be gone because your parts have the company of you, always. You will finally be able to go BIG and dream BIG and make it happen. Because all of your parts are so happy with you now, they are saying:

Go! Go! Go! You can do this... we're rooting for you. You are the bomb, you can get that pretty girl. You can date that cute guy. You deserve that promotion. You deserve good health. You deserve to be in your skinny jeans. We know you are beautiful. We believe in you. Now be fearless, jump in and do it. The real you is in charge now. We are your parts that will always be cheering you on to your greatness. You have healed us. We have no reason to hold you back. We know we are loved by you so we are setting the real you free to self-actualize and wake up with a smile every day on your journey. You're awesome and amazing! You have brought so much love to others and have made such a difference in this world with your charisma, compassion and purpose.

In the end, you're only going to regret the chances you didn't take. "I coulda', I shoulda', I woulda'.... if I weren't so afraid." If you "don't do emotions," you'll never feel fully alive and fulfilled and you'll forever be chasing the horizon, thinking that happiness is out there after the arbitrary goals are reached.

One of the most powerful and moving song about self-actualization is Beyonce's "I Was Here." I recommend you watch the YouTube video of this song when she sang this at the United Nations World Humanitarian Day. It will send chills up your spine.

I wanna leave my footprints on the sands of time
Know there was something that,
meant something that I left behind
When I leave this world, I'll leave no regrets
Leave something to remember, so they won't forget
I was here, I lived, I loved, I was here . . .

You are not average. You are extraordinary. You will believe how extraordinary you are when you decide to invest the time and energy to do the inner work to erase the negative self-talk and limiting beliefs. You are the one all of your parts have been waiting for to rescue them out of the past so they can give you the strength and permission to be whole and show up as the most extraordinary version of you. When you end the inner conflict and erase the negative self-talk, you can be unleashed and become unstoppable and live happily ever after!

Please drop me a line to let me know what opens up for you after reading this book. Emily@BeMoreExtraordinary. com Twitter: @EmilyFilloramo ☺

Appendix A

What's in the Way of Happiness and Living to Your Potential

"You will never rise above how you see yourself."

– Oprah

The first step to becoming the best version of you is **awareness** of the obstacles you may not even realize you have. The answers to the questions below will allow you to see the gap of where you are now versus where you want to be. The answers will also allow you to see how your thoughts and feelings about the past could be keeping you stuck. Use your instincts to answer the questions—no need to overthink what your answers should be.

Once you are **aware** of what could be keeping you stuck, the next step is to make a **decision** that you are going to do whatever it takes to get yourself to a better place.

"Pleasure Island"

1. What do you want? What are your soul's deepest desires and vision?
   (Losing 10 pounds is not a vision. Wanting health so you can play with your grandchildren is. You have to know where you want to drive the bus of your life. If you don't have a vision, you'll stay exactly where you are because you haven't plugged in the destination into your life's GPS.)

2. Do you know what the **purpose of your life** is?

3. Finish the sentence "I'll be **happy** when . . . " or "My life would be **perfect** when . . ."

4. Describe your life as if you **weren't afraid** and have **already achieved your goals**. What would it **look** and **feel** like? What would you be doing, who would you be with?

5. Why is it **important** for you to achieve what you want? What **values** are you expressing when you get what you want?

6. Who would you have to **become** in order to achieve your goals?

7. On a scale of 1-10, (10 being very worthy) do you believe you are **worthy** of getting what you want?
   (If not, the exiles that don't believe they are worthy are holding you back.)

8. Are you willing to take **risks** and face the **fear of the unknown** in order to get what you want?

9. Please finish the sentence: "If I were _____,
   I would be _____."
   (Examples: If I were prettier, I would be more popular. If I were thinner, I'd be more courageous about networking. If I was nicer to myself, I would be happier. If I were less fearful, I would go out there and make myself known. (Put down as many phrases as you can think of.)

10. Do you really **want** this or is this something you **should** do?
    (If this is something you should do, then the results will not be sustained. You're doing it for the wrong reasons and you'll sabotage yourself back to the old state.)

11. What's the **first thing** that will let you know you are moving forward towards solving this problem?

"Pain Island"

12. Now that you see and feel what it's like to live on "Pleasure Island," how do you **feel** about **not** having that right now?

13. How badly (on a scale of 1-10) do you want to take **action** to solve that problem **NOW** and get off of "Pain Island" and go to "Pleasure Island"?

(If the answer isn't a "10," you are probably not ready to take scary action to change yet. What would make it a "10?" You need to address the parts of you that are afraid to change. What is it that they are afraid of if you do change and go to "Pleasure Island?" When their fears are addressed then these parts may allow you to take the scary steps to move off of "Pain Island.")

14. What exactly are you **struggling** with? What keeps you up at night?

15. How are you **showing up** *now* that has you frustrated?

16. What are the **fears and concerns** that **stop** you from doing the work or from believing in yourself? What keeps you from changing?

17. What do you **need** in order to move forward?

18. Is the pain of staying on "Pain Island" **greater** than the pain of the fear of change and the fear of the unknown when you do get everything you want?
    (If being in the pain is not great enough, this "nail" of pain you have been sitting on hasn't gone deep enough—you hardly feel it anymore. It's easier to live with the devil you know than to live with the devil you don't know, of being in your spotlight of greatness.)

19. Have you made the decision to do whatever it's going to take to get out of this pain?

(If the answer isn't "yes," you are not ready to move forward. There's a part of you that would rather stay small, go unnoticed and hide behind excuses.)

20. How does being stuck affect your **relationships**?

21. How does being stuck affect your **financial situation**?

22. How does being stuck affect your **health**?

23. How would you **feel** if you were still stuck in the same place six months from now? One year from now? Two years from now? Ten years from now? How **badly** do you want to **prevent** this from happening?

24. What is the **biggest pain** you want to **avoid** at all cost? *(Examples: financial failure, divorce, loss of love, loss of friendships, dying from ill health.)*

25. Have you hit **rock bottom** yet with regards to where you are right now?

26. What do you think **will happen** to you if you do **not** do the work to solve your challenges? *(Examples: My spouse will divorce me, I'll have to close my business and I'll be a failure, I'll leave this world depressed and full of regrets, etc.)*

27. What will you **miss out on** if you stay where you are?

28. What are you **willing to do** to achieve your goals? Are you willing to get uncomfortable? *(You must have the courage to go through the "breakdown" to get to the breakthrough.)*

Fears

29. What **fears** are coming up as you think about achieving your ultimate goals and being in the spotlight of your greatness?
    (Whether you like it or not, when you are showing up as the greatest version of you, you will be noticed.)

30. Are you afraid of **failing**?
    (Examples: If you felt humiliated when people watched you gain all the weight back, you're less likely to go through the humiliation of failing again. You have to address the exiles that make you unable to sustain weight loss. If they feel worthless, they won't believe you deserve to be slimmer. They will sabotage you and make you fail and get fat again.)

31. What are you **afraid** of if you do succeed and get **what you want**?
    (Examples: My husband might divorce me if I'm too attractive, my girlfriends won't like it, I'll be all alone because everyone will be jealous of me.)

32. Do you have a **vested interest in staying the same**?
    (Examples: If I remain heavy, I won't have to have sex with my husband. If I remain depressed, I won't have to go out, be visible and be accountable to do something with my life.)

33. What about the fear of "What will **they think of me** if I accomplish my goals?" Who are "they" that you are concerned about and why do you care what they think of you?

34. Is the thought of **succeeding** and getting what you want **more frightening** than your current state of being?

35. What would make your fears decrease or disappear?

Emotional State

36. On a scale of 1-100, where are you on the **Happiness Scale**?
   (1=ready to jump off a bridge, 100=very happy)

37. On a scale of 1-10, where are you on the **Self-Esteem** Scale?
   (1=very low, 10=very high)

38. On a scale of 1-10, where are you on the **Confidence** Scale?
   (1=very low, 10=very high)

39. On most days I am . . . (there can be more than one emotion)

   -Sad
   -Glad
   -Mad
   -Afraid
   -Angry
   -Irritated
   -Numb/Indifferent

40. What, if any, **resentments and anger** are you holding onto?

41. Who do you **need to forgive**?

42. Were you ever inappropriately touched and/or sexually abused as a child and/or young adult? *(If you are still holding onto the burden of shame from sexual abuse, this exile can hold you back in some part of your life.)*

43. Have you ever been in counseling? Were your challenges ever "resolved" from going to counseling?

Parts that are in Conflict with One Another

44. What's **not in alignment** with the decision to move forward to solve the challenge you are in right now? *(Examples: I'll be a bad mom if I am successful, I won't have as much time with my kids; my family believes rich people are not nice; my husband won't like it if I make more money than he does; if I'm healthier and thinner than my friends, I'll be made fun of and get kicked out of our circle of friends.")*

45. What **difficulties do you foresee** if you do get what you want? *(Examples: If I lost 3 dress sizes, I'd have to buy a new wardrobe and I don't have the money for that now; I might get more attention if I am successful and I am not ready to be in the spotlight.)*

46. What **relationships might be affected** if you achieved your desired outcome? Or, who might be **jealous** if you get what you want?

47. What might you have to be **accountable for** that you are not accountable for now *if* you get the outcome you want? *(Examples: I don't have to get a job now because I am "sick and depressed." If I get well I would be expected to contribute financially.*

48. Who would you allow yourself to be if the **opinion of others** were **no longer important** to you?

46. What *if anything* might you **lose of value** if you followed through with doing the work to get achieve your outcome? *(Examples: Freedom to travel, the comfortable paycheck and benefits from my employer, the freedom to not have to think about work after 5 pm.)*

Parts of You

49. Please describe the **"parts" of you** (i.e. the voices in your head) that are **holding you back** from reaching your full potential.

50. Where do you think those **parts** are from in your childhood? Young child, teenage years and/or young adulthood?

51. How have your parents, caretakers, teachers and your peers at school contributed to your self-image and how you think about the world?

52. Please list and describe the **most significant painful memories** from your young childhood, teenage years, young adulthood, and adulthood that contributes to negative thoughts and feelings.

53. When you hear **voices inside of you** that say or make you **feel**, "You are not good enough" or "Who do you think you are?" or "You are worthless" whose voice(s) are you hearing (mother, father, teacher, kids on the playground, etc.)

54. What were your parents like? How would you **describe your childhood**? *(Loving, tense, full of conflict, I couldn't wait to leave or go off to college and be away from the drama, etc.)*

55. How big, on a scale of 1-10, is the **"charge" of negative emotional burdens** you are holding onto from the past? *(1 is not much of a 'charge', 10 is a very big 'charge' and runs my feelings and gets in the way of doing and being more in my life.)*

56. If you do know the **source of the major negative emotional charges**, please share them . . . they could be people and/or events.

57. What do you do, if anything, to soothe the pain of the emotional baggage you carry around? *(Examples: Eating, shopping, drinking, gambling, working, getting angry, being controlling, etc.)*

58. Picture the "future you" that has already achieved what you want. What advice would the future you tell your present self in order to live his/her life fully?

59. Please share anything else about your life experiences that are keeping you from feeling and thinking and being the best of who you want to be.

Core Beliefs

"You become what you believe."

Core beliefs are like **energy magnets. They** attract what you believe right into your life. Law of Attraction works positively or negatively—depending on what your beliefs are. Core beliefs are usually formed by age seven. **Whatever comes after the words "I am…" will come looking for you in adulthood.** When you change your beliefs (by changing the beliefs of the exiles), your self-image can soar and your life can positively change. *(Note: Even saying "I am tired of being fat" or "I am tired of being poor" will result in you staying fat or poor because you have said those words after the "I am…" statement and the brain can't understand the negative part of the sentence. In order to change the belief, it has to be stated in the positive: "I am wealthy" or "I am trim.")*

What are your current CORE beliefs: It's what you feel in the pit of your stomach about who you are.

"I am…" *(Examples: Not lovable, not good enough, not trusting enough, not wanted, intelligent, dumb, a loser, ugly, fat, worthless, beautiful, eccentric, not that smart, stupid, a procrastinator, shy, outgoing, not the best but second best.)*

"I am . . ." (list as many as you'd like)

Can you or have you ever been able to say to yourself in the mirror **without** adding a "**BUT**..." at the end of the sentence: *"I love you. You are perfect the way you are. You are beautiful inside and out."*

Yes or no? (If the answer is no, it means there are exiles that don't believe you are the greatest thing ever.)

"I believe..." (*Examples: I won't amount to anything, I'm not as smart as my peers, I'll never be as pretty as my sister, I'll never be a millionaire, I'll never make as much money as my brother, I can accomplish anything I set my mind to, I am usually the most attractive person in the room, I will become a millionaire in the next 5 years, I will be successful.*)

Whatever your beliefs are, the Universe will more than likely conspire to make it happen. If you want to change anything negative, the beliefs of the exiles need to be changed.

I believe . . .

~

~

~

~

~

~

"I want..." (*Examples: To marry Prince Charming, to have $1 million in the bank, to leave my spouse, to be famous, to be a rock star, to be financially free, to be really happy, to have children who love me, to be slim.*)

~

~

~

~

~

~

What **new beliefs** would have to be in place in order to get what you want?

"I am..." (*Examples: Usually the smartest guy in the room, the most humble person in the room, the friendliest person in the room, the next GURU in my marketplace, so unique that I can only deliver the goods in the way my market wants them, going to buy that second home in the Hamptons, damn good in sales, one of the most LOVABLE and charming people I know, worth my weight in gold, loved unconditionally by my parents, someone with a lot to offer, a person who everyone likes.*)

~

~

~

~

~

~

~

~

Global beliefs:

"Life is… "

~

~

~

~

~

"People are... "

~

~

~

~

~

Ranking of your values:

Rank the following in order of importance. "1" is most important.

Success
Family
Adventure
Love

I hope that this worksheet has given you some insights on what could be keeping you stuck from getting what you want. My ideal one-on-one clients are people who already know they are extraordinary and they know their lives can be even better. They want to take quantum leaps personally and professionally because not doing so would be the ultimate pain. If you fit this profile and would like to have an exploratory consultation, please send me an email at Emily@ BeMoreExtraordinary.com.

Please go to my website www.BeMoreExtraordinary. com to learn about programs to help you get started on the journey to erase negative self-talk and becoming your most extraordinary self.

Appendix B

Get Unstuck and Unleashed
Internal Family Systems Healing Steps

Internal Family Systems is a very powerful modality for getting unstuck and unleashed, and the steps I've shared in the case histories are more or less linear. These steps work for some people, but if you find that you get stuck because your mind throws in all sorts of things to block the process, then your situation is more complex. Your mind doesn't want you to shift so quickly and get out of the habit of being who you are. And the protectors don't want you to shift either. They think bad things will happen if you do change and if you are able to retrieve the exiles. It's essential to get to know these protectors and address their fears first so they can allow you to go deeper. These are some of the challenges that can come up when you want to get to know your parts. The steps of getting through the complexities are myriad and beyond the scope of this book.

As I stated in the beginning of the book, reading this book will not solve your problems overnight. The purpose of the book was to give you insights on what keeps you stuck from extraordinary. You can start the healing process on your own by getting to know your protectors. In order to transform into your best self, it is imperative that you seek guidance from an Internal Family Systems psychotherapist or coach so they can safely take you through unburdening your exiles. Go to www.Selfleadership.org to find an IFS therapist in your area. Many of them work virtually via Skype.

The most important aspect of healing is finding a therapist/coach you feel connected with. If you don't feel connected, your parts are certainly not going to feel comfortable opening up. Keep looking until you find someone you feel comfortable with. Also, finding someone that works in 1.5-2 hour blocks would be very beneficial. This means you will have the time to go deeper during each session and you can make faster progress.

Please note that in the healing steps below, it is safe to get to know your protectors on your own. It is NOT safe to go into the memories and vulnerable feelings of the exiles on your own. Healing the exiles must be completed with a trained professional. (I'm including the steps to heal the exiles just so you know what the IFS practitioner will take you through.)

If you have been through therapy, self-help workshops or programs and feel you have unleashed about 80-90% of your full potential (but you still have that residual bit that's keeping you stuck), then the IFS process can be relatively linear. Your system is used to experiencing the efforts you make towards positive change and it should allow you to go further.

If you have never worked on yourself or have made little or no progress in the few therapy sessions you've had, the journey may take a little longer. If you try to force your system to change drastically and you haven't taken the time to get to know your protectors, your mind may freak out from attempting to change their roles.

These steps are not meant to be a substitute for psychotherapy but can be a good complement to psychotherapy. Please seek the help of a mental health professional if you are not emotionally stable.

Visualization to Get Started

You can record this visualization into your phone and then play it back to get yourself "in the zone" to get to know your parts. (Courtesy of Richard Schwartz, PhD)

> *Imagine you are at the base of a path. It can be any path, one you are familiar with or one you have never been on before. Before you go anywhere on the path, meet with you emotions and thoughts (these are your parts) at the base and ask that they remain there and allow you to head out on the path without them.*
>
> *If they are afraid to let you go, reassure them you won't be gone long and that both they and you will benefit from the experience. See if you can arrange for any scared parts to be cared for by those that aren't scared.*
>
> *If parts remain afraid to let you go, don't go, and instead spend some time discussing their fears with them. Exactly what are they afraid will happen if they allow you to go off on your own?*
>
> *If, however, you sense permission to go, head out on the path. Notice as you go whether you are watching yourself on the path or whether you are on it such that you don't see yourself—you just see or sense your surroundings.*
>
> *If you are watching yourself, that's a signal that a part is present. Find the part that's afraid to let you proceed on*

the path and ask it to relax and return to the base. If it won't, spend time exploring its fears.

As you continue on the path, notice whether you are thinking about anything. If you are, ask those thoughts to return to the base as well so that you increasingly become pure awareness. As you continue on the path, check periodically to see if you are thinking and, if so, gently send the thoughts back.

As each part leaves you, notice what happens to your body and mind. Notice the amount of space you sense around you and the kind of energy that flows in your body.

When it feels as if you have spent enough time on the path away from your parts, begin to return to the base. See if it is possible to hold the spaciousness and energy you feel even as you get close to your parts again. When you arrive at the base, meet with your parts and see how they fared without you and what they might need from you.

When that process is complete, thank your parts for letting you go if they did. If they didn't, thank them for letting you know they were afraid to let you go. Then take some deep breaths again and follow your breath back to the outside world.

Whatever parts held you back from letting you loose on the path to your ultimate journey to your spiritual Self are parts you will want to consider getting to know.

The steps below are adapted from Richard Schwartz, PhD's *Internal Family Systems* protocol for healing and Self-leadership.

Getting to Know Protectors

1. Finding the Target Part
- Find the protector you want to get to know. (*"Sad part."*)
- How do you experience this part?
  - In and around your body, an image, a thought? (*"Heaviness on chest."*)

2. "Unblend" from this Part and Get Access to Self
- How do you **feel** towards this part? (*"I want to get to know it."*)
(You need to see that you are separated enough from the part to want to get to know it. If you get answers such as "I *hate* this part, I'm *frustrated*," ask these additional protector parts that just jumped in to step back.)
- How do you feel towards this part now?
(When you feel curious, compassionate, connected or calm towards it, this means you are separated enough to get to know it and the Self is present.)

3. See if Part is Aware of You and How Old You are Now
- How does this part respond to your presence? (*"It's telling me it likes that I'm getting to know it. It's been so alone all of these years."*)
- How long have you been in my life? (*"Since seven years old."*)
- Is it aware of how old you are now? (*"No, it has no idea I'm 40 years old." "Hey, it's me, the adult version of*

you, I'm 40 now. A lot has happened.)
(If not, update this part on how old you are today
and what your life is like now.)

4. Hear the Protector's Story and It's Job

- What's your job? *("To keep you safe from criticism.")*
- Invite this part to tell you more of its story, its job
  and its concerns. *("Mom has a habit of always picking
  on me whenever I seem happy, happy with my grades,
  happy with friends, happy playing with my dolls. So if
  I remain sad, she's less likely to criticize because she's
  usually in a depressed state and can't stand it when she
  sees other people happy.")*

5. Uncover Protector's Fears if It Didn't Keep Doing Its Job

- What are you **afraid** of if you don't do your job?
  *("Mom would go off the deep end and be so jealous of my
  happiness that she might threaten and commit suicide.
  Happiness = Danger.")*
  - o Then what? *("Then I would have no mom.")*
  - o Then what? *("Then I would be abandoned because
    dad lives in another state with his new wife.")*
  - o Then what? *("Then I would be all alone and I
    wouldn't be able to take care of myself and I might
    die.")*

6. Show Appreciation for How Hard It Has Worked to Protect You

- Let this part know how much you **appreciate** what is
  has done for you in protecting you all of these years.

("Thank you for protecting me from death. If I remain sad, Mom will criticize me less, I won't be as hurt, she won't threaten to take her life, and I won't be alone and abandoned if she did the worst thing of taking her own life. Thank you for keeping safe and from being alone.")

- What would this part rather do if it didn't work so hard? *("It would rather be carefree and happy and play with my friends.")*

- Does this part know that it is not helping you in your life right now to be sad? *("No, let me update you. This sadness keeps me unproductive and holds me back from making friends because people don't want to be around my sad energy.")*

- What does this part need from you in order for it to feel safe, not be afraid anymore and relax and let go of some or all of its roles? *("It needs to know that I won't be criticized if I'm happy. I'll let it know that.")*

- Is there anything else this part wants you to know? *("No.")*

- Is this part willing to show you the exile it has been protecting all of these years? *("Yes.")*

- (If no, then ask what it is afraid of if the exile is revealed. It might be afraid that the emotions could be too overwhelming. In which case you can reassure it that you can ask it to dial down the emotions.)

Getting to Know Your Exiles

Please do NOT take yourself through exile work. You MUST seek the guidance of an IFS professional. The following steps are an illustration of what your IFS therapist will take you through.

1. Access the Scene

- What scene or image comes to you when you see this exile?

- Where she? (*"In the kitchen when I'm happily playing with the new dolls that grandma got me for my birthday."*)

- What is he/she wearing? (*"She has pigtails and a red and white dress on."*)

2. Making Sure You are in Self and Separated Enough from the Exile

(If you are too blended with the feeling and emotions of this part, then it's hard to get to know it and let it tell its story to you. The Self needs to be separated from the exile so it can be the healer.)

- How do you feel towards her? (*"I feel connected to her."*)

    (If you don't get the feeling of curiosity, compassion, connectedness, caring or calmness, and you feel *sorry* for this exile, then ask sorry protector part to step aside. Once that protector has stepped aside, ask again, "How do you feel towards him/her?" When you feel compassionate, curious, connected, caring or calm toward him/her, then it's safe for you to get to know the exile.)

- How old is this part of you? (*"Seven years old."*)

- How close or far are you from this exile? Can you get closer? (*"I'm standing a few feet away from her."*)

- Does the exile recognize you? (*"Yes."*)
(If not, tell this exile who you are and how old you are and what you've been up to. If you feel vulnerable emotions coming up from this exile, you can ask this part not to overwhelm you.)

- How is it reacting to your presence? (*"She's running towards me and wants to sit on my lap."*)

3. Witnessing What the Exile Went Through

- Invite this exile to tell you or show you what it wants you to know. What happened? (*"Mommy just yelled at me to pick up my dolls. I set up house and spread the pots and pans around to play being a cook."*)

- What is the burden or belief that this part took on as a result of the bad experience? (*"I must be bad, I must not be lovable if mom is criticizing me like this. It's not safe to be happy, Mom just gets mad at me. If I remain sad, maybe she won't be as mean to me."*)

- Is there anything else that this part would like to share with you or show you? (*"How Mom hates it when she is jumping up and down on the couch because she's happy. She gets criticized to stop doing that."*)

- Does this exile feel understood by you? (*"Yes."*)

4. Self-led "Re-parenting" of the Exile

- What does this exile need from you in order for it overcome this negative experience? (*"She needs to be told that she is not bad, she deserves to be happy, she is lovable, she doesn't deserves to be criticized. I'll tell her how mom is emotionally unstable and that's the reason why she blows up at her."*)

  (Be with this exile the way that he/she needed at the time of this wounding experience. Be that protective adult who can make the situation all better so she feels whole and worthy.)

- Does this part need to be taken out of the scene of this memory to someplace safe? (*"Yeah, I'll take her to the park with me."*)

  (Take it someplace safe, into the present with you or to the beach or the park, whatever feels right.)

- Does this part feel fully heard? (*"Yes."*)

5. Unburdening the Extreme Feelings and Beliefs of the Exile

- Is it ready to unburden itself of the faulty beliefs it has taken on as a result of that devaluing experience? (*"Yes."*)

- How would it like to rid itself of the burden? Burn it up? Release it to the light? Let the wind take it away? Let the water wash it away? Whatever feels right to you. (*"Put it in a bottle and let the ocean wash it away."*)

6. Reintegration with Protector

- Ask the protector that stepped aside (*"Sad protector"*) to come back and tell you how it feels about what just happened with the exile since it has been rescued out of the dungeon. Is it ready to let go or relax its extreme feelings, behaviors and emotions? If it's okay with what you just did but it is still not ready to release and take on more positive roles, it means that there are more exiles being protected that you haven't addressed yet. During your next session, go through the steps again and talk to the protector and ask it to reveal more exiles. (*"Yes, it's ready to let go of some of its sad feelings but not all because there are still others exiles in hiding."*)

- When the protector sees that the exiles are no longer stuck in the past and that they are safe with you, then it will relax and allow them to take on more positive roles to help you move forward.

7. Appreciation for Your Parts

- Conclude by thanking all of your parts for letting you get to know them. (*"Thank you for letting me get to know you and for all the hard work you have done to protect me all of these years."*)

- How is that heaviness in the chest feeling now where you felt the sad part? (*"It feels lighter now."*)

Appendix C

How to Find the Love of Your Life Who Treats You Right

The type of person you attract is a reflection of your own self-image. Deep down inside, if you don't think much of yourself, you can end up attracting someone who doesn't think much of him or herself either. This will more than likely lead to conflict. If you want to break out of this pattern, you need to work on yourself first.

Here are the suggested steps to take to break out of the pattern of attracting lovers who invite conflict and abuse. If you want to have the prince charming/fairy princess type of "happily ever after" relationship, then you must become the best of who you can be to attract that head-over-heels partner, and a relationship full of sizzle and emotional intimacy.

I highly recommend you buy Dr. Richard Schwartz must read book on relationships, *You Are The One You've Been Waiting For: Bringing Courageous Love To Intimate Relationships.* This book is only available at www.Selfleadership.org. Go to the "IFS Store" tab.

* * *

Step 1:

Raise Your Self Image So You Can be Full of Self Love

Nothing is more magnetic than someone who exudes the confidence that radiates from self-love. In order to be irresistible, do the inner work to understand your parts and unburden them of negative beliefs that you might not even know you have. Many of us unknowingly possess exiles that hold certain "I'm not lovable, I'm not enough, I'm worthless" burdens. (Some of the most successful and seemingly confident clients I've worked with had these burdens and that's why they were having difficulty in some area of their lives.) These exiles can unconsciously attract a partner that may not be able to fulfill your emotional needs.

Your partner will not "complete" you, **you** will complete **you** by being the primary caretaker of your parts. That's why when you work on yourself first, your self-image rises and you'll be able to magnetize a better partner than the last time. That's because your energy will be more positive and nothing is as attractive as someone who radiates that magical aura.

Step 2:

Be Vulnerable, Share Your Past

After about the third date, test the waters to see how comfortable your date is with sharing emotions. Share yours first. When you have released the past and are full of self-love, you will be comfortable sharing what you learned about yourself. You're not living in your story anymore, you're past all that. Just as famous people like Oprah openly share old baggage, ask yourself if you can do the same. We don't think any less of Oprah for sharing, in fact most of us love the fact that she is open and not drowning in her old memories. Start with sharing small stuff and then if your date is intrigued and wants to hear more, share more. Invite them to share their memories too. This will create instant intimacy.

If you want a cheat sheet of how to really get to know someone quickly and develop a deep connection, Google "36 Questions to Bring You Closer Together." Some of the people in the study actually got married.

Step 3:

Inquire About Your Date's History with Doing Inner Work

Everyone has exiles, even if you had perfect parents. Some exiles are more traumatized than others. If the date says that they are over the past (because they have consciously willed it away), you know now from reading this book that they very well may not be over their past. If they show any signs of negativity, anger or bitterness when they make statements such as "My mother was crazy and my dad was a depressed alcoholic and a womanizer, " or "I was teased a lot in school," then you'll instantly recognize that there are exiles associated with the incidents they describe. Notice *how* they say this. Is it with hate and bitterness or is this with a neutral energy? Sometimes people look back with amazement at what they endured. They express a considerable amount of emotion, but it is the emotion of compassion for themselves. However, if they are visibly upset or angry, they have a lot of work to do with getting over the past. If they express their story with neutrality, they could be in total denial or they have worked through it. However, if they have never worked on themselves and they are saying it nonchalantly, they have exiles that have been pushed out of their consciousness. It will show up in some way later on, perhaps in the way they treat you.

These "skeletons in the closet" are going to show up in the relationship because your date hasn't done any inner work. If they have never gone to therapy or worked on themselves and it seems like they are not even open to talking about it, then run away. Their baggage will eventually show up in the relationship.

If you are so attracted to the new prospect that you find yourself making all sorts of excuses for their bad behaviors, that is a red flag. Just let your former exiles know that "We are not falling for that again!" Run away before you repeat the same patterns.

* * *

What if I Don't Want to Leave my Relationship But it Lacks Sizzle and We're Just Bored with One Another?

If one partner is dead emotionally, it will drive a wedge in the relationship and you'll end up like roommates, unsatisfied. Lots of couples fall into this pattern. Many men are reluctant to go to therapy because they think it makes them look weak. Others dislike the idea of revealing their private thoughts and emotions. If that is the case, then finding a coach trained in IFS would be ideal for you. Go to www.Selfleadership.org to find one. If your partner won't go, go by yourself and get to know your protectors and exiles. When you feel really good about yourself, you'll be able to decide if you are willing to put up with living with an "emotionally dead" partner or whether you are strong enough to end the relationship. For some, the situation isn't bad enough to warrant a breakup. In this case, you may have to decide what you need to add into your life to make it more exciting. Maybe it's picking up a new hobby or spreading your wings by making more friends who will satisfy your emotional needs. Those solutions are fine, but having an affair often creates many more problems that tend to blow up in your face.

Only you will know what's right for you. If nothing else changes, at least you have changed for the better and that is the first step towards doing the scary things you need to do to take your life to the next level.

Partners Who Work on Themselves Stay Together—with Sizzle

The more you can share your vulnerabilities and relate to each other through your true Selves (instead of through your protectors and exiles) the more exciting and emotionally intimate your relationship can be. After all, emotional intimacy is the key to a sizzling sex life.

ALSO FROM
NEW CHAPTER PRESS

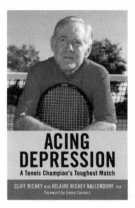

Acing Depression: A Tennis Champion's Toughest Match
by Cliff Richey

Chronicling the tumultuous life of the original bad boy of tennis, this engaging and inspiring memoir describes one man's public battle with clinical depression. Describing torturous days in which he would place black trash bags on the windows and lay in bed crying for hours, this brutally honest narrative stresses that depression is a mental disorder that can affect anyone.

Macci Magic: Extracting Greatness From Yourself and Others
by Rick Macci with Jim Martz

Through anecdotes and more than 100 sayings that exemplify his teaching philosophy, this inspirational manual helps pave the way to great achievement not only in tennis, but in business and in life